DISCARD

Realism and the
Explanation of Behavior

THE CENTURY PSYCHOLOGY SERIES

KENNETH MacCORQUODALE, GARDNER LINDZEY, & KENNETH CLARK
Editors

MERLE B. TURNER
SAN DIEGO STATE COLLEGE

Realism and the Explanation of Behavior

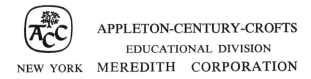

APPLETON-CENTURY-CROFTS
EDUCATIONAL DIVISION
NEW YORK   MEREDITH   CORPORATION

711-1

Library of Congress Card Number: 73-137640

PRINTED IN THE UNITED STATES OF AMERICA

390-88879-6

ACKNOWLEDGMENTS

Pages 8, 9. Quote from Thomas Kuhn, *The Structure of Scientific Revolutions,* by permission of the University of Chicago Press.

Pages 19, 20. Quotes from F. C. Bartlett, *Remembering,* by permission of Cambridge University Press.

Pages 35 (quote), 53 (table). Reprinted with permission from Mario Bunge, *Scientific Research II: the Search for Truth.* © 1967, Springer-Verlag New York Inc.

Pages 56, 57, 59. Quotes from K. J. W. Craik, *The Nature of Explanation,* by permission of Cambridge University Press.

Pages 60, 61. Quotes from J. von Neuman, "The General and Logical Theory of Automata," in L. A. Jeffress, editor, *Cerebral Mechanisms in Behavior,* by permission of John Wiley & Sons, Inc.

Page 76. Quotes from J. A. Deutsch, *The Structural Basis of Behavior,* by permission of the University of Chicago Press.

Page 126. Quote reprinted by permission of the publishers from *Gödel's Proof* by Ernest Nagel and James R. Newman, published by New York University Press and by Routledge & Kegan Paul Ltd. © 1958 by Ernest Nagel and James R. Newman.

Pages 146, 147, 148. Quotes from J. R. Lucas, "Mind, Machine, and Gödel," by permission of the Editor of *Philosophy.*

Pages 149, 150. Quotes from P. Benacerraf, "God, the Devil and Gödel." Reprinted from the *Monist* with the permission of the author and publisher.

Pages 168, 169. Quotes reprinted with permission from D. M. MacKay, "Cerebral Organization and the Consciousness Control of Action," in J. C. Eccles, editor, *Brain and Consciousness.* © 1966, Springer-Verlag New York Inc.

Pages 204, 206, 207, 208, 209, 210. Quotes from *Psychological Explanation,* by Jerry Fodor. © Copyright 1968 by Random House, Inc. Reprinted by permission.

CONTENTS

PREFACE

NEITHER PRACTICE nor performance will sustain defense of the idea of scientific reductionism. Our sciences are seldom static, their conceptual frameworks hardly final; the changing apperceptive manifold does not conduce the prospects of finished sciences and ordered hierarchies. Even our exemplars of reduction are a source of embarrassment. Phenomenal languages of the sciences are matters of concept, not raw sense data. Seeing a complex event as a behavioral action is not the same as being witness to a furtive concert played by neurones.

Still I wish to maintain that reductive explanation in science is a defensible tactic. To the extent that there is synthetic unity among the sciences, that unity is secured by common heuristic bonds. What may be hypothesis and improvisation in one science may provide the base for phenomenal reification in another. One does not search for scientific realism through ontological spectacles but rather through convergent operations as occasioned by the sharing of a conceptual focus. To be sure, one seldom makes a scientific discovery or adds to the observational base of his science without knowing what to look for. And one may sharpen his focus or expand his horizons as much by stressing the autonomy of his discipline, as much by a free commitment to inventiveness as by reduction of a "higher" to a "lower" order discipline. However, the unity of the sciences (except perhaps as to method) would be dissolved by instrumentalism. The realism of scientific discovery would succumb to the pragmatics. And one might indeed lose sight of the fact that it is the substantive aspects of mediating process (call it "materialism," if you will) as much as method that bind the sciences together.

There is, however, a pragmatic aspect to the argument. Not only is reduction intrinsically, substantively feasible in our conception of mediating process, but it is heuristically so. That is, not only do we visualize the dependence of the reduced discipline upon the reducing one, but also the reverse; not only do we seek reduction (in kinship to simplicity) as criterial for selecting among alternative theoretic conceptions, but we take that reductive rubric as heuristic for the development of relevant hypotheses in the basic reducing science. Thus psychology needs a conceptually significant neurophysiology, but no more than neurophysiology needs a conceptually relevant psychology.

The explanatory rubrics defended here are the traditional deductivistic ones. Undoubtedly the language of explanation embraces a broader purview than that of the scientific traditionalist. The language of intention, of offering reasons for behavior from the vantage of the active agent rather than in accordance with a deductive rubric, may indeed provide the rubbery grist for the mills of the language analysts. But "intention" that is not translatable into behavior or into causal rubrics does not promise to enrich the language of science.

This admittedly is a dogmatic position, but not so dogmatic that we foreclose persuasion that the introduction of subjectivistic predicates may supplement the language of science without, at the same time, our surrendering the historic advantages gained through the formalization of theory and the objectification of observation. Yet we must be convinced of the advantages of mentalism. Mentalism may indeed provide useful access to mediating processes, but the predicates of the mental language are least refractory when we can tie them to an objectifiable base.

In the meantime there are the arguments to the effect that significant predications of psychological phenomena are logically incompatible with reductive rubrics. Psychology may warrant a broader intentional base, but not, so far as I can see, on "logical" grounds that psychological explanation as presently conceived by behaviorists is methodologically deficient.

I wish to acknowledge an abiding indebtedness to the late Professor Norwood R. Hanson for initiating an interest in many of these inquiries. I wish to thank Stanley N. Weissman, Charles R. Burton, and Michael J. Carella for their critical reading of parts of the manuscript. And I wish to thank Anita Smith for undertaking the ordeal of transcribing my pencilled script.

M. B. T.

Realism and the
Explanation of Behavior

CHAPTER 1

Introduction

THERE ARE occasions when the votaries of any given science reflect upon the future directions of their discipline. For a science caught in the clutch of tradition, the occasions are infrequent and polite. For a science caught up in conceptual revolution the occasions are exciting, heady ones. And for a science weighted down by tradition, yet struggling for new paradigmatic expressions, the occasions become contentious ones. Psychology, I think, is of the last genre. And in large part, the contention centers around the issues of reductionism and explanation.

The thesis to be examined in this essay is the early Hobbesian one of biomechanics, namely, the idea that the behavior of organisms is both describable and explainable in terms of functional relations that structure the succession of observable states. This thesis combines the ideas of hypothetico-deductive explanation and reductionism. Implicit within it are two fundamental premises: one, the referents of observation terms in the language of behavioral science must be extrinsic to the observer; and two, process functions interconnecting the observable states of the organism should be implemented by material systems or by hypothetical constructs compatible with possibility of material realization.

Insofar as this program for a behavioral science is achievable, then the science itself belongs to the family of all "physicalistic" sciences. It embraces the common deductivist tradition of scientific explanation as first formulated in the physical sciences. It holds to the precept of logical empiricism: there is, or rather should be, a unity among all the sciences.

The thesis of the biomechanical explanation of behavior obviously implies reductionism. That, however, does not constitute a denial of psychology as an autonomous discipline. Psychology developed as an offshoot of epistemology, not biology. Hence its language and concepts bear the imprint of cognition and awareness as much as they do of organic mediation. Autonomy is the characteristic of every science. It allows the theoretician to invent and to improvise in his construction of explanatory rubrics. It licenses him as instrumentalist and pragmatist.

Still, there is something more to this role of the creative scientist than mere pragmatics, more to the enduring substance of scientific ideas than their workability, or their elegance, or their simplicity. There is the sense of scientific realism, that where two disciplines focus upon a common domain of "process functions," or better, where it is legitimate for them to do so, the explanatory concepts and the hypotheses should be clearly relevant, existentially relevant, to the two disciplines.

Psychology is not about to become an adjunct of neurophysiology. Even such obvious candidates for reduction as learning and memory remain typically "psychological" in their conception. And the empirics of these subjects represent a domain unto itself. Still, laws of learning and retention, the meticulous spelling out of the phenomenological laws, are not sufficient. We require explanations of our laws; we need theories and hypothetical fabrics that will permit the deduction of our laws. To be sure, ultimate reduction may be a will-of-the-wisp, but brusque and impatient challenges to produce will not carry the argument.[1]

Prima facie, reductionism in psychology is a plausible doctrine (if for no other reason than mediation takes place between the observable environmental and response states). What is required of the argument against reduction, if it is to be convincing, is that we demonstrate a logical incompatibility between the concepts and languages of psychology and neurophysiology. Are the languages of the two disciplines, in some sense, incompatible? Are there possible explanations in psychology logically, not just technologically, recalcitrant to interpretation in the language of neurophysiology?

These are the questions we should examine. Rather than a review of some compendium of successful biomechanical explanations (this would hardly be persuasive) we should examine those arguments which suggest a logical incompatibility as between the languages of our two sciences. In the chapters which follow, we shall first establish a methodological prospectus for reduction, and then turn to those issues which suggest that even this ideal prospectus may be insufficient to the task of comprehensive reductive explanation.

METHODOLOGICAL BEHAVIORISM

Psychology, to be sure, has its roots in the study of mental life. From a science of mental life, *per se,* to perceptual phenomenology to behavioral

---

[1] For example, Abraham Kaplan writes: "It may well be that the psychologist can derive the whole of his discipline from neurology, biochemistry, and the rest; it is not destructive skepticism but productive pragmatism to say, 'I'd like to see him

intentions, psychology has indeed taken note of referents in the intrinsic domain of consciousness. As such, this historical precedent represents neither the affirmation nor the denial of the Hobbesian theme of biomechanics. The tactic of biomechanical explanation asserts only that all phenomena and all constructs in the domain of psychology should be representable and interpretable in the extrinsic biophysical domain.

But what of the involuted, self-contained aspects of raw conscious experience? What of feelings, pure images, pure sentience, as such? If they are to be proscribed from behavioral science, the proscription must be regarded as a methodological one, stemming not from an implicit denial of consciousness but from our incapacity concertedly to make sense of inner reference in any way comparable to the sense we make of outer reference. Thus, the tactic of methodological behaviorism is to translate all self-reference constructs into explicit behavioral ramifications. By virtue of this tactic alone we are assured styles and types of explanation compatible with those of the physical sciences.

Yet this methodological tactic, it may be argued, makes for a relatively trivial science of behavior. Restricted as it is to simple stimulus-response paradigms with limited behavioral options and simple reinforcement contingencies, psychology has retreated from the problems of intention and conflict—problems, we may add, that endow behavior with purpose, foresight, and striving. But need this be so? If it is possible to adopt behavioral translations of intentional concepts, then a genuine purposive behaviorism compatible with the idea of biomechanical explanation is plausible. The defense of our concentrating upon relatively simple observational paradigms is then the tactical one: every future science requires its prolegomena of first principles.

But shouldn't we be more skeptical? A science of behavior restricted to simple input-output rubrics, to simple choices and reinforcement contingencies, indeed degenerates into trivial subject matter. Human endeavor, at least, boasts of larger dimensions—of goals, purposes, and intentions, of perceptual construction, anticipation, and evaluation—none of which, we are told, are to be objectified by convenient dispositional translations.

The most we can offer against this catalogue of complaints is that there is nothing incompatible between behavioristics and the idea that organisms display intention and purposive striving. The tactic of behaviorism is to treat these concepts as dispositional, to translate them as situational behaviors. What other alternative is open to the behavioral scientist?

Let us assume for the moment that behavioral intentions are irreducible. If these "intentional" entities, such as they be, are to be integrated into our explanatory rubrics then symbolically either they fall within the

---

do it!' " (1964, p. 125). And quoted by Howard Kendler (1968) in his own examination of the thesis of reductionism.

causal nexus, or they emerge to designate a set of predicates uniquely dissimilar to those of the traditional behavioral language. Assume the first case, that ideas, thoughts, intentions, *per se,* are causal. Then either we must come up with the ingenious explication of psychophysical transmutation, or we are thrown back on the traditional mind-body muddles from which we, as objectivists, have taken grateful leave. Such ingenious insights are wanting despite our wistful wonderments after emergent entelechies. In the second case, the presumptive significance of intentional terms implies that a new science waits its borning, a science unique unto purposively involved organisms, and one whose terms do not and cannot translate into behavioral predicates. Of this we have had the critique, and the calling, but as yet no promise, no science, no systematic corpus of knowledge that carries us beyond the reminder that the individual as executor of his own action looks from a vantage no scientist in the established practice can bring to bear in his own objectivistic descriptions. But this turns out merely to be a reminder that objective science does not say all there is to say about human experience, a point which any behavioral scientist would be foolish to deny.

Yet in acknowledging this, or rather in accepting the reminder, we need not plead our remissions for not fulfilling expectations that fall beyond the purview of our science. If indeed there are alternatives to scientific explanation, such as intentionalistic ones, so be it; but we need not confess to ineptness, obtuseness, or to any other calumniated penchant, merely because there is a mentalistic language in some sense correlative to that of scientific explanation.

Thus the issue is not one of alternative languages, one semantically anchored to consensual protocols, the other to the vagaries of private experience, but one of whether there is any phenomenon in the behavioral context which cannot in principle be explicated in the explanatory rubrics of an objectivist behavioral science. If the answer is affirmative to this query, then there is a case for some essential incompleteness of that objective behavioral science. But it is that *in principle* phrase which requires emphasis. If something is *in principle* not describable, not expressible, not representable, then the expression of that something, however it be, is incompatible with our objectivistic explanatory rubrics. Our purpose therefore should be to examine those arguments that have been offered as *in principle* objections to our biomechanical rubrics for explaining behavior.

At the outset, however, we should remark that reductionistic explanation as here implied is not that "vulgar" kind which it has become fashionable to eschew (e.g., Polanyi and Bar-Hillel in Coulson and Rogers, 1968). A strictly reductive operationism that explicitly translates all mediating variables as intervening variables, as logical constructions of object-data statements, leaves the organism a hollow entity emitting responses in the presence of its stimulus situations. This radical empiricism leaves nothing to hypothesis, nothing to neurological speculation, and nothing to those intentional states that are the basis for purposive descriptions. Rather, what is proposed in this essay is that mediating states, both mental and neuro-physiological, are subject to descriptions as process functions, the implications of which are subject to detailing in the objective observational language. We may accept the critic's judgment that strict operationism is passé; it has been from its symposiastic beginnings (Bridgman, 1954; Feigl, 1945). The freedom to conceptualize from any source, mental or physical, is to be insisted upon. But for the methodological behaviorist this means simply that he must take cognizance of phenomenologically meaningful mediational states, and that he must formulate these in terms that translate into a public observation language. What is disavowed is not the "reality" of phenomenology and intention, but rather the proposition that these realities are intractable to interpretation within that observation language.

PARADIGMATIC AND NORMAL SCIENCE

In spite of its long history and established traditions, psychology is an immature science—this is an observation with the status of a truism. But it is the immaturity of quandary and contentiousness rather than youth. The focal issue is that of the character of explanation. In no other science are we so argumentative as to what is the scientific credo. In no other phenomenal domain does the natural language so favor conflicting classes of explanation. In no other area of scientific endeavor are we so likely to counterpose the intrinsic and the extrinsic.

As yet we have received no mandate as to how we should go about explaining psychological events, no covenants as to what constitutes a universal explanatory language. To be sure, directives and patterns of explanation have emerged. For most of us, psychology is in the fold of the empirical sciences. But the issues of instrumentalism vis à vis alternative explanations remain unresolved. If the thesis to be maintained in this essay (viz., the legitimacy of biomechanical explanations of behavior) is a defensible one, then we ought to be able to reveal some promise that an encompassing view of life science will nurture psychology along to its comparative maturity.

In science, promises are often difficult to fulfill. However, it may be helpful if we look at scientific development from the perspective of Thomas Kuhn's provocative analysis of scientific revolution. In *The Structure of Scientific Revolutions* (Kuhn, 1962), he argues that science develops in a relatively nonlogical fashion from one revolution to another. Each revolution is to be distinguished by its *paradigm*, usually the product of scientific genius. Against the backdrop of a preparadigmatic state of the science, or of some previous paradigm, the emergent paradigm prescribes new ways of conceptualizing the structure of events, new ways of perceptual reification, new ways of actually doing science. The impact of the paradigm is that of achieving "a change in world views." Thus effectiveness of the paradigm is achieved only by subsequently winning support within the community of scientists. Such support is contingent upon the paradigm's success in resolving quandaries over phenomena that prove anomalous to the established theory. However, in light of the entrenched tradition, persuasiveness and charisma have as much to contribute to the acceptance of the paradigm as any sentimental myth about the pursuit of enduring truth.

Now paradigms, the ingenious contributions of a Copernicus, a Newton, a Lavoisier, an Einstein, are relatively rare. In great measure, scientific endeavor is engaged in the activity of "normal science." By *normal* science Kuhn means the activity stimulated by the paradigm and directed to securing and enhancing the foundations of that paradigm. Thus normal science is engaged in fact finding, in seeking confirmational support of the paradigm, and in the possible reformulation of the paradigm in more manageable or more elegant form. In brief, the paradigm provides the conceptual foundations for experimental work. Once the paradigm is rooted, normal science takes over. The normal experimental work (much of it ingenious in itself) is designed to obtain support for the paradigm.

A salient aspect of Kuhn's thesis is that there is no systematic logic of scientific development.[2] He makes much of the principle, the priority of paradigms: the paradigm is prior to rules. The rules of the new science emerge only informally in the practice of normal science. Thus, borrowing from Wittgenstein, Kuhn visualizes the paradigm and subsequent practice of normal science as generating families of usage and meaning in the scientific language. Only by playing the language game and noting family resemblances and by modeling these resemblances are we able to develop the characteristics essential to classifying objects. There is no *natural* science, as such, based on natural kinds—only an emerging science contingent upon a flexible apperceptive mass.

Kuhn amply demonstrates his argument with historical examples. Among the paradigms, he mentions the contributions of Galileo, Copernicus, Newton, Franklin, Maxwell, Lyell, Lavoisier, Einstein. At no place does he exemplify a paradigm with mention of a psychologist, or for that matter a physiologist. Perhaps that is understandable, Kuhn is trained as a physicist and historian of physical science. But we also note that the physical sciences are distinguished by their reliance on mathematics and a common reductive bond. Could it be that psychology remains in a preparadigmatic state? Does psychology stand in need of a paradigm?

[2] In this he agrees with Hanson (1958) and Feyerabend (1962) who also favor a kind of conceptual realism. For a counter argument concerning a logic of scientific development, see Sheffler (1967) and Purtill (1967).

PSYCHOLOGY: SEARCH FOR A PARADIGM?

Undoubtedly Kuhn's thesis of scientific revolution is as meaningful to psychology as to other sciences. It is relatively easy, within the historical framework of psychology, to visualize its own paradigm cases; the works, say, of Freud, Pavlov, Thorndike, Watson, Skinner, will surely come to mind (cf. Note 1.1). The rich heyday of formal learning theory was distinguished by its charismatic theory founders and their loyal followers. But do these people and their ideas represent paradigms, in the sense that their contributions punctuate a continuum in the development of behavioral theory? Before offering an opinion we should first examine more closely what Kuhn means by the preparadigmatic state of a science.

Although Kuhn refrains from giving us an explicit taxonomy, we can glean from his argument three features of preparadigmatic science. One, science, in its preparadigmatic state, is frequently hampered by ties to traditional metaphysics. Two, it suffers for the lack of any systematic corpus of constructs integrating its diverse subject matters. And three, it reveals no systemic continuity in the development of conceptual frameworks.

On all three counts psychology experiences embarrassment. Of the first, psychology still suffers conceptually from its ties to dualism (cf. Kantor, 1947). As yet, logical behaviorism remains only a recommendation to a very large group of practitioners. As a credo it is proscriptive; otherwise any consideration of cognitive constructs is an invitation to interpolate a domain of mental processes and entities between objectively observable states. To the extent we insist upon two domains of reference, the mental and the physical, psychology is open to the charge of dualism and is subject to all the quandary of that philosophical heritage. Still, it can be countered, we may engage the tactics of methodological behaviorism without confronting two domains of reference within the scientific language, *per se*. If cognition and intention are given behavioral interpretations then we are freed of metaphysical involvements, if not ties; and we may leave mind-body to critical philosophy. In effect, psychology can dissolve its metaphysical ties by virtue of a methodological gambit.

On the other two counts, however, psychology does not fare so easily. Consider first the question of a systematic set of concepts and constructs underwriting an integrated treatment of diverse subject matters. Psychology does not suffer for a lack of general textbooks. And if one surveys the contents of these texts, he will observe remarkable agreement as to subject matters and organization. It is seldom clear, however, that the subject matters are systemically integrated.[3] Learning, memory, perception, motivation, emotion are all there; but each of the subject matters is treated to a profusion of concepts more or less unique unto themselves. There are, of

---

[3] For exceptions see Hebb (1966) and the old textbook of Muenzinger (1942).

course, records of our efforts to integrate motivation and learning, motivation and perception, learning and memory, learning and perception, and so on; but as often as not the professional investigator is concerned with a unique subject matter and with the task of improvising constructs that provide vehicles of description and inference appropriate alone to the given subject matter. Consequently, a search for paradigms in psychology turns up a number of ingenious schemata for treating distinct subject matters in learning (e.g., operant conditioning), in perception (e.g., signal detection theory), in cognition (e.g., a theory of cognitive dissonance), but seldom a schema that will encompass all of these subject matters into a comprehensive theory of behavior. This is not a complaint, it is an observation on the state of a science.

Or, for that matter, consider an isolated subject matter in itself, for example, the area of learning. Here, if we cannot boast of paradigms proportionate to Kuhn's sense of revolution, at least we have "paradigmettes." But as has been frequently observed (e.g., Gibson, 1960; Turner, 1967), a profusion of theories of learning has produced a profusion of definitions in the basic language of stimulus and response. Even with so solvent and pervasive a subject matter as learning, we have no integrative paradigms to command anything like consensus among the practitioners.

This diversity of conceptual frameworks within a given subject matter exemplifies another feature of preparadigmatic science, namely that of schools. Of the phenomenon of schools in preparadigmatic science, Kuhn has this to say:

> These transformations of the paradigms of physical optics are scientific revolutions, and the successive transition from one paradigm to another via revolution is the usual developmental pattern of mature science. It is not, however, the pattern characteristic of the period before Newton's work, and that is the contrast that concerns us here. No period between remote antiquity and the end of the seventeenth century exhibited a single generally accepted view about the nature of light. Instead there were a number of competing schools and subschools, most of them espousing one variant or another of Epicurean, Aristotelian, or Platonic theory. One group took light to be particles emanating from material bodies; for another it was a modification of the medium that intervened between the body and the eye; still another explained light in terms of an interaction of the medium with an emanation from the eye; and there were other combinations and modifications besides. Each of the corresponding schools derived strength from its relation to some particular metaphysic, and each emphasized, as paradigmatic observations, the particular cluster of optical phenomena that its own theory could do most to explain. Other observations were dealt with by *ad hoc* elaborations, or they remained as outstanding problems for further research.
>
> At various times all these schools made significant contributions to the body of concepts, phenomena, and techniques from which Newton drew the first nearly uniformly accepted paradigm for physical optics. Any definition of the scientist that excludes at least the more creative

members of these various schools will exclude their modern successors as well. Those men were scientists. Yet anyone examining a survey of physical optics before Newton may well conclude that, though the field's practitioners were scientists, the net result of their activity was something less than science. Being able to take no common body of belief for granted, each writer on physical optics felt forced to build his field anew from its foundations. In doing so, his choice of supporting observation and experiment was relatively free, for there was no standard set of methods or of phenomena that every optical writer felt forced to employ and explain. Under these circumstances, the dialogue of the resulting books was often directed as much to the members of other schools as it was to nature. That pattern is not unfamiliar in a number of creative fields today, nor is it incompatible with significant discovery and invention. It is not, however, the pattern of development that physical optics acquired after Newton and that other natural sciences make familiar today. (1962, pp. 12–13)

Doubtless psychology is further along than optics was just prior to Newton. No serious theoretician in learning or perception is "forced to build his field anew from its foundations." Rather it is the case of his presenting alternative explanatory rubrics for a given domain of phenomena (as in learning theory of the two previous decades) or a case of his providing different formulations of what substantially amounts to a single paradigm (cf. Note 1.2). In either case, one might argue, the emphasis is upon pragmatics and representation. Rather than integrative paradigms commanding a consensus and cutting new pathways in a wilderness, we have new maps for traversing what, for the most part, is familiar terrain.

One might, of course, suggest that a plethora of paradigmettes betokens gamesmanship in the competition of paradigms. However, the gamesmanship among schools, i.e., the gamesmanship of alternative explanations, is not quite the kind which Kuhn visualizes for the competition among paradigms. According to Kuhn, paradigms signify consensus and the prevalence of world views. Anomalies arise as the result of the activities of normal science. It is emergent phenomena, so to speak, which prove refractory to the established paradigm and which invite the invention of new paradigms. Although the rules are not so clearly stipulated that we may invariably resolve the issue of competing paradigms by crucial experiments, there is a sense in which crucial experiment is a meaningful scientific exercise. It may present a clear indication as to where the new paradigm offers a sufficient explanation of the "anomalous" phenomenon and where the older paradigm fails.

Yet there is another feature which distinguishes the competition of paradigms from that of schools. Acceptance of a new paradigm invariably involves a paradigm which is more inclusive than the one it replaces. Hence there is continuity predicated of the history of paradigms not unlike that which finds expression in the correspondence principle of Niels Bohr. Ideally, the new paradigm replaces the old paradigm only if it is the case that the old paradigm is derivable under special limiting conditions within the new paradigm (as for example, celestial mechanics within relativistic mechanics, classical mechanics within quantum mechanics).

Historical continuity of paradigms points to the third feature of pre-paradigmatic science, the lack of systemic continuity in the development of theory. Psychology boasts of no historical continuity such as that we attribute to physics, chemistry, astronomy, or even genetics. Rather, it is almost as if we can tout an ironic advantage over these sciences. We in psychology can turn back to history in search of a paradigm, to the reading of a Herbart, or a James, or a Brentano. Where, in what science, does history offer such heuristic riches?

But there is a melancholy note to this lack of continuity. The heyday of hypothetico-deductive learning theory ("psychology's rococo period," as one able psychologist has put it) is in decline. Psychologists turned from theory construction to technology, simulation, and mathematical representation. (Hilgard's three editions of *Theories of Learning,* the last with Bower, chronicle the change.) Competition among learning theories epitomized the age of schools. Normal science abounded in support of paradigmettes, but no systemic paradigm emerged to integrate the schools. No paradigms emerged to synthesize those anomalies of mid-century learning theory: latent learning, discontinuity, one-trial learning. Consequently we find that creative scientists turned to the development of "paradigms" that were matters more of methodology and technology than of conceptual revolution.

Consider two of these "paradigms," the development of operant conditioning technology and the development of mathematical models. Treating Skinner (1950) as the spokesman of the operant conditioners, we observe that the move toward technology carries with it an antitheoretical bias. Emphasis is placed upon empirical laws expressed according to the now familiar paradigms of instrumental conditioning. To be sure, operant conditioning reflects a heuristic paradigm of sorts, a conceptual framework, but it is a framework that is taken as an experimental rubric for empirical observations and not one which affords us perspectives for integrating diverse fields of psychology, or even a diversity of empirical laws. The ascetic disavowal of hypothetical constructs betokens the return to Bacon and the inductive principle: we must first have laws before we can build a theory.

From the paradigmatic point of view this emphasis is in error. Without the conceptual framework, paradigm or paradigmette, we would have no perceptual rubric for observation. As Kuhn said of Bacon, natural histories and the recording of lawful relations produce a morass of information, useful perhaps as content for an encyclopedia, but not in providing an understanding of the connection between empirical laws.

As to the role mathematics plays in the tactical retreat from systematic learning theory, we must be more cautious. Mathematical models and mathematical learning theories have generated interesting normal science. As a result they serve the functions of paradigms. But here we must be careful not to confuse the syntactical with the semantical functions of a theory. Mathematics, as such, tells us nothing of experience, nothing of the material world. Syntactically, the mathematization of science simply aids us in the process of drawing precise inferences from the postulational structure of a theory. In a sense the mathematics of stimulus sampling theory, information processes, stochastic learning models, and signal detection theory provide very little in the way of new conceptual paradigms. Rather the mathematics generates precise vehicles for drawing conclusions within a theory, the hypothesis of which has already been established in broad conceptual terms. The mathematics may be useful in the construction of a paradigm, but the mathematical rubric itself is never the paradigm.

But again we must be careful, for in another sense a mathematical model, as a coherent set of equations, may generate a conceptual focus which is novel to a particular scientific discipline (Hesse, 1953, 1963). For example, information theory appropriates the equations of thermodynamics (Shannon and Weaver, 1949). In turn we see an analogy between the empirical relations of the parent application (mechanical communications) and the empirical relations of some other discipline (description of perception; cf. Miller, 1953; Attneave, 1959). Consequently, since the mathematical argument presents the logical map of structure and process, we look for analogies between the worlds of its primary and its derivative applications. Indeed, the mathematical argument may provide a science with a "new" paradigm, but that is only because the mathematical argument has been previously interpreted in another material domain.

One should not be categorical as to the priority or posteriority of mathematics in scientific creativity. However, I do think it justifiable to conclude that for psychology the stressing of mathematical reasoning and mathematical modeling has done much more for tidying up the statement of theories, hypotheses, and their deductive implications than it has for generating paradigms that are conceptually revolutionary. Mathematics has been most effectively applied where we already have explicit descriptions of behavior and of mediating processes in fairly traditional molds.

We should be reluctant to claim that the mathematization of learning theory or of perception, as such, has generated any conceptual innovations that have proved world-revolutionary. Rather what we have are new ways of representing what essentially are established paradigms. Mathematics may very well prove indispensable to future developments in theoretical psychology, but the mathematics itself is not sufficient for assuring paradigmatic evolution (cf. Note 1.3).

INSTRUMENTALISM

So what is the paradigmatic status of psychology? As yet we have little promise of a breakthrough such as that recent one in genetic coding, a breakthrough, incidentally, that has sent biologists out for refresher courses in biochemistry. For psychologists the spirit of the times remains essentially pragmatic, instrumentalist, conventionalist. Prediction more than enduring understanding dominates the philosophical credo. Accordingly, if we can build more explicit, more logically rigorous predictive models then we should not be overly concerned with how the intricacies of the black-box process are implemented. We need assess our theories only in terms of their workability, their scope, and perhaps their conceptual simplicity.

Psychology, to be sure, is not unique in adopting the tactics of conventionalism. For the most part, the details of the doctrine were spelled out initially for physical science by Duhem (1914) and Poincaré (1905, 1913). Moreover, the pragmatics of pure description were exhaustively surveyed in the analytic writings of Ernst Mach (1883). Therefore the conceptual history of physics, like that of psychology, can be conceived along conventionalistic lines. There is, of course, a difference; physics presents a continuity of development not to be found in psychology. New paradigmatic developments are always directed toward absorbing emergent anomalies into the deductive fabrics of increasingly comprehensive theories. In physics, the correspondence principle has been applied as a meaningful criterion for the evaluation of paradigms; in psychology the applications are nil. For physics the trend is always toward inclusiveness and unification, in spite of the fact that lasting conceptual frameworks and enduring truths are ever evasive.

We suggest here that the implications of instrumentalism have not been the same for the two sciences. In physics, instrumentalism has frequently been directed toward a more explicit detailing of physical structure. Hypothetical constructs as to structures and processes are implemented to explicate lawful relations among physical events. Although microrepresentations become increasingly abstract and decreasingly concrete, the abstraction as such is coerced by the impact of observation. Howbeit, a sense of realism pervades all; one, because in the microstructure rests the clue to an understanding of observable phenomena, and two, because the representation is just that, a representation of a real process, the abstract description being coerced by the inseparability of object and observation.

For psychology the case has been different. As often as not, instrumentalism has been defended by persons opposed to microreduction as a tactic for psychology (e.g., Kessen and Kimble, 1952; Kendler, 1952; Kaplan, 1964). As in physics, observable phenomena constitute the explananda, the subject matter of the discipline. However, by focusing upon molar events to the exclusion of detailed microreductive processes one tends ultimately to consider phenomena generatable alone by manipulations of the extrinsic environment. Anomalies, if such occur for a theory, are anomalies arising only in the molar settings in which experimentation and observation take place. Now manipulation of molar variables (e.g., environmental variables and constructive intervening variables) could conceivably prove a rich heuristic resource for an evolving behavioral science. But such, we observe, is hardly the case. Contrary to much popular opinion, focus upon molar behaviorism, as supported by instrumentalism, often proves to be a conservative influence.

Nonreductively oriented, instrumentalism takes two directions; one, that of radical empiricism; the other, that of theoretic constructionism. In the one case, the instrumental rubric is that which we formulate for the observation of behavior. Thus various performatory paradigms are imposed in learning and retention situations. What the investigator is concerned with is the development of a corpus of laws, with presumed generality. Skinnerian learning paradigms are a case in point. They are extended to cover a wide variety of subject and environmental manipulations. And from them a remarkable technology of learning has arisen. But as we noted before, what is missing programmatically is any systematic effort to integrate a diversity of laws into a comprehensive theory. Nor is there a curiosity as to why the laws are as they are.

The antitheoretical bias in psychology is nonetheless limited. In the case of constructionism we find instrumentalism in its pure pragmatic form. The investigator is free to invent theoretical constructions without regard to an ontological precept. Hence the emphasis is upon the intervening variables which are heuristically limited (when not conceived as real mediators). Or instrumentalism falls prey to hollow constructs which, though serving an inferential function, betoken neither sensible nor reductive hypotheses as such.

But there is another emphasis which we should not overlook. In the defense of pragmatism Abraham Kaplan (1964) refers to the "principle of autonomy of inquiry." This principle represents a "declaration of scientific independence," the freedom from preconceptions. But there is an important corollary: "the autonomy of the conceptual base." In this context Kaplan writes:

> To the principle of autonomy of inquiry we may add the corollary principle of *autonomy of the conceptual base*. A scientist *may* use whatever concepts he *can* use, whatever ones he finds useful in fact. The restriction to which he is subject is only that what he says be capable of being checked by experience, or alternatively, capable of providing some guidance to action. To be sure, the choice of one conceptual base rather than another may make more readily available the findings of other sciences. . . . The choice of locus is subject to the demand of empirical anchorage,

but not necessarily to that of physicalistic reduction. The "behavior" in "behavioral science" does not serve to limit the science's choice of conceptual base but only to emphasize its ultimate empiricism. (1964, p. 79)

Though certainly richer in the inferential fabric than Skinner's radical behaviorism and more heuristically conjectural, the instrumentalism of autonomous theoretic construction suffers on several counts:

One, an emphasis upon pragmatics and autonomy makes it difficult to prescribe criteria for assessing alternative theories. Crucial experiments are invariably meaningless since *ad hoc* adjustments can always be made within the disfavored theory. There is no sense of convergence of concepts, no sense of semantical or scientific realism.

Two, such an emphasis leads to a fractionation of the scientific discipline into special areas and special languages having limited generality. Thus instrumentalistic psychology becomes parochial through the quest for *ad hoc* theories, model making, and computational gimmickry.

Three, the license to be free with theoretical language results in a plethora of reformulations of a basic paradigm out of proportion to the contribution such formulations make to the articulation of the paradigm. The temptation is great to take as paradigmatic the reformulation of an established paradigm. Genuine paradigms are rare (cf. Note 1.2).

Four, the limited variety of possible material mediators is belied by the proliferation of hypothetical mediators that presumably require no interpretation in a material medium.

Five, emphasis upon autonomy and inventiveness, *per se,* removes psychology from checks and balances imposed by related disciplines.

And six, emphasis upon autonomy, to the exclusion of an idea of unified science, results in the fractionation of psychology into substantively different disciplines. Instrumentalism encourages methodological disagreements over the nature and scope of psychology as a scientific discipline. In large part, claims that psychological explanation is incompatible with the physicalistic tradition stem from a failure to distinguish subject matters which are amenable to treatment in the reductive hierarchy in science from representations that are not.

Now upon initial indulgence there is something refreshing about instrumentalism in science. For one thing it emphasizes inventiveness: it generates a certain spiritedness not to be found in the routines of fact-grubbing, it brings science into the self-conscious fold of creative disciplines. And for another thing, it affords succor to those of us who have been disenchanted by the fact that scientific theorizing is not the route to Platonic reals and enduring truth. Coupled with experimental inference and hypothesis testing, instrumentalism invites us to engage in creative work in which the rules and stipulations as to what is acceptable and what is good are more clearly defined than they are in any of the creative arts.

In brief, instrumentalism has freed us of the bonds, the indefensible tenets, and the embarrassments of scientific rationalism.

However, the freedom of instrumentalism, the freedom to be inventive, is more limited than many of us are inclined to think. The principle of limited variety (Keynes, 1921; Broad, 1918, 1920; Jeffreys, 1939) has application other than to probability domains. For example, if we consider black boxes in general as the template for theoretic enterprise, then there are really but three hypothetical possibilities: amplification, damping, and straight line transmission (Bunge, 1963). In perception, we may visualize realistic, constructual, or filter processors. In memory, decay, associative, or intrusive processors, and so on. It is just this principle of limited possibility that led Kenneth Craik and subsequent cyberneticists to construct material models as a source of hypothesis for psychology.

Conceding the point of limited variety, we must then reiterate that self-conscious instrumentalism encourages redundant formulations of substantially identical paradigms. Cognitive theory is a case in point (cf. Note 1.2). The basic paradigm presents a clear prospectus as to the limited possibility of cognitive systems. But rather than directing attention to the material realization of these limited possibilities, instrumentalism frequently leads to the seeking of different constructual expressions of the basic paradigm.

REDUCTIONISM

If we consider unqualified instrumentalism to be the freedom to invent constructs without regard to their possible reification, then we may consider reductionism to be a case of qualified instrumentalism. Reductionism embraces the precept of scientific realism, namely, there are fundamental conceptions, changing and evolving as they may be, which establish the communalities and interdependencies among all scientific disciplines. Thus, if we think of mediating constructs as being hypotheses concerning real processes, then possible reification of these constructs is visualizable for the related reductive discipline.

We may mention three implications of our treating reductionism as qualified instrumentalism.

One, it is assumed that hypothetical invention is limited by physical possibilities appropriate to the physical medium in which the mediating constructs of our focal science are set. The principle of limited variety implies that mediational process is ultimately to be restricted to mechanical possibilities as defined for the reductive discipline.

Two, heurism is in the direction of reduction. We are encouraged to hypothesize mediating processes which are consonant with the generic principles and processes of the reducing science.

Three, paradigmatic developments ought generally to be compatible with reductionism. Implicitly, a directedness resides as inherent within the collective disciplines of science. A sense of scientific realism emerges as we seek to establish consistency among our disciplines, by taking constructs of one science as possible existential hypotheses in another science.

Now reductionism, I submit, is a very plausible doctrine for behavioral science. It is just that it promises so much and delivers so little. Indeed, point three above prejudges the issue.

Does reductionism offer the prospect of distinguished paradigms? For the present it would be far too wistful of us to assert that it does. There are precedents, however. Just as statistical mechanics provided a paradigm for thermodynamics and just as biochemistry provided a paradigm for genetics so it is not inconceivable that psychoneurology will provide major paradigms for integrating our molar theories of learning, perception, and memory. Since the paradigm to prove this conjecture is yet to emerge, two alternatives remain open to us. We can speculate on the nature of possible paradigms, on the possible material realizations of psychological processes. Or, we can examine the possibility of reduction critically, to see if what may be cognitively plausible is also logically tenable.

For the most part, the chapters that follow concern this second matter. We shall address ourselves to the following questions:

If neurophysiology is to be a paradigmatic resource for psychology, can we be assured that there is no logical incompatibility as between the languages of the two disciplines? Is the phenomenological language of psychology uniquely nonreducible? Is there something about human computability and human problem-solving not realizable in principle by material, mechanical, or, for that matter, biomechanical systems? Does man, particularly, enjoy a privileged status so that he stands apart in controlling his actions? Do we witness in him a participation in events, a self-engagement not appropriately assigned to other organisms, to other events? These, after all, are the issues that must decide the fate of reductionism, not the argument over our proprietary rights to be inventive.

Finally, from our involvement in experience as subject as well as object, we observe that human behavior reflects a diversity of purposive tactics and vantages, the variety of which is captured in ordinary language. Our misgivings concerning reduction and the explanation of behavior arise in part from the questions we have as to how well expressions in the ordinary language of explanation can be accommodated by the scientific language. Methodological behaviorism is a hygienic, a refreshing, a heuristic doctrine, but it is a defensible one only if it can accommodate this complexity and richness of behavior. We can gain very little from the paradigms of neurophysiology, if in the process we cut the heart out of our curiosity.

NOTES

NOTE 1.1

Out of curiosity I asked a group of my colleagues to list what they considered to be paradigms in psychology. Two of Kuhn's phrases were used as reference: paradigms are represented as "changing world views" and as occasions "for a significant turning point" in the history of scientific knowledge. Responses ranged from the denial of any significant paradigm to a veritable catalog of recent developments in psychophysiology. The most frequently mentioned name was Freud, followed by Pavlov and Skinner, sometimes with only a hyphen separating the two. Galton, Binet, Thorndike were also mentioned frequently. As the reader will surmise, respondents favor the contributions in their own fields of interests.

The sample was small, the question too tersely phrased. But what sets the response off from that which we would anticipate for physics is its variety and lack of agreement. Psychology has not suffered for lack of theory-builders. What is missing in psychology is any well-formalized theory enjoying consensual status. First, there has been no pervasive logical formalism to capture consensual agreement akin to that found in physics. And second, attention to phenomenological schemata and laws encourages pluralistic theoretic formulations without regard to existential substructures. The pluralism is inseparable from the pragmatic roots; so long as we are concerned primarily with the prediction and control of molar behavior then psychology is prone to be inventive without the constrictions of microreduction.

NOTE 1.2

A case in point is that of contemporary cognitive theory. Do the theories of cognitive dissonance (Festinger, 1957), cognitive congruity (Osgood and Tannenbaum, 1955), and cognitive balance (Heider, 1946) represent distinguishable paradigms, or do they represent efforts in "normal science" to reformulate a traditional paradigm? This second alternative is not an implausible one.

Let us pick up the paradigm with the notion of apperception. The idea of cognitive relativism is an old one, at least as old as the bifurcation of epistemology: either empirical knowledge is generated from the *tabula rasa,* or it is generated in the context of transcendental apperception. In the one case we have naive realism and in the other, conceptual realism. However, as stated in such general terms the idea of cognitive relativism can hardly be taken as paradigmatic. For the paradigm theory we turn to the work of Johann Herbart (1834).

Human perception is not a straight-line recording of what is out there. It is a matter of perceiving-now against a backdrop of past experience. Emphasis is placed on assimilation, accommodation, harmony, equilibrium as between what is perceived and what constitutes the cognitive residue of prior experience. The act of perception is really one of apperceiving; the object as presented in the senses is perceptually assimilated according to the person's conceptual structures.

In the opening paragraph of his *Textbook in Psychology*, Herbart writes: "Concepts become forces when they resist one another. This resistance occurs when two or more opposed concepts encounter one another." (1834, p. 9) For "concepts" (Vorstellungen) read "ideas" and "representations." The problem of apperception is that of arriving at a concept from an instantaneous act of sense perception. Concepts resist one another, they stand in opposition to one another as contrasts. When the opposition is well established, they are said to be in equilibrium. But concepts not in opposition may occur together. In this case they become part of an associative complex. Thus apperception involves concept opposition, the blending or fusing of these concepts, and the formation of complexes. An apperceptive mass constructed of a network of oppositions, blendings, and complexes constitutes a stable cognitive structure by which the individual classifies and construes the perceived world.

This much constitutes the statics of perception, the aspects of "mediate reproduction." What of immediate reproduction, what of the "mechanics" of apperception? Here we touch upon familiar aspects of the paradigm. The apperceiving ego strives to maintain a unity in perception. It may handle a limited number of concepts in opposition; but with increasing numbers, some are suppressed below the threshold of consciousness. By immediate reproduction Herbart means reproductions which arise upon a resolution of conflicting concept forces (a "yielding of the hindrances").

> The ordinary case is that a concept gained by a new act of perception causes the old concept of the same or of a similiar object to rise into consciousness. This occurs when the concept furnished by the new act of perception presses back everything present in conciousness opposed to the old concept. . . . (1834, p. 70)

A concept furnished by an act of perception is the occasion for the rising of an old concept. The concepts now blend in the act of apperception according to a twofold process: vaulting and tapering. Let the new concept be P and the older concept be the schema Π. Then elements P^+ and Π^+ are common to both. But there are some elements in Π, say Π^-, that are not common to P. The vaulting (arching) principle then implies that properties Π^- are suppressed such that some common element Π^+, or some combination of such elements, arches forth to become the salient element in assimilating P to Π. Vaulting thereby implies assimilation to the salient elements. By tapering (or pointing) Herbart means that from a set of heterogeneous concepts those features are isolated which point toward a homogeneous concept, while discordant elements are suppressed.

In brief, the apperceptive system is one that operates under the constraints of similarities and contrasts. If disharmony arises among concepts or if concepts compete against one another, then an equilibrium is achieved either by blending the new and old by way of vaulting and tapering, or by outright suppression of discordant elements. Herbart's theory of apperception thus sets the pattern for the later reformulations: one, perception takes place in the context of an established conceptual rubric; two, apperception is a process of emphasis and editing; and three, apperception occurs in the affective context of harmony and disharmony.

The theory of apperception had considerable influence upon Herbart's contemporaries. Later it influenced Wundt and James in their respective treatments of perception. By the twentieth century it had become a historical note, but its substance had been absorbed into the conceptual language. A clear expression of this substance can be found in the Gestalt theory of perception (Koffka, 1935) and in Bartlett's schematic theory of reproduction.

For Gestalt phenomenology, the vehicle of apperception is the trace system. We distinguish between a geographic environment and the behavioral one, the latter being the phenomenological environment as constructed in apperception. Besides the classical Gestalt laws of perceptual construction (the autochthonous factors) we find functional laws operating in the context of apperception. Although Koffka does not use the term "apperception," kinship to the paradigm is especially evident in the description of reproduction. Rather than the apperceptive mass, we now have the collective of dynamic trace systems. The familiar forces are operative: normalizing (modification of reproduction toward the familiar), pointing (emphasizing of detail), and autonomous changes.

Clearly unique to Gestalt theory (as made explicit in the physiological idealism of Kohler) are the concepts of field dynamics. Apart from the excursion of some Gestaltists into speculative physiology the experimentalists agree that an apperceptive process is operative in reproduction whether it is a function of unique physical processes (Kohler, 1947), or of associative ones (Gibson, 1929; Carmichael, Hogan and Walter, 1932).

The idea of an associative, apperceptive mass is elaborated in Bartlett's classic work on remembering (Bartlett, 1932). Here the emphasis is upon mnemonic reproduction and recognition but the implications for perception or immediate reproduction are obvious. The focal concept is the *schema:*

> 'Schema' refers to an active organisation of past reactions, or of past experiences, which must always be supposed to be operating in any well-adapted organic response. That is, whenever there is any order or regularity of behaviour, a particular response is possible only because it is related to other similar responses which have been serially organised, yet which operate, not simply as individual members coming one after another, but as a unitary mass. Determination by schemata is the most fundamental of all the ways in which we can be influenced by reactions and experiences which occurred some

time in the past. All incoming impulses of a certain kind, or mode, go together to build up an active, organised setting: visual, auditory, various types of cutaneous impulses and the like, at a relatively low level; all the experiences connected by a common interest: in sport, in literature, history, art, science, philosophy and so on, on a higher level. There is not the slightest reason, however, to suppose that each set of incoming impulses, each new group of experiences persists as an isolated member of some passive patchwork. They have to be regarded as constituents of living, momentary settings belonging to the organism, or to whatever parts of the organism are concerned in making a response of a given kind, and not as a number of individual events somehow strung together and stored within the organism. (1932, p. 201)

Of perception Bartlett writes:

Perceptual process, in fact, involves two different, but related functions: a) that of the sensory pattern, which provides a physiological basis for perceiving; and b) that of another factor which constructs the sensory pattern into something having a significance which goes beyond its immediate sensory character. (1932, p. 188)

This latter function is a strictly psychological function that Bartlett describes as "effort after meaning."

For social psychology we pick up the paradigm again in a somewhat improbable place, in Walter Lippmann's early book, *Public Opinion* (1922). In this work he introduced the concept of stereotype into social science. Perception is not a case of faithful construction of what is out there, but the resultant of experiential input and what is already in the mind.

For the most part we do not first see and then define, we define first and then see. In the great blooming, buzzing confusion of the outer world we pick out what our culture has already defined for us, and we tend to perceive that which we have picked out in the form stereotyped for us by our culture. (1922, p. 61)

Here the emphasis is upon our cultural inheritance. But Lippmann goes further. For the integrity of the stereotype, the conservative influence in perception is maintained by means of exclusion and assimilation.

The Lippmann theory, a journalistic expression, was adopted by Katz and Braly (1935) in the formulation of a stereotypic theory of racial perception; the stereotype provides the perceptual frame of reference. The Gestalt and associationist traditions were amplified in a number of ways. In an eclectic defense of perceptual relativism Krech and Crutchfield (1948) emphasized the protective roles of similarity and contrast. Helson (1959) formulated the general theory of perceptual adaptation. Most significant perhaps was the tying in of values and affect to the apperceptive function. Hence the self-conscious identification with the "new look" in perception and the wealth of experiments and controversy stimulated by Bruner and Goodman (1947).

I am not arguing that these various efforts to improvise upon the paradigm of apperception are in any sense trivial or noninventive. Collectively they represent the extension of a paradigm. What deprives them of the status of reformulations, in the sense of Kuhn's usage, is that they are the works of individuals going their own way within a diffuse tradition rather than efforts to support and enhance a formal paradigm.

When we turn to the more recent expressions of the apperceptive paradigm, we do observe rather profound analogies in form and application. The terms dissonance, congruity, and balance could very well have come out of Herbart. A review of these recent theories would take us far afield, but, as Zajonc (1960) notes, theories of dissonance, congruity, and balance are all ramifications of a perceptual consistency paradigm. (See also McGuire, 1966.) The occasions for their systematic reformulations are ones seeking explicit predictive applications. They reflect a need to spell out the conditions and ramifications of perceptual stability in well-defined behavioral settings.

Finally, I should not wish to argue that these efforts of improvising on the basic paradigm are either stultifying, unimaginative, or redundant. But granting to apperception the status of a paradigm, they are a part of what Kuhn would call normal science. Lacking either the occasions or the incentive for development of new paradigms, social psychology has recently concentrated on refining and refurbishing the traditional paradigm of apperception.

For psychology, the multifarious ramifications of cognitive theory may very well suggest that Kuhn's essay on scientific revolution is a simplification—applicable perhaps to highly formalized theories such as physics, but not to the behavioral sciences. For the latter, may we not speak of paradigms within paradigms, rather than of normal science, or demeaningly of preparadigmatic science? Indeed, in light of the limited possibility of phenomenological paradigms, this might be the appropriate tactic.

There is, however, an unfortunate implication of this tactic. Because specific applications of the paradigm are practically unlimited, there would hardly be a limit to the paradigmatic formulations. The result is parochialism and schoolsmanship. In such a context any commanding paradigm would have to bear other than pragmatic credentials. Might we not then suggest reductive credentials?

As yet neurophysiology is not an indispensable part of the social psychology curriculum. It is wishful to most, depressing to some, to think it will ever be so. But for the basic paradigm of apperception the case is different. We do have neurophysiological speculations (e.g., Pitts and McCulloch, 1947; Hayek, 1952; Pribram, 1960; Rosenblatt, 1958, 1967) as to implementation of the apperceptive system. Should such speculations ever generate experimentally supported paradigms in neurophysiology then we would understand why the phenomenological laws of apperception are as they are. A paradigm within a paradigm in this reductive sense would then indeed become a paradigm in the Kuhn sense.

NOTE 1.3

In the introduction to *Mathematics and Psychology*, Miller writes:

"Mathematical psychology is more an attitude than a topic" (1964, p. 1). By and large this distinction sets mathematical psychology apart from mathematical physics. In physics the language of mathematics and the language of the science are all but inseparable; in psychology the mathematics presents itself as a tool for expressing and detailing substantive ideas for the most part independently developed. There are exceptions no doubt, as in psychophysics, just as there have been exceptions in physics. Newton's calculus was invented to afford explicit representation of acceleration and momentary change of states. Probability theory was developed initially for the description of random physical events. It is even a matter of conjecture that geometry was invented to facilitate geodetic survey. But in so many cases of application, the mathematics had been initially developed in purely abstract form. Gifted people then saw in the mathematics formal means of representing extant substantive ideas.

The question for us is whether mathematical argument itself constitutes a scientific paradigm. I think the answer must be that it does not. Only as substantively interpreted can a mathematical theory be considered a paradigm. This of course is not to undermine the importance of mathematics. The more complex our behavioral or neurophysiological descriptions are and the more complex the hypothetical structure of our theories, then the more rigorous must be our logical calculi. It is a truism to say that the language of a mature science must be a mathematical one.

It is interesting to note that in organizing his anthology of mathematical psychology, Miller (1964) adopts the categories of *discursive, normative, functional,* and *structural* uses. Discursive uses involve "mathematical notation as a convenient extension of natural language." Normative uses concern rational inferences, rational consequences. They relate to making rational decisions, drawing rational conclusions. Thus statistics and rational decision procedures fall in this purview. Functional uses concern the description of lawful relations, either statistical or determinate, between physical, psychophysical, and constructual variables. Structural uses of mathematics intend to map or represent behavioral processes and psychological characteristics isomorphically. Structure itself becomes a primitive concept to be explicated in the language of logical form and isomorphic relation.

Of these uses, perhaps only the structural is inseparably caught up in paradigmatic thinking. To conceive is to conceive structurally. Thus the examples Miller takes—the factor analytic structure of intelligence (Thurstone and Spearman), linguistic structure (Chomsky), the functional role of the human operator (Craik)—are at least token paradigms in which the mathematical and substantive components of the argument are inseparable.

Structural uses apart; however, what passes as mathematical psychology deals for the most part with normal science. The mathematical argument is frequently devoted to articulation and reformulation of established paradigms.

Reduction

A THESIS maintained throughout this work is that scientific explanations of behavior are in principle reducible to the more basic discipline of neurophysiology. Reduction implies that the theoretical, mediating constructs of one science are ultimately realizable in the language of an adjacent science. And as a scientific credo, reductionism incorporates (1) the idea of a hierarchy of sciences, and (2) the thesis of the pervasive unity of all scientific disciplines within the fabric of objectivism.

Contrary to the fears of provincials, the credo of reductionism does not require that we surrender our regional specialties. It does not require of psychologists, for example, that they become neurophysiologists. Rather, the theoretical constructs of one science become concrete hypotheses for another. Ultimately, the explication of the theoretical constructs of one science becomes the subject matter of another. Hence reduction leads to hyphenated disciplines—neurophysiology, biochemistry, molecular biology, social psychology. The proper calling of the theoretical scientist is not merely to construct theoretical explanations of phenomena that are phenomenologically unique to his own discipline, but to propose hypotheses that (1) are consonant with adjacent sciences and (2) to the extent those hypotheses are unique, provide a heuristic for those sciences.

MECHANICAL EXPLANATION

Since much of the argument that follows hinges upon the ideas of machines and simulators, let us introduce the idea of mechanical explanation. By mechanical explanation we should mean no more than the description and explanation of behavior in terms of a sequence of processes implemented by systems with objectifiable structural properties.

Doubtless the use of the terms "reductive" and "mechanical" interchangeably indicates a broadening of the base of classical mechanics.

Such a practice is not uncommon among writers who wish to emphasize that organismic behavior is to be understood in a causal nexus analogous to that of the physical sciences. Thus we may use "mechanical" in its generic sense, not because the organism resembles a simple machine composed of material masses and functioning under momenta exchange, but because in our behavioral descriptions we move systematically from input processes to output processes without recourse to supraphysical entities or to inexplicable lacunae in the chain. We need not, of course, rule out alternative descriptions of behavior, descriptions, for example, of valuing and of intending as seen from the focal vortex of the participating ego. But such alternative descriptions are complementary accounts of events taken from the internal rather than the external reference. As interesting as these intentional accounts may be in their own right, they prove refractory to scientific description and explanation, unless, of course, we attempt to reformulate them in the objective behavioral language of dispositions.

Historically, mechanics has dealt with the movements and interactions of physical bodies. Thus, Newtonian mechanics is able to explain a host of terrestial and celestial phenomena by laws of motion and gravitation in which state conditions are expressed in terms of time, space, and mass. Changes of states of the system (process functions) are expressible in differential equations, where, for example, if we can solve certain second-order differential equations, we can ascertain the effects of acceleration on the system. As Nagel (1961, p. 170) points out, the classical treatment of mechanics in terms of mass and force does not differ substantially from the more simplified discussions in terms of matter and motion.

It is obvious that our use of mechanics is more comprehensive than the description of catapults, pendulums, and billiard balls. We do not suggest that the organism is a "machine." Nor need we imply by "mechanism" and "mechanical" any metaphysical commitment concerning the nature of reality. A mechanical explanation is one which entails a specific type of schema for description and inference. In brief, it provides a logical rubric in which theoretical constructs are regarded as being interpretable in terms of explicit observational consequences. Thus, emphasis is placed upon mediating structure. If there is anything metaphysical about behavioral mechanics, it is the assumption that if any theoretical term is interpretable at all, it is interpretable as a physical process.

In developing a generic treatment of behavioral mechanics we need, however, to be more explicit. For a mechanical explanation we initially stipulate the following conditions.

(a) The operation of the behavioral system is contingent upon a finite set of definable resources.

(b) Conservation principles applicable to any and all physical systems must necessarily apply to the behavioral system.

(c) No behavioral process, no matter how fine, stands in physical isolation from antecedent events.

These propositions are somewhat obvious. Perhaps only the last calls for comment. The implication of this proposition is that it allows for no intrusive factors which are themselves not of a physical character. Thus, although psychophysical parallelism would not be ruled out in the description of behavioral action, we at no time propose that thought, as a nonphysical mental stuff, activates the nervous system. Indeed interaction between body and mind is already rendered suspect by virtue of the conservation principle.

In addition, we note the following properties and assumptions of mechanical explanations of behavior.

(1) Mediation between any two observable states in a behavioral or physical process is itself a physical process. This proposition has two immediate implications. One, it rules out intrusive nonphysical influences such as disembodied mind, thought, intuition, intention. And two, purely fictive mediators, calculational devices as it were, are proscribed in favor of processes and structural entities capable of implementing those processes.

(2) Physical structures and their associated process functions are sufficient to account for observable behavior. That is to say, the scientific explanation of any behavior, if realizable at all, is also realizable in terms of structures and process functions of the viable physical organism.

(3) Any behavioral language is translatable directly into terms of the physical language and any nonbehavioral, cognitive, or intentional language can be translated into the behavioral language by means of dispositional terms.

(4) The medium of any process function is a biophysical medium; for behavioral descriptions the appropriate process functions are interpreted in terms of the biophysical media of the organism.

Finally, let us take note of what is meant by a *process function*. In general, a process function is any functional relation that is utilized in the explanation of a behavioral phenomenon. To be more explicit, a process function involves (1) a description of the system which is the object of our observations, (2) a state description of that system at some specified time, and (3) a functional law that enables us to make an inference from our knowledge of (1) and (2) to the state of a system at some subsequent time (Bergmann, 1957). Such functional laws bear the aura of causal laws, but that connotation is not necessary to their explication. Our assumptions regarding mechanical explanation imply that between any two cognitively isolable state descriptions in the fine grain of time there is in principle a process function which ties the two together in an inferential bond. That is to say, taking Δt as small as we wish in the separation of state descriptions, then in principle we may bond the two without recourse to extra physical predicates or principles.

Obviously here the question of how fine we make the grain of time for specifying distinct state descriptions is partly methodological and partly technological. In classical mechanics the grain of time is made infinitesimally dense, and the functional relations are frequently articulated as differential equations of the second order. In our behavioral studies and intraorganismic theories, we seldom encounter such refined functional laws. Although fine grain laws are perhaps conceivable over continuous ranges of amplification and damping effects, we are often forced to plot quantal outputs against continuously graded inputs (e.g., classical psychophysics). However, regardless of such difficulties, we expect the observable flow of events to be describable in principle by process functions in the physical medium (cf. Note 2.1).

LOGIC OF SCIENTIFIC EXPLANATION

The request to offer an explanation is satisfied contextually by several types of response. Thus, the word "explanation" belongs to the common language, and acquires semantic precision only as we prescribe a context. I may provide an explanation by offering reasons for my actions. Thus the context is intentional, and it might be inappropriate to suggest that an explanation of my action is to be found in the schemata of stimulus and response. On other occasions, I may refer simply to analogy or to what is familiar. Thus to explain my malaise I may propose that I have been victimized by a virus. Both my malaise and my absenteeism are thereby explained. Or I may explain my poor reflex action at guarding the net in tennis as being due to my growing old. After all, aging is one of the catchall explainers for a host of familiar malfunctions. These are familiar refrains in explanatory discourse. Or then, out of my species-specific proclivity for first cause, I may comply with the explanatory request by providing a panoply of agents, of unexplained explainers. The ontogenetic quest may end eventually with the intonation of "God," or it may end much sooner with cryptic allusions to conspirators, to conservatives, the establishment, communists, the Mafia, and the like. From the Hyperion heights of first cause to paranoidal preoccupations with conspiratorial agents, explanations are offered by casual reference to personified forces.

Doubtless most of us learn to speak each of these languages in context, but none of the locutions satisfies the accepted formats of scientific explanation.

In scientific explanation we follow what is now the classical paradigm. In this scientific context, an event is explained if a statement of that event is shown to follow as a logical consequence of a complex of statements involving laws and other statements of the situational conditions. Thus, if a statement of the event to be explained is designated the *explanandum,* and the complex of statements which constitute the substantive aspects of the explanation is designated the *explanans,* a scientific explanation is one in which the explanandum is shown to be a logical consequence of the explanans.

There are, however, stringent requirements imposed upon the explanans. The laws are either postulational in character (such as the laws of motion, or the laws of one-trial bonding) or they are empirical (such as the laws of phenomenological thermodynamics, or the law of effect). And the situational factors are represented by statements of the relevant physical conditions prevailing in the given event context. It is obvious that a purely deductive requirement will not suffice. We can always adduce irrelevant or meaningless postulates sufficient to permit the deduction of the explanandum. Also, we note that from a set of inconsistent postulates we may deduce the statement of any event. The content of the explanans must therefore be empirically relevant, and for the lack of any more specific criteria, it must be scientifically relevant. That is to say, the content must be relevant to what we concertedly hold to be our scientific traditions.

Admittedly our scientific traditions are poorly defined. Tradition often proves misleading, and subsequently erroneous. The substantive emphasis, however, is upon empirical laws and upon integrating and relating laws through theoretical constructions. Empirical laws themselves are subject to explanation (such as Kepler's laws of planetary motion, the law of reinforcement, psychophysical law, and so on). In this case we seek their explanation as deductive consequences of a more synthetic theory. There are, in a word, no enduring first causes, no unexplained explainers. The kind of answers that may satisfy a metaphysical cosmologist or a theologian is not the kind of answers called for in scientific inquiries.

But note here that we have touched on two quite separable levels of explanation. On the one hand, we have explanation by instantiation, whereby an event is explained if within the logical rubric it can be shown to be an instance of a law. On the other hand, a law itself is subject to explanation in that we may show it to be a logical consequence of a theory that integrates several laws into a deductive system. Thus there are lawful explanations and there are theoretic explanations, both utilizing the deductive schemata of explanation.

In this context of scientific explanation, it is well to distinguish between the "phenomenological" state of a science and its more mature "theoretic" state (e.g., Bunge, 1967). That is, a science belongs to the former state when the substantive content of the explanatory rubric is constituted solely of phenomenological (empirical) laws. Thus we may have phenomenological thermodynamics contingent alone upon laws of gases *sans* any theoretical constructions relating these laws to molecular structure and kinematics. We may have a corpus of laws relating to forgetting and memory, without having a theory of memory as such. (Indeed, Skinner [1950] has argued that the aims of psychological science should be, for the present at least, to develop its phenomenological status.) However, a science achieves theoretic status when, by means of postulates and theoretical constructions, it is able to provide explanations of the empirical laws themselves. Hence the kinetic theory of gases provides theoretical constructs sufficient for us to deduce the significant laws of gases. Hebb's (1949) theoretical constructions of phase cells and reverberatory circuits enables him to deduce certain lawful generalizations of long term and short term memory.

To be sure, both levels of explanation may prove cognitively satisfying to the investigator. However, it is clear that theoretic synthesis enables us to pull initially unrelated laws together into a unified deductive schema. The role of theory, as it were, is to establish the communality between what initially are disparate subject matters. Thus, a synthetic theory provides means for understanding not only that a law holds, but indeed why it does hold (Sellars, 1961; Rozeboom, 1961).

No formal discussion of scientific explanation is intended here (cf. Note 2.2). The thesis embraced is the now classical one of hypothetico-deductive explanation. To be sure, there are other forms of explanation, but they are scientifically relevant only to the extent they are rendered amenable to deductive rubrics. However, there are two issues that we need briefly to consider. One is the issue of theoretical constructs, the other is the related issue of instrumentalism in scientific invention.

Theoretical constructs

The classical distinction between intervening variables and hypothetical constructs (MacCorquodale and Meehl, 1948) has now, it would appear, passed into the domain of the commonplace. Still there are purists who believe that intervening variables are strictly reducible to logical operations performed on observation statements. There is no question of ontological status or semantic reference, for the intervening variable postulates no entity, involves no referential thing. It is a convention, an operational definition or a logical construction, facilitating the generalizability of empirical laws. In a sense, then, intervening variables are not theoretical constructs at all, for according to their semantic status they are explicit definitions anchored to indubitable observation statements. Drive can be explicitly defined in terms of ecological conditions, maintenance schedules and the like, without pretentious reference to tissue needs or neural states. Hence the function of the intervening variable is to qualify laws of reinforcement, extinction, response rate, and the like. In a word, they provide an index for selecting appropriate members from a set of laws (Turner, 1967).

Hypothetical constructs, on the other hand, carry "surplus" meaning. Only partially interpreted in terms of observation, they provide hypotheses for a fuller articulation of mediating process functions. They are heuristic; they provide direction for intraorganismic researches. And according to the conceptual foundations of observation, they provide the reference for our literally visualizing data as factual entities. Thus the strong argument for hypothetical constructions is the heuristic one of developing the parent theory, say psychology, in such a way as to provide direction to the related reductive discipline of neurophysiology.

Instrumentalism

Although hypothetical constructs have usually carried the connotation of reductive hypothesis, this need not be so. Theorists committed to instrumentalism and pragmatic tactics have often emphasized that reductionism is too restrictive, if not downright stultifying (e.g., Kessen and Kimble, 1952; Kendler, 1952; and Kendler and Kendler, 1962). This is a defensible argument. For psychology, premature speculation in neurophysiology is as much in the realm of "as if" as any apparatus of purely symbolic mediators or cognitive functions. Yet one should not lose the sense of realism. Where mediating processes are predicated, the organism itself must be the medium. A commitment to mechanical and reductive explanation is an article of assurance that wherever a mediating process is fully articulable, it should be compatible with corresponding mechanical and reductive realizations. One argues not that cognitive theorists and person-oriented theorists are wrong or are in the limbo of scientific respectability, but only that their theoretical constructs should be logically compatible with reduction.

There is, of course, the problem of alternative theories and alternative representations. Having lost the faith in the ideal of crucial experiments, we seek other criteria for the evaluation of theories—criteria like simplicity, comprehensiveness, heurism. Yet even the right to pragmatic license should not repudiate reductionism. Just as there need be nothing logically incompatible between molar and molecular behavioral descriptions, so there need be nothing incompatible between synaptic and cognitive models of neural function. The reductive criteria for the evaluation of theory specifies only that once the mediating process is fully articulated then its description must be compatible with a realization in the language of neurophysiology. If intention, insight, transference, inhibition, expectancy, r_g and s_g are articulable process constructions, then their viability will be contingent not alone upon their confirmational implications but also upon their providing a conceptual reference to reductive realization.

Too often the argument against reductionism rests on the premise that the psychologist need not concern himself with neurophysiological descriptions. And indeed he need not. According to the thesis defended here, there is a hierarchy of sciences such that the higher order (reduced) science should provide a heuristic for the lower order (reducing) science. Yet the inventiveness of the psychologist should not be circumscribed either by his concern for, or knowledge of, neurophysiology. One can agree with Deutsch (1960), that in psychological theorizing, one need only be concerned with structural descriptions of behavioral systems and not with their embodiments in neurophysiology. But this is quite another matter than that of suggesting there is a logical incompatibility between psychological descriptions and those of neurophysiology (Jessor, 1958). It is this point which I wish to emphasize: there is no logical incompatibility between psychological explanation and neurophysiological reduction.

We need also to emphasize the heuristic implication of the reductive thesis, not from the lower to the higher discipline, but just the reverse. However, the proposition that in the long term neurophysiology will decide the mediational issue is, at best, a truism. For the psychologist, the neurophysiology is yet to be done. And he can leave it at that. But he is arguing for a radical revision of our conception of scientific explanation if he maintains that psychology is somehow logically differentiable from the hard sciences.[1]

PARADIGMS OF REDUCTION

"Reductionism" is a term most of us understand without the help of logical exegesis. One science is reducible to another if the explanatory concepts of the one are expressible in the language of the other. The reducing science is generally considered to be more basic in the sense that it purports to study the material medium in which the hypothetical constructs of the reduced science portend reification. Thus sociology reduces to psychology, psychology to physiology, physiology to biochemistry, and so on. The demarcations between disciplines are not always clear, to be sure. They reflect the traditional academic departmentalizations of scientific pursuits as much as they do profound substantive differences in subject matters. Therefore, it is not at all surprising that scientific creativity is frequently to be found at the interface of related disciplines where the hypothesis of one level of theory provides conceptual, fact-finding direction for another.

In perspective, we find one science is reducible to another if logical equivalencies can be established between the exhaustive sets of concepts of the two sciences (Woodger, 1952, and Nagel, 1949, 1961); or if one science (the reducing one) can be regarded as a subtheory of the other (Bunge, 1967); or if the theories of two related disciplines provide alternative explanations for what are phenomenologically the same set of observations (Kemeny and Oppenheim, 1956). The defense of such perspectives

[1] I have reviewed elsewhere the methodological and phenomenological argument against reductionism (Turner, 1967). One can hardly quarrel with methodological rejections, since these deal with the tactics of research and not of explanation. The only telling argument against reductionism is that of putative logical incompatibility between psychological explanation and reduction. Subsequent chapters are directed to this issue.

implies one of two commitments; reduction is to be defended either on methodological or on ontological grounds.

Methodologically, reduction is regarded as instrumental in the evaluation of theoretical constructs. Assuming methodological reduction, one selects theoretical constructs which offer a potential for reification in the reducing science. There is an arbitrary commitment to the idea of the unity of science; the agreement is contractual, so to speak, such that in the competition of instrumental ideas, those are retained which are subject to reductive affirmation.

However, instrumentalism is a two-edged weapon. Granting the emergence of higher order constructs and the higher order factual language, nothing logically precludes our articulating a theory in a language unique to the given discipline (e.g., Woodger, 1952; Kessen and Kimble, 1952; Kendler and Kendler, 1962). In fact, if the thesis of reduction is defensible alone on methodological grounds, then we should indeed be pressed to demonstrate that reductive programs are more fruitful for the given science than purely instrumental ones which are assessed on their explanatory and predictive utility.

Ontological reduction, on the other hand, suggests that the foundations of a scientific realism are embedded in the language of science as such. Scientific disciplines do not develop in isolation. Although the concepts of a "higher" order discipline are emergent in the sense of their being unique to that discipline, they are tied to an observational and factual language common to "lower" order disciplines.[2] Thus in psychology we may develop cognitive concepts for mediating between the variables of input and output. However, the object languages of physics and physiology are necessary to the articulation of the theory. Otherwise cognitive organization, selectivity, sensing, and so on, would have little relevance in the environmental and intraorganismic setting. Moreover, the hypothetical constructs of a given science are introduced in settings that are clearly mediational. Thus between the reduced and the reducing science, there is always the relation of macro and microphenomena. The questions we ask of mediational processes are always the queries that are answerable in terms of microreduction.

In large part then, the relevance of microreduction rests in the language common to all sciences, the physical language. Conceptually, the traditions of physical sciences determine our factual probes. Just as we are epistemologically limited by our sensory-perceptual apparatus, so are we factually limited by our factual potentialities. Method alone does not dictate our seeking reductive explanations, but the broad scope of our scien-

---

[2] "Higher" here means more complex. The designation of orders is arbitrary. Whether the hierarchy of sciences is taken from physics up or physics down is a matter of expositional preference. The present designation is just the reverse of that used in an earlier work by the author (Turner, 1967).

tific tradition does coalesce to produce a rare sense of unity, the realization that all scientists share in a common discipline and a definable hierarchy of phenomena. Yet what is perhaps more significant is the realization that there is something natural about reduction. In an indubitable sense, mediation just is microreductive. One can offer higher order explanations by recourse to instantiation of phenomenological laws unique to the given discipline. However, curiosity does not rest here. We seek lower order explanations through the invention of hypothetical constructs, and subsidiary hypotheses (Bunge, 1967) in principle reifiable as microreductions. These lower order explanations provide the basis for our understanding why phenomenological laws do in fact serve as explainers (Sellars, 1961).

Woodger-Nagel Paradigm

This paradigm rests on our establishing equivalencies between the explanatory concepts and hypotheses of one science with predicates and concepts of another. Let us visualize two systematic theories in which the higher order discipline T_2 is to be reduced to a lower order discipline T_1. Thus T_2 is secondary to T_1 and T_1 is primary to T_2. Since T_1 and T_2 are members of a common scientific tradition stressing logic and basic observation, many properties and propositional forms will be common to the two disciplines. However, T_2 is higher order with respect to T_1, in that it includes certain predicative expressions which are emergent so far as concerns T_1. This is emergence purely in the epistemic sense; for in the incipient development of T_2, the predicative expressions which are apparently unique to T_2 designate concepts and perceptual constructions which are molar relative to T_1. Hence behavioral intentions are more molar than reflexes; and, as between psychology and, say, neurophysiology, intentional constructions are emergent.

Let us now visualize the following sets of predicates:

$a, b, c, \ldots \ldots$ those belonging to the language common to all sciences
$A, B, C, \ldots \ldots$ those which are alone common to T_2 and T_1
$\mathcal{A}, \mathcal{B}, \mathcal{C}, \ldots \ldots$ those unique to T_2

Thus for the sets of predicates assignable to the two sciences we have

T_1: $a, b, c, \ldots$; $A, B, C, \ldots$
T_2: $a, b, c, \ldots$; $A, B, C, \ldots$; $\mathcal{A}, \mathcal{B}, \mathcal{C}, \ldots$

First we note that the vocabulary of T_1 is a subset of T_2, and if T_2 is reducible to T_1, it is reducible to a subtheory within itself. Thus the reduction represents a simplification of the explanatory concepts in the secondary theory. Second, there are two formal requirements for successful reduction: one proposes the *connectibility* of theoretical concepts and terms in the two sciences; the other proposes that all theorems in T_2 should in fact be *derivable* from postulates, primitive predicative expressions, and observational statements in the primary science T_1 (Nagel, 1961).

At first glance it would seem that these two requirements are redundant. That, however, is not the case. Connectibility assures similarity in structure, an isomorphic mapping, as between the explanatory concepts of T_2 and T_1. Derivability merely assures that T_2 and T_1 offer corresponding explanations over the same domain of experimental hypotheses. Derivability is the looser condition, so to speak, for it allows for alternative theoretical explanations of a common set of facts. Connectibility assures isomorphic theoretical structure. Thus, for strict reduction, connectibility is the focal issue.

Now, this isomorphism of theoretical structure is assured if every propositional expression in T_2 not in T_1 can be satisfied in T_1 by biconditional constructions. Thus let $\mathcal{A}x$ be a propositional expression in T_2 but not in T_1. Then connectibility is assured if for every such expression

$$(x)\,\mathcal{A}x \equiv Px$$
$$Px \equiv (x, a, b, c, \ldots, A, B, C, \ldots)$$

That is to say, every predicate in T_2 not in T_1 is constructible from the set of predicates in T_1 (Woodger, 1952).

There are three tactics for establishing these biconditionals. One, $\mathcal{A}$ and P may be regarded as synonymous, thus the biconditional is a matter of logical equivalence. Two, the connection between the two may be purely conventional, so that reduction is shaped by a kind of Procrustean bias. And three, and most important heuristically, the two may be connected empirically. This would be the case, for example, if say a concept of reflex reserve were connected empirically with physiological mechanisms of long term memory.

It must be emphasized that a rigid adherence to this reductive paradigm is more an ideal, and perhaps a crippling one at that, than a program of directed research. Even in the case of phenomenological thermodynamics (the familiar paradigm case, Nagel, 1961), certain ergodic propositions concerning closed systems cannot be resolved by the reduction of thermodynamics to statistical mechanics (e.g., see Bunge, 1967, p. 43).

Bunge Paradigm

Although it is doubtful that Mario Bunge (1967) intended to construct a paradigm of reduction as such, his treatment of the subject represents a tactical improvement over the strict logical format of Woodger and Nagel. In a word, Bunge embraces the ontological notion that reduction gives substantive direction to theory and research, without at the same time holding to the ideals of exhaustive connectibility and derivability. He structures his account of reduction on a distinction between phenomenological explanation and theoretic explanation, between lawful explanation and "interpretive explanation by representational theory."

By lawful or "subsumptive" explanation, he alludes to the practice of explaining an event by subsuming it under a phenomenological law. In more familiar terms this is simply a matter of explanation by instantiation. Although subsumptive explanation satisfies the logical paradigm of explanation (the explanans, therefore the explanandum) the explanation is, in a sense, an empty one. The law stipulates some functional relation between properties (e.g., distance of free fall and time, pressure and temperature), but the functional relation is not explained. Thus the event is explained by an unexplained law, such that all events like the observed event have, according to the law, just the phenomenal properties they do have. Why does a given response occur in the given situation? Because responses of the given type tend to occur in all situations like the given situation (e.g., according to the reinforcement paradigm). To take a superficial tack, suppose we are to explain a unique behavioral relation $sRr;$ then we explain the s–r relation if we can find a class of similar events, all of which display the property as expressed in sRr.

A more sophisticated level of explanation occurs when we can intercorrelate laws in a nomological net. Here subsidiary hypotheses (intervening variables) are interjected to set up families of laws in a way that facilitates the application of specific basic laws. Thus, for example, we may have laws interrelating primary and secondary reinforcement such that specific extinction rates are explained in the context of specified stimulus situations. Or, to take another example, we may introduce motivational states to accommodate selective application of laws of extinction.

But even here the formulation of nomological nets, sophisticated as they may be, does not eventuate in a representational theory yielding interpretive explanation. The goal of interpretive explanation is to articulate the *modus operandi* of the referents of theoretical constructs. Interpretive explanations are forthcoming when the theoretical constructs of a secondary theory are reduced to predicative expressions in the primary science. Thus, from the nomological net interrelating primary and secondary reinforcement and implicit stimuli and responses, we proceed to the reductive detailing of mechanisms sufficient to implement the theoretic principles.

There is a sense of scientific realism which pervades this interpretive approach—one, because it is the nature of scientific quest to seek "deeper" understanding as to why phenomenological laws hold; and two, because, wherever subsidiary hypotheses are introduced, we attempt to visualize them as referring to mediational processes, themselves subject to scientific understanding and perhaps to mechanical description.

In this context Bunge mounts an attack on the theses of radical descriptivism and conventionalism. Bunge remarks that radical descriptivism is "preposterous." First, without theory we would not know the what and how of description; an exhaustive recording of "all" the data would be a meaningless jumble. And second, the doctrine of conventionalism and its cousin black-boxism essentially propose that "science cannot represent reality." There are lacunae, as it were, to be filled in by black-boxes, undetailed except for their role in bridging the connection between input and output. Bunge maintains that black-boxes are empty mediators, instrumental afterthoughts for qualifying input-output contingencies. Thus, blackbox tactics are little better than phenomenological explanations. They offer no models for realizing the mediating linkages in mechanical terms. They offer no heuristic for scientific research. And they offer no explanation at all as to why a phenomenological law does hold.

As an example of the restrictive nature of descriptivism, Bunge mentions the discovery (1821) by Seebeck of the relation between the heating of a circuit and its magnetization. Electric current was not then known to be the mediator; hence the phenomenological law is simply: "The heating of a circuit containing the different metals is accompanied by the magnetization of the circuit." It was only when the connection between electric current and magnetic field was introduced that we began to understand that magnetism is not simply a function of heat. Or, to take an example closer to home, our understanding of kinesthesis and its role in motor control was limited indeed until we succeeded in interpolating the structures of neural feedback.

Turning to social phenomena, Bunge writes:

> No social fact, let alone a social function, is ever observed by a theoretically unprejudiced scientist. All we do observe is a few active individuals and crowds; the rest is conjectured or inferred. An adequate description of a social institution requires a handful of ideas just as an adequate description of a cloud requires a handful of theories; and the more representational the theories used for the description the more profound the latter will be (1967, pp. 57–58).

How empty conventional constructs can facilitate research or new factual conceptualizations is not clear. This is the weakness of the most inventive of instrumentalisms. On the other hand, a theoretical construct that hypothesizes a physical mediator does define for us a prospectus for experimental search. Since the medium of process functions is the physical medium then there is some prospect for factual reification.

Kemeny-Oppenheim Paradigm

Whereas Bunge's treatment of reductionism focuses essentially on the condition of connectibility, an earlier treatment by Kemeny and Oppenheim (1956) exploits the condition of derivability. And whereas Nagel would argue that the condition of connectibility is necessary but not sufficient to assure derivability, Kemeny and Oppenheim would argue just the reverse. Connectibility assures reduction, but it is not necessary for it. Thus reduction is achieved when alternative disciplines in the hierarchy of sciences are sufficient to derive a common set of theorems.

Let us again assume two disciplines T_2 and T_1, with T_1 at least as well systematized as T_2. Then T_2 is reducible to T_1 over a set of observations O, if

(1) Vocabulary of T_2 contains terms not in vocabulary of T_1.

(2) Any part of O explainable by T_2 is explainable by T_1.

(3) T_1 is at least as well systematized as T_2.

Furthermore T_2 is internally reducible to T_1 if

(3') The vocabulary of T_1 is a subset of the vocabulary of T_2.

Note that Kemeny and Oppenheim build upon the arguments of Woodger and Nagel. However, propositions (1), (2), and (3') require that reduction is epistemologically embedded in the secondary science T_2, whereas (1), (2), and (3) assure us only that T_2 and T_1 offer alternative theoretical rubrics for explaining observations in the set, O. Heuristically, (1), (2), (3) is the weaker set of propositions. It specifies only that reduction is a possibility, not that it is particularly germane to the development of T_2.

Feyerabend–Shaffner Paradigm

Following Shaffner (1967) we turn now to an evolutionary paradigm of reduction. According to Feyerabend (1962, 1965), formal paradigms of reduction are indefensible for two reasons: one, reductive synthesis of two theories is impossible without imposing methodological and empirical restrictions on the domains of the two theories; and two, the meanings of observational terms are not invariant in the context of the reductive program. These are important criticisms. We must amplify upon them if we are to appreciate Shaffner's attempt to bring Feyerabend's critical analysis into the fold of the reductionist paradigms.

First, let us consider what Feyerabend (1962) calls a pragmatic theory of observation. In substance this theory states that the meaning of a set of observations is to be found in the theoretic context in which those observations are embedded. It follows that we must distinguish between the raw data of observation (e.g., pointer readings) and their factual interpretation in the context of a given theory. Thus the same raw data of observation may, in the context of two different theories, yield disparate factual interpretations. The facts, so to speak, will not decide an experimental issue, since in their respective interpretive formats, the "same" raw data will support different theoretic hypotheses. The reason for this is that there is always an openness of meaning in factual accounts of data: one, the theory itself is generally in a state of incompleteness, i.e., refinements and innovations are always in order; and two, all observations are subject to errors of measurement, thus allowing for flexibility in the interpretation of data.

The gist of these comments underscores the proposition that the scientific meanings of basic data are not invariant. This being the case, the deductive paradigms of explanation and reduction become suspect. First, consider explanation. Assume that novel or anomalous events arise and call for explanation. Generally in such cases we either attempt to deduce the appropriate observational statements within the formal language of the finished theory, or we seek to modify the theory so as to make the anomalous events logically compatible with the theory. However, it is seldom, if ever, the case that we have a finished theory. The act of explanation invariably involves our modifying the theory and hence our interpretation of the observational terms. The deductive paradigm of explanation serves only to codify the routine of scientific inference within relatively well-developed theories; it provides neither insight nor method on how to proceed in the development of the scientific theory. The resolution of an explanatory problem comes in giving an observation a factual interpretation in the modified theory.

It is of interest that both Nagel (1961) and Feyerabend (1962) allude to the fact that the phenomenal meaning of terrestrial data underwent a change when the mechanics of Galileo were reinterpreted so to be included in those of Newton. For Nagel, this reinterpretation, or reduction, appears to be hardly more than the development of a comprehensive theory of mechanics. But for Feyerabend, it suggests that attempts to extend the generality of mechanics called for modifications in the theory requiring a reinterpretation of the data, the reinterpretation being incompatible with the prior state of the theory. As an example from psychology, consider the state of reinforcement theory at the time latent learning phenomena were anomalous to the theory. Initially, reinforcement theorists responded either by questioning experimental design, or by looking for as yet unspecified reinforcers rendering the data compatible with theory. However, as anomalous experimental results persisted, it became incumbent on the theorists to modify the theory by interposing mediational constructs which preserved the major reinforcement postulates of the theory. And as the theory was modified, the data of latent learning experiments were structured in a different interpretive frame. The meanings of observational terms changed. For Hull (1952), for example, response defined initially in terms of reinforcement contingency was subsequently modified in terms of incentive. Accordingly, it would appear that a simple Hempel-Oppenheim paradigm of explanation fails to account for either the psychological or epistemic factors of scientific invention.

But a critique of deductivist paradigms of explanation is not the issue. We need to consider reduction as such. Doctrinaire reductionism is at fault, because in initially treating the observation language as having meaning invariant, it proposes that a theory T_2 and a theory T_1 in the reductive hierarchy must be mutually consistent. According to Feyerabend this requirement of consistency is stultifying. Both the deductivist paradigm of explanation and the consistency requirement fail because *"one and the same set of observational data is compatible with very different and mutually inconsistent theories"* (1962, p. 48). The observational data of the two theories may be the same, but the "facts" differ. Emphasis upon consistency and reducibility necessarily places a restriction upon scientific creativity, and hence upon the potential for factual interpretation.

Shaffner reformulates Feyerabend's critique of deductivism into a dynamic, as opposed to static, reductive paradigm. Let T_2 again be the secondary science with at least one predicative expression not to be found in T_1. Then a theory T_2 can be "explained" by or reduced to T_1 in a "nonformal sense" if T_1 will yield experimentally verifiable predictions (i.e., deductive consequences) which are "very close" (numerically) to the predictions of T_2. Moreover, these predictions of T_1 should serve as a corrective of T_2 in that they should improve upon the corresponding predictions of T_2. And they should point to essential modifications of the theoretical variables in T_2.

It is not clear that Feyerabend would agree to the reformulation of his argument as a reductive paradigm. He insists that competition among nonconsistent theories provides a potential for the growth of scientific realism not to be found in our commitment to invariance in the observation language. What Shaffner's interpretation does point out, however, is the heuristic relation between the primary and the secondary science. The primary science becomes a source of hypotheses; for the secondary science, it generates hypotheses now expressible in the language of the secondary science.

Thus Shaffner is led to formulate a "general reduction paradigm." Reduction is achieved if, and only if:

(1) All predicative expressions in the corrected secondary theory T_2' are to be found in T_1 and all (logical) constructions of predicates in T_2' can be set up in one-to-one correspondence with constructions of predicates in T_1 (i.e., empirical support of identity of reference);

(2) contingent upon (1) T_2' is derivable from T_1;

(3) T_2' is a corrective of T_2;

(4) T_1 should "explain" T_2' in the sense of providing predictions very close to those of T_2'; and

(5) there should be strong positive analogy between T_2' and T_2.

Emphasis here is to be placed on the heuristic function of the reducing science. For example, in genetics the constructs of genetic coding and trait determination should provide experimental hypotheses in biochemistry which, upon verification, lead to the modification of the language of genetic determination in the new molecular genetics. Or in psychology, verification of hypotheses concerning arousal and awareness in neurophysiology should lead to modification of the treatment of functional awareness in psychological theory.

A Heuristic Paradigm of Reduction

The Shaffner-Feyerabend paradigm of reduction represents a clear improvement over what appears to be the static implications of earlier paradigms.[3]

But where I believe it to be deficient is in the directional implications of the heuristic function. According to Shaffner and Feyerabend, it would appear that the seed and potential for theoretic modification rest primarily in the impact that the primary science has upon the meaning and structure of the secondary science. Thus our efforts at reduction would seem to imply a rather passive reliance upon the state and development of the primary science. In terms of maturity we proceed up the hierarchical ladder of the sciences. And although each secondary science proceeds initially in its own formulation of premises and predicates, its mature modifications occur as a function of reductive undertakings.

Doubtless some notable modifications of theory have followed this paradigm (Shaffner, 1967a, b). However it is essential that we modify the dynamic paradigm of reduction to be bidirectional. As often as not, it is the secondary science which serves a heuristic function with respect to the primary science. Its hypotheses may provide the conceptual vehicle for modifying the premise and the factual interpretation of the primary science. It is not so much the case that the secondary science relies upon the mature state of the primary science as it is that the primary science requires the heuristic stimulation of a sophisticated secondary science. Thus, biochemistry looks to biology, neurophysiology looks to psychology, and so on; not, of course, for empirical support, but for hypotheses as to theoretical constructs which might lead to empirically verifiable hypotheses in their own respective domains.

Let us now adopt a modified paradigm of reduction.

(1) Let T_2 have the set of predicative expressions

$$q_1, q_2, \ldots, q_n, \ldots$$

and T_1 have the set

$$p_1, p_2, \ldots, p_m, \ldots$$

with the set $\{p_i\}$ being a possible subset of $q_1, q_2, \ldots, q_n, \ldots$.

(2) There is at least one complex expression generated from the predicates of T_2 not included in the predicates of T_1.

---

[3] This is somewhat unfair to Nagel, since he describes in detail the changes of meaning in the concept temperature which were due to the reduction of thermodynamics to statistical mechanics (Nagel, 1961).

(3) Neither T_2 nor T_1 are complete, formal systems; hence the openness concerning the sets of predicative expressions in the two theories.

(4) Let Hq_j be a construct (logical or hypothetical) generatable in T_2; let Hp_i be a construct generatable in T_1.

Then a reduction of T_2 to T_1 occurs if, and only if, for every Hq_j in T_2 there is a substitutable Hp_i in T_1, that is,

$$Hq_j \equiv Hp_i$$

where Hp_i is generated by suitable modifications or extensions of the set of predicates in T_1.

Now, since the set of predicates $q_1, \ldots, q_n, \ldots$ is an open set, nothing precludes the modification and augmentation of this set on the occasion of heuristic interchange between T_2 and T_1. Hence the modified theory may be akin to T_2' as prescribed by the Feyerabend-Shaffner paradigm. But note that $p_1, \ldots, p_m, \ldots$ is also an open set. Hence nothing prohibits the augmentation of this set of predicates in the primary science by our theoretical and experimental efforts to establish the equivalence between Hq_j and Hp_i. That is to say, a synthetic reduction may be achieved by our first stipulating a construct in T_2, and in such a way that it leads to a modification of T_1 sufficient to establish the empirical equivalence between Hq_j and Hp_i.

It is significant that both theories, T_2 and T_1, are incomplete. The predicative expressions in T_1 which also are a subset of T_2 are in a sense the same for the two sciences. They constitute the partially interpreted data rubrics of the two sciences. Variance in meaning arises, however, when we put constructions on the data; that is to say, although Hq_j and Hp_i may be empirically equivalent expressions, their meanings are contextually bound to their respective theories. What ties them together is the factor of heuristic interdependence. Since the reductive program calls for equivalent mappings of occurrences and structures as interpreted in two theoretic domains, the formulation of an Hq_j in T_2 but uninterpreted in T_1, leads to an extension of the predicates and constructs in T_1 in such a way as to accommodate the missing interpretation.[4]

---

[4] I believe the notion of the openness in the predicative expressions, both for the reduced and reducing science, meets two objections to reductionism mentioned by Beloff (1965). From the logical point of view strict operational reductions are rejected on the grounds that higher-order concepts do not entail any conjunction or disjunction of lower-order concepts, nor conversely can any set of lower-order concepts be rendered equivalent to a higher-order concept. Perhaps so, but this is a telling argument only if we consider the sets of predicative expressions of the higher and lower order disciplines closed ones. From the epistemological point of view, it has been argued that molar phenomena cannot be understood solely in terms of molecular constituents since the element of "tacit inference" is indispensable to the understanding of the molar events (Polanyi, 1962). But note that tacit inference is a psychological agent of understanding, and that is not at all at issue. And the openness of predicative expressions will allow for any emergent phenomena that are presum-

It should be obvious from this that we do not mean to assert that T_2 and T_1 are identical, or that T_2 should in any event be an expansion of T_1. Rather it is the case that reduction provides epistemic guidance. The constructions of T_2 should be such that they provide heuristic direction in T_1. Then new constructs in T_1 will be reductively significant for T_2 yet will remain uniquely interpretable and meaningful within T_1. It is not the case that one science should become another, or that meaning invariance should exist as between factual interpretations of the data, but rather that the attempted reduction should give direction to both disciplines within their respective domains. It is in this context that we propose reductionism as a criterion for selecting among alternative theories. We do not say select T_2 such that it reduces to T_1, but that between two theoretical alternatives in the domain of T_2 select that alternative which proves most heuristically fruitful in the development of T_1. Similarly, it is defensible to say that between alternative conceptions in the domain of T_1, that alternative will be selected which proves most fruitful to the development of T_2.

According to our heuristic paradigm of reduction, the predicate set $\{p_i\}$ in T_1 is a subset of predicates in T_2. Thus, although there may be meaning variance in the language common to both theories, as for example, with terms such as "stimulus" and "inhibition," the meaning of a term in T_2 should be compatible with the meaning of the terms and constructs in T_1.

Finally, in this context, the argument that psychologists can proceed to develop mechanical descriptions and explanations independently of realizing their descriptions in biological terms can be an entirely defensible one (e.g., Deutsch, 1960), but only if the mechanics of behavioral description are compatible with those of the machinery of the body. There is a sense in which alternative descriptions are descriptions of the same thing, the basic uninterpreted data. Reductionism implies and assures that alternative descriptions need not be, indeed must not be, incompatible. The fact that our observational and theoretic perspectives are convergent affords us the basis for a conception of scientific realism.

COMMENT

In psychology, the critique of reductionism devolves, one, upon our failure to achieve significant reductions and, two, upon our pragmatic tactics for developing concepts and perspectives unique to psychology. Such criticisms are trenchant ones, but they should not be construed as indicating that two theories, T_2 and T_1, are logically incompatible. Too often the general critique of reductionism fails to distinguish between the logical and the epis-

---

ably the product of tacit inference. The psychology of invention is not at issue so long as the paradigm of reduction allows for invention in both the reduced and reducing sciences.

temological aspects of the issue. Just as some individuals have been critical of the deductivist schema (Hempel-Oppenheim) of explanation on grounds that such a schema does not represent the way scientists do science, so others are critical of reductive paradigms on the grounds that no scientist proceeds systematically according to reductive paradigms. In scientific explanation, rigorous inference chains are frequently found wanting, since many of the observational and theoretical terms are either ambiguously or partially interpreted (Körner, 1964, 1966). Witness the quandaries over fundamental entities in quantum physics. Putative reductions of one science to another are found just as wanting. However, the failure to achieve either ideal explanations or ideal reductions does not rule out the need to formulate in crisp, formal terms what an explanation or a reduction ought to be. Nor does this failure of ideal reduction rule out our formulating epistemological paradigms of reduction that are programmatic for scientific undertaking, even though we may reject the notion of complete reduction as a realizable ideal.

We observe that Woodger, perhaps the first person to give us a formal paradigm of reduction, was himself an "antireductionist." Among other disaffections, he did not believe that the "person language" of psychology was logically reducible to the language of biology. As the languages stood at the time of his writing (1929, 1952), this conceivably was the case. At any rate, it was important for him to develop a normative reductive paradigm in order to show what conditions ought to be fulfilled if we are to have a biological theory encompassing psychology (cf. Note 2.3).

Later in this work we shall be responding to selected arguments in the personalistic critique of reductionism. For the present, however, we point out that subsequent paradigms of reductionism have served to explicate the epistemological role of reductive undertakings, even in those contexts in which the ideal of complete reduction is unrealistic. Indeed, if the thesis of the essential incompleteness of theoretic systems is a reasonable one, then achievement of the normative paradigm of reduction is unrealistic. At no time is the set of predicates within any given science complete, nor is the set of its theoretical constructs. But for any given time, and for any of the given states of the sciences, we may examine the question of whether a T_2 reduces to a T_1. Thus, we do make use of our normative paradigms of reduction.

There is an obvious sense in which we may reject the thesis of reductionism outright. It is never the case that T_2 actually reduces to T_1; the respective theories are incomplete. In certain domains, within our respective theories, we may carry out successful reductions, as in the case of thermodynamics and statistical mechanics; but then anomalous phenomena arise (Kuhn, 1962) which become problematic for both reduction and explanation. The theory then requires modification. We, of course, do not reject the hypothetico-deductive paradigm of explanation in the face of anomalous events. Rather, utilizing all the inventive resources at our command, we proceed to improvise upon our theory or even to replace it with another. Our goal is again to satisfy the normative paradigm of scientific explanation. Nor does the freedom to invent theoretical constructs in the secondary science, T_2, preclude our seeking eventual reductions as befits the normative paradigm of reduction. If reduction is to be an epistemological guide, then a paradigm of reduction is useful in evaluating our work.

In brief, we should not ask whether one science reduces to another, but rather, does reduction provide a useful paradigm for convergent descriptions and explanations of phenomena. Two theories related in the reductive hierarchy offer alternative perspectives, descriptions, meanings, and explanations. Their conceptual frameworks differing, two theories do promote meaning variance in the observation language. However, so long as the program for establishing the empirical equivalencies between the constructs of two theories is a legitimate one, then meaning variance need not imply logical incompatibility. In the main, reductive enterprises serve an epistemological function. They give direction to the developments of both the reduced and reducing sciences.

It should be illuminating now to exemplify the various paradigms introduced in the preceding discussion and to illustrate the diverse functions these paradigms perform. The example offered by Nagel in behalf of the Woodger-Nagel paradigm of reduction is the familiar one of thermodynamics and statistical mechanics. Although the reduction is a comprehensive one, it is by no means complete (Bunge, 1967, p. 44). Nagel confines himself to the simple gas laws of Boyle and Gay-Lussac relating pressure and temperature.

Historically, temperature has been associated with expansion of gases and solids (Galileo) and with the atomic structure of material bodies and their media (Democritus, Leucippus, and Gassendi). Boyle himself adopted an atomic theory of gases in order to explain the relation of pressure and volume. However, contributions by Daniel Bernoulli, Clausius, Joule, Maxwell, and Boltzmann led to the derivation of heat phenomena within classical mechanics. By simplifying our assumptions concerning number, distribution, and velocities of the molecules of a gas, we postulate that temperature is equal to the mean kinetic energy of the constituent molecules. Since kinetic energy of the molecule is a function of mass and the square of velocity, and since the masses of the molecules are assumed equal for an ideal gas, then temperature may be regarded as proportional to the average velocity of the molecules. Furthermore, we take pressure to be proportional to momenta transfer as imparted by the molecules to the container wall. And since momenta and kinetic energy involve the same variables, we are able to derive the relationship between pressure, temperature, and volume as stipulated in the Boyle-Charles law. Moreover, the assumptions of the kinetic theory of gases enable us to deduce properties of gases relating to specific heat, condensation, and evaporation.

This example appears to fit the requirements of the formal paradigm of reduction to the extent that all variables in the phenomenological gas law (pressure and temperature) are replaceable by variables specifying mass and velocity. Furthermore, it sets the epistemological pattern of reductive undertakings in that the reduction of the secondary science is a mediational one; it is microreductive. Yet equally important, even in Nagel's treatment, is the realization that meanings of terms do not remain invariant. Phenomenological temperature, as visualized in early thermometry and calorimetry, is hardly the concept that we now visualize in terms of mean kinetic energy. Extremely low and extremely high temperature states had no place in the earlier treatment; and heat, a property we initially assigned to objects, now becomes inseparable from the state of molecular structure itself. Again, to misconstrue reduction as implying the static state of terms and concepts, is to overlook the epistemological impact of that reduction.

The Feyerabend-Shaffner paradigm of reduction is clear in its rejection of meaning invariance. Feyerabend, a skeptic, is critical of Nagel's example of reducing Galilean science to Newtonian mechanics (cf. Note 2.4). Newtonian science entails idealizations not strictly meaningful in terms of Galilean notions of vertical acceleration. Since Galileo assumed that acceleration was constant over a finite distance and since the gravitational principle makes acceleration a function of that distance (and air resistance), the Galilean law of free fall is not strictly deducible from Newtonian mechanics. We would in fact derive another slightly altered law which would serve to modify the prior theory. In this case, a precise reduction is not possible, but an attempted reduction results in the amelioration of the prior theory.

Shaffner is more explicit in the heuristic role of attempted reductions. As an example, he treats the reduction of genetics to biophysics. Discovery of the coding and duplicative functions of DNA has indeed been dramatic (Watson, 1968). Subsequent developments now suggest that genetic determiners are neither simple nor independent as once was thought. Rather, we distinguish among the smallest mutational unit of the chromosome (muton), the smallest unit subject to crossing over (recon), and the smallest unit for character determination (cistron). Obviously, the new molecular genetics entails a modification of the theory of phenomenological genetics as initially conceived by Mendel. In each of the foregoing examples it is apparent that reduction has enriched the meanings of terms in the fundamental disciplines.

Still it is not clear in any of these examples that the heuristic impact of reduction is bidirectional. The Feyerabend-Shaffner paradigm emphasizes modification of meanings in the secondary science. We must now emphasize the heuristic contribution that the secondary science makes to the primary.

This contribution becomes especially significant when the two sciences considered are psychology and neurophysiology. Note what Lindsley writes at the beginning of his 1955 article for the *Annual Review of Physiology:*

> Electrophysiology, together with increasing knowledge of brain structure and chemistry, has provided neurophysiology not only with the working tools and methods, but with materials for fashioning testable hypotheses and for the development of new theories of brain function. But these gains in neurophysiology might go for naught, were it not also for the gradual, but systematic, accumulation of knowledge concerning behavior and its adaptations. Learning how we learn, whether by psychological, neurophysiological, biochemical, or other approaches, must be one of our main goals. With increasing knowledge of the finer structure of the central nervous system, and particularly with improved electrical means of tracing and plotting the course, magnitude, and temporal relations of events throughout the nervous system from receptors to effectors, there has come an increasing demand for comprehensive theories which, in part at least, will encompass the facts observed, but perhaps more importantly will serve to guide future research. (1955, p. 312)

Stellar writes at the beginning of his 1957 article for the *Annual Review of Psychology:*

> Not only has the physiological psychologist been afforded new techniques and new concepts of neural function, but it has become abundantly clear to neurophysiologists themselves that behavioral techniques and behavioral concepts are essential in the analysis of the complexities of the nervous system. (1957, p. 415)

The two sciences, psychology and physiology, become integrated in the classical discipline of psychophysiology. Developments in physiology, so to speak, would be inconceivable without the substantive and conceptual focus of psychology.

In general, there are two ways in which psychology serves as a heuristic to research in neurophysiology. One, psychological description, both introspective and behavioral, provides an observational base for identifying functional systems and processes within the organism. Thus, studies making use of ablation, microstimulation, and electroencephalographic techniques are effective only to the extent that their consequences are associated with descriptions of psychological functions. The refinements of functional analysis and the conjecture are contingent upon the refinement of behavioral description. Two, the detail, complexity, and organization of systematic psychological descriptions provide a model for isolating and interrelating neurophysiological concepts into functional schemata. Without this tie to psychology, neurophysiology would be limited to the study of involuntary life-maintaining functions.

This thesis, namely, that psychology is a heuristic to neurophysiology, is so obvious to the psychologist as to border on the trivial. Historically, the inceptions of psychophysiology and experimental psychology are inseparable. The physiology of sensation and perception would be unstructured were it not that the relevant external-internal parameters had been identified in classical psychophysics. Far amiss as phrenology and early efforts at brain localization were, they would have been inconceivable without prior conceptualization of psychological faculty and function. And it would be inconceivable today that psychopharmacology could have emerged as a discipline without behavioral parameters and the experimental methodology being developed in psychology.

The heuristic contributions of psychology to neurophysiology are expressible in terms of parametric identification and systemic construction. In the development of psychophysics and psychophysiology, parametric identifications are inseparable from the emergence of experimental psychology itself. Reductions, as it would appear, were more in the way of constructions of the essential physiology. Classical conditioning is another case in point. The great tradition in the conditioning paradigm was instigated by Sechenov, Pavlov, and Bechterev. All were physiologists or were medically trained. The science of reflexology, both conditioned and unconditioned, was realizable only in the format of classical associationism. Thus, Sechenov sought to establish the physiological (reflex) foundations, indeed the reduction, of psychic life. For both Sechenov and Pavlov, the idea of substitute stimuli became the physiological analogue of associative processes. And for all of these Russian scientists, the neurological speculations and hypotheses were structured according to the classical descriptions of psychological processes, even though the emphasis was to be on neurology (cf. Razran, 1965). Moreover, it is significant that Hull's modifications of classical conditioning paradigms in terms of drive and drive reduction led, in turn, to speculations on how to realize principles of reinforcement and drive in physiological terms (Hebb, 1949; Milner, 1957; Rosenblatt, 1958; Glickman and Schiff, 1967).

Another area in which psychology plays a significant role in parameter identification is electroencephalography. The EEG record offers relatively crude data; but with electronic averaging of the potentials over time, we are now able to isolate salient patterns of evoked response as separable from background noise. The significance of the record, crude as the record is, is tied almost exclusively to psychological variables. Thus, we associate EEG records with states of sleep and dreaming, with consciousness, with types of visual experience, with muscular response, even with personality dimensions. In a word, the psychological variables provide the perspective for reading significance into gross brain activity.

In the area of systemic construction we mention two cases in which psychological concepts have contributed significantly to the substantive developments of neurophysiology. One case concerns conceptualization of the memory system; the other, essentially the role of "awareness," attention, and similar psychological functions in the organization of brain function.

From the time of Hebb's reformulation of the two-process memory hypothesis (Hebb, 1949), psychologists and neurophysiologists have renewed their efforts to isolate separable brain systems for short-term and long-term memory. Thus, short-term memory is conceived as reverberatory circuits (Hebb, 1949, 1958; Milner, 1957; Lorente de Nó, 1938) with the "trace" being carried by perseverating intercellular excitation. Long-term memory is conceived as synaptic consolidation (cf. Hudspeth and Gerbrandt, 1965, for review) or as molecular change (cf. Gaito and Zavala, 1964; Landauer, 1964; Booth, 1967; John, 1967, for review). In either case, the separation of relevant mnemonic behaviors has been propaedeutic to neurophysiological speculations. Behavioral studies made independently of physiological speculations have, as a matter of course, established the rubrics for the neurophysiological systems implementing the behavioral phenomena.

Apropos of the molar functioning of the nervous system, we mention two conceptual developments, both of which have borrowed from formulation of psychological processes. By virtue of the work of Magoun, Lindsley, and others, it has become apparent that within the brainstem the reticular formation plays a significant role in arousal, sensory selectivity, and inhibition, all operative in attentive behaviors. Thus, systematic psychological descriptions of awareness, attentiveness, and sensory selectivity have now been articulated in terms of the ascending reticular arousal system. Such a system implements both diffuse cortical preparation and specific excitation of the cortical centers. It accounts for the diversity of arousal functions, response reinforcement, efferent feedback, and motivation. The neurophysiological system, one might say, is structured to well-established constructs in the language of psychology.

Pribram's (1960) conceptual system is considerably more ambitious. First, visualizing detailed descriptions of the behavioral system (arrived at in part through introspection), he proceeds to develop representations of the referent processes. These representations can either be metallic in character (e.g., computer models) or neurophysiological. The essential referent, however, is the behavioral system. Analogy, of course, is presumed to exist between two representations of the given behavioral referent. Thus cybernetic modeling of sensory and motor feedback, memory, and homeostasis provides hypotheses as to how a neurophysiological system may be structured to achieve analogous functions. Here again, the lower centers of the brain play an important role in complex intelligent behavior. Also, descriptions of psychological functions are epistemologically prior to those of the neurophysiological system.

Whether any of the foregoing speculations in neurophysiology will stand up to ultimate experimental confirmation is beside the point. The fact remains that the psychology and behavioristics are inseparable from the neurophysiology. Even with the highly tentative speculations of Hebb, Magoun, Pribram, and others, we see the pattern of cerebral structure and function beginning to emerge. And without our becoming involved in the traditional philosophical squabbles, we can see that clear "mind-body" conceptualizations are essential to researchers in neurophysiology (cf. Note 2.5).

In conclusion then, it is curious that the heuristic service that the reduced science provides for the reducing science has not been emphasized in literature on reduction. The usual tactic in defense (or rejection) of reductionism in psychology is that the latter science awaits the development of a comprehensive neurophysiology. Thus it is claimed that the reductionist program is premature, or that it must await the development of the primary science before defense of reductive theory building in psychology may be undertaken. What we are apparently reluctant to consider is the fact that neurophysiology awaits the development of a conceptually sophisticated psychology. Only with such a psychology will the neurophysiologist be able to conceive both the structures and the functional rubrics that will provide direction in his own substantive researches.

The psychologist then provides the neurophysiologist with the rubrics for reifying his observations and his constructs. In the language of his own discipline, that of attitude, set, drive, inhibition, memory trace, conflict, and so on, the psychologist provides the neurophysiologist direction as to what kind of neurophysiological systems are sufficient for implementing behavioral functions. Without these hypotheses from the secondary science, investigations in the primary science would indeed be blind. A nerve cell, a synapse, even a neural circuit would be meaningless without the constructual framework for organizing them into functional systems.

The moral of our addendum to reduction is not that the theoretical psychologist should proceed self-consciously as the guiding light for the neurophysiologist. Nor is it that he should wait for the development of a mature primary science in the reductive hierarchy before he proceeds to the development of theoretical constructs in his own discipline. Rather, the psychologist should recognize his responsibility to those working in the discipline reductively primary to his own. He has the responsibility of generating hypotheses that are heuristically compatible with related disciplines. Perhaps only as an afterthought need the psychologist consider that the durability of his own theoretical work will be contingent upon its fulfilling that heuristic function. But surely he cannot deny that the psychological construct which endures is the construct that leads to a corresponding reification in the domain of neurophysiology.

NOTES

NOTE 2.1

Process and process functions have been extensively analyzed by Bergmann in his *Philosophy of Science*. Besides stipulating what a process is, he amplifies on the methodological aspects of process analysis by introducing the notions of *closure, completeness of the set of relevant variables,* and *imperfect knowledge.*

By *closure* Bergmann means that what happens within the phenomenal context subject to description by a process function is not in any way affected by phenomenal factors outside that context. Thus, process functions are descriptive of closed systems and represent idealizations subject to the stipulations of boundary conditions. Therefore, a statement of a process function is subject to inaccuracy as concerns actual phenomena. There are intrusive factors impinging on the closed system as well as errors of measurement.

By *completeness* of the set of relevant variables, Bergmann means that the set of variables for state descriptions within the closed system is a sufficient set. That is, one may distinguish within the closed system factors which are relevant and those which are irrelevant for the stipulation of process laws.

By *imperfect knowledge* Bergmann intends to make room for developmental laws (i.e., time sequences) and stochastic laws, both of which express relations that are less than determinate. Whereas for perfect knowledge, a process law establishes both necessary and sufficient conditions between E_{t_1} (event at time t_1) and E_{t_2}, with imperfect knowledge E_{t_1} is merely sufficient for E_{t_2}. Our knowledge of behavior and psychology being what it is, we settle for imperfect knowledge. The possibility of perfect knowledge as against imperfect knowledge implies, however, either that the system is not a closed one as our ideal process laws require, or that the set of all relevant variables has not been completely established within the closed system.

Thus our uncertainty effects and our indeterminancies are included within this purview. And they are compatible with the idea that determinism in principle can be accommodated within a causal theory of probability and indeterminacy (see for example, Poincaré, 1905; Birkhoff and Lewis, 1935; Hawkins, 1964).

Doubtless indeterminacy effects are problematic for a program intent on writing explicit process laws. Although uncertainties arise in our efforts to establish the boundary conditions of our closed systems (Hawkins, 1964), there may be "indeterminancies in principle" due to measurement and specification of microstates (i.e., the indeterminancies of quantal states). But even these need not and perhaps should not provide license for going outside the physical medium of the closed system. For example, in the well-known addendum to *The Neurological Basis of Mind,* Eccles indicates that uncertainty effects may prevail in our efforts to ascertain neuronal transmission at synaptic junctures in the cortex. Moreover, it is conceivable to him that such uncertainty effects may, collectively combined, provide a sufficient base for free will. This conjecture, however, is a nonscientific aside. In a subsequent comment Eccles (1966) attests that his function as a scientist is to consider only what we call process functions irrespective of extraphysical surmises.

NOTE 2.2

The now classic paper on hypothetico-deductive explanation is by Hempel and Oppenheim (1948). In summary the schema of explanation is as follows:

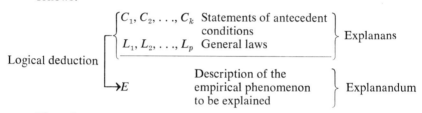

The adequacy of the explanation is attested if the following conditions are met.

$R(1)$, The explanandum must be a logical consequence of the explanans.

$R(2)$, The explanans must contain general laws and these must actually be required for the derivation of the explanandum.

$R(3)$, The explanans must have empirical content; i.e., it must be capable, at least in principle, of test by experiment or observation.

$R(4)$, The sentences constituting the explanans must be true.
(1948, p. 137)

The schema covers both lawful and theoretic explanations. In the latter case the postulates of the theory are included among the general laws.

Less formal discussions of hypothetico-deductive explanation are to be found in Campbell, N. R., *Physics, the elements* (1920), reprinted as *The foundations of science* (1957); Nagel, E., *The structure of science* (1961); Popper, K., *The logic of scientific discovery* (1959). A sophisticated elaboration of the deductive apparatus in scientific explanation is to be found in Braithwaite, R. B., *Scientific explanation* (1953). The author's own discussion of these matters is to be found in Chapter 10 of *Philosophy and the science of behavior* (1967).

NOTE 2.3

Woodger distinguishes four different languages: the phenomenal sensible object language, the physical language, the person language, and the community language. Psychology deals with persons and the person language. Since the person is the totality of many functional systems and yet an identity in the person language, it would be an error to reduce the person that includes all systems to a subset of neurophysiological process. Thus the person is more than his brain.

This is both straightforward and convincing. But it is also misleading, for it implies that the person, the particular identity, must be reduced to sets of properties if reduction is to be possible. This, however, is not what a program of reduction requires. It commands only that the properties we assign to persons be reducible to "matrices" of properties in the reducing science. Furthermore, the issue of reductionism arises almost solely in the context of amplifying upon and interpreting mediational processes. The person may love, hate, inhibit, vacillate, recognize, and so on; each of these terms is a behavioral or dispositional property. The task of reduction is not to find a complex of properties substitutable for the person, but rather to find a set of properties in the language of the reducing science which is substitutable for mediational properties expressed in the person language. The person language is in its way unique, person identity being what it is. However, it is uniquely nonreducible only if the person-attributes of the person, and the processes mediating those attributes, are in fact nonreducible.

There is, however, another feature of Woodger's argument that needs emphasizing. Persons have feeling, knowing, awareness, and so on. There is an element of sincerity in feeling, say feeling love, not detectable alone in behavioral reference. Dispositional translations of "feeling love" will not suffice, for although a person may appear in his behavior, even his verbal behavior, to feel love, the essential sincerity is implicit alone within the feeling.

In and of themselves these observations enable us to differentiate between genuine acts and pretending. However, awareness of this distinction does not preclude the possibility of behavioral criteria for distinguishing between, say, loving and pretending to love. Woodger writes:

> But for behaviorism the sincerity requirement cannot even be formulated, because it essentially involves person language. Incidentally, I may point out that in a properly formulated scientific theory the word 'love' would not enter as the name of a feeling, but as a shared name of each couple x,y such that x loves y. (1952, p. 309)

Now it is just the incidental remark, it seems to me, that renders the language of love amenable to behavioral translations. True love may be hard to detect through our behavioral spectacles, but the relevance of sincerity versus insincerity is often realized in our ability to discriminate between those who behave (love) in a genuine fashion and those who do not. And suppose we are to insist on the feeling itself: can we then be sure that we are escaping the trap of insincerity? There are manifest feelings and there are latent feelings that belie the manifest experience. Just as it is possible to question the sincerity of behavior, so it is possible for the person to question the feelings he experiences. Does John love

Mary? We may question the sincerity of John's behavior; but we may also counsel John to question the genuineness of his feelings.

NOTE 2.4

This is not entirely germane to Nagel's argument or support of reduction, *per se*. It should be noted that he makes a distinction between reducing one theory to another, and deriving one theory within another. Thus we find that thermodynamics is reduced to statistical mechanics, but Galilean mechanics and the Keplerian laws of planetary motion are derived within Newtonian mechanics. In such derivations, say of deriving T_j within T_k, T_k is simply the more general theory. The Galilean law of free-fall, $s(t) = \frac{1}{2} gt^2$, is derived within the laws of motion and gravitation. The Keplerian laws and the orbital motion of the moon about the earth were derived within Newtonian mechanics. Moreover, Newtonian mechanics is then derivable within relativistic mechanics. In all such cases T_k represents the more comprehensive theory; T_j represents a subset in the set of postulates and provable theorems in T_k.

Consider Table 2.1 as prepared by Mario Bunge (1967).
Here the development of optics encompasses more and more phenomena. The classical optics of, say, Huygens accounted for many optical phenomena. However, as optical theory developed and fundamental conceptions changed, new phenomena were discovered and were included within the scope of the theory. One would say that basic laws of refraction and rectilinear propagation, and so on, are now derivable within quantum theory rather than being reducible to it.

The distinction between reducibility and derivability is not easily made. At first glance, we see that in derivability T_j is essentially included in T_k, hence derivable in a trivial sense. But according to the paradigm of reduction, T_2 is not essentially included in T_1, since according to Nagel and Woodger, T_2 contains functors (predicates) not in T_1. It would appear that T_2, the reduced science, would be a more comprehensive theory since it includes all of the functors of T_1 and some unique unto itself. Thus the paradigms of reduction and derivation would appear to differ. Although this may be helpful in distinguishing between T_k and T_j, which traditionally relate to the same corpus of theory, and T_2 and T_1, which do not, it is not clear that a profound logical distinction is involved.

Consider that within the Woodger-Nagel paradigm, T_2 contains a set of functors not included in T_1. Then Nagel's condition of derivability (reductive) is assured if such functors are empirically or logically equivalent to a subset of functors in T_1. But also note that all functors of T_1 are contained in T_2. Is it not the case then that T_2 is more comprehensive than T_1, hence T_1 is derivable (nonreductive) within T_2? This confusion, it appears, stems from our adopting derivability as a trivial property of inclusion. It does make sense to say that optics is included in quantum physics hence derivable, but that sense of derivability is meaningless when applied to the proposition that physics is derivable in psychology because the language of physics is a sublanguage of psychology. In the one case derivability signifies the expansion or inclusiveness of the theory, in the other, that one science may utilize the language of another where appropriate.

Despite the inclusion of the language of T_1 in T_2 it can still be maintained that T_1 is the more "inclusive" science. And no paradox is involved. To say that the language of T_1 is included in T_2 is to say only that certain subsets of functors in T_1 will be utilized in deriving the set of functors unique to T_2. That does not suggest, however, that all functors of T_1 will be utilized in T_2. What distinguishes T_2 as a unique science is its set of unique functors. Its subject matter, as it were, is determined by this set of functors. Hence, in effect, the reduction of T_2 to T_1 implies that the whole of T_2 can be generated out of a subdomain of its functors (concepts, constructs, observational predicates).

TABLE 2.1

Typical facts and laws	Ray optics (Hero)	Hydrodynamic aether theory (Descartes)	Corpuscular theory (Newton)	Longitudinal wave theory (Huygens)	Transversal wave theory (Fresnel, Cauchy, Green)	Electromagnetic theory (Maxwell)	Electromagnetic theory without aether	Electromagnetic theory with curved space	Electromagnetic theory and electron theory	Quantum electrodynamics and nonrelativistic Q.M.	Quantum electrodynamics and relativistic Q.M.
1. Rectilinear propagation	×	×	×	×	×	×	×	×	×	×	×
2. Reflection	×	×	×	×	×	×	×	×	×	×	×
3. Refraction	×	×	×	×	×	×	×	×	×	×	×
4. Extremal travel time	×	×	×	×	×	×	×	×	×	×	×
5. Dispersion	×	×	×	×	×	×	×	×	×	×	×
6. Superposition				×	×	×	×	×	×	×	×
7. Double refraction				×	×	×	×	×	×	×	×
8. Decrease of speed in transparent media				×	×	×	×	×	×	×	×
9. Diffraction				×	×	×	×	×	×	×	×
10. Interference				×	×	×	×	×	×	×	×
11. Doppler effect				×	×	×	×	×	×	×	×
12. Polarization					×	×	×	×	×	×	×
13. Radiation pressure		×				×	×	×	×	×	×
14. Anomalous dispersion									×	×	×
15. Invariant speed light							×	×			×
16. Change of frequency in gravitational field								×			
17. Light scattering									×	×	×
18. Blackbody spectrum										×	×
19. Photoelectric effect										×	×
20. Compton effect										×	×

Thus, psychology, to the extent it reduces to physiology, is derivable within physiology, and not vice versa. Furthermore, many phenomena explainable within physiology (e.g., circulatory, nutritional phenomena) are of no substantive interest in psychology.

The distinction Nagel makes is one which enables us to bring reductionism into the deductivist rubric of explanation. Whether a reduction is an explanation of one science by another, or whether it represents the broadening frontiers of the reducing discipline, is more a partisan than a penetrating question. Is genetics now reducible to and explainable by molecular biology, or is it a subdivision of biology? Perhaps the departmentalization of science favors the former response; but it may very well be that the reducible aspects of genetic coding will become a chapter in biochemistry.

NOTE 2.5

On at least three occasions Pribram (1960, a,b, 1962), a neurophysiologist, has alluded to the significance of traditional mind-body conceptualizations for the structural development of neurophysiology. Less methodologically inhibited than many of his contemporaries, he adopts a position of subjective behaviorism, namely, that the significant behavioral descriptions subject to ultimate reduction are themselves derivable in introspection. Thus the observational and experimental data are to be compatible with phenomenologically given experience. The relation between the strictly observational (physicalistic) data and the phenomenological data is hence epistemological. Awareness of such a relation stems from our concern over the etiology of objective descriptions. Questions of etiology are irrelevant to the descriptions. However, they do remind us that a science of neurophysiology cannot develop in isolation from psychology, or perhaps even from our introspective penchants.

In the 1962 article, Pribram makes an interesting observation. The discipline of neurophysiology has developed among departments of psychology, anatomy, physiology, and pharmacology, but not where we might think that it would be most appropriate, among "medical schools and psychiatric institutes." The reason for this, Pribram maintains, is that such schools have been conceptually tied to medical practice and not to disciplines wherein behavioral descriptions constitute a basic language.

CHAPTER 3

The Cybernetic Hypothesis

BEFORE TURNING to theorems of incompleteness as the logical grounds for rejecting reductionism, we need first to review some results concerning complex descriptions and concerning the possibility of simulation. By the cybernetic hypothesis we mean that if any perceptual-behavioral phenomenon can be described in lawful, causal terms, then it is possible to construct another material system which constitutes a model of the theory of the phenomenon. We should note, one, that the term "causal" does not preclude probabilistic relations existing between states of the system, and two, that the theory of the original phenomenon and the cybernetic model of the theory usually, but not necessarily always, involve entities in different physical media (cf. Note 3.1).

What is of interest in this hypothesis is not its acknowledgment of our ingenuity at simulation for its own sake, but the fact that the cybernetic system, in terms of its own functional components, provides a rubric of hypothesis as to how the object system in the primary theory functions. The cybernetic hypothesis states that material modeling of functions in a scientific theory of behavior is possible; it is not an epistemological statement of how we proceed initially to develop theories. Rather than our beginning with a finished theory and then proceeding to a cybernetic model, or rather than our beginning with a model and then proceeding to the development of a theory, we first seek to describe the primary phenomena in functional detail sufficient to facilitate the construction of the cybernetic model. The model then becomes the epistemic guide for amplifying the theory. As concerns feedback systems, for example, we begin with certain functional descriptions of motor control. A cybernetic model may then be composed to provide the functional, though not necessarily the biophysical, detail as to how the feedback mechanism works.

It should be emphasized at the outset that robotism, or mere effective simulation, is not the issue. A machine M may provide a faithful simulation of behavior in its gross detail, for example, punch hole cards as a system of memory, without the mechanics of *M* providing any useful hypothesis as to the character of organic memory. Emphasis must be placed on criteria for reaching "optimal" positive analogy between the phenomena and the cybernetic model (cf. Note 3.2).

PIONEER SPECULATIONS OF KENNETH CRAIK

Although the discipline of cybernetics is usually associated with the names of Norbert Wiener (1948) and his co-workers, and with W. R. Ashby (1952, 1956), a more explicit and earlier statement of the cybernetic hypothesis can be found in the remarkable but tragically terminated writings of Kenneth Craik. Craik published his cybernetic prospectus for a science of behavior in his book, *The Nature of Explanation* (1943).

This essay begins with a critique of logical formalism (Russell), logical positivism, and Humean skepticism. Logical formalism is rejected as a language for behavioral analysis because it is too committed to exactness ("a garden where all is neat and tidy but bearing little relation to the arbitrary tangle of experience from which the experimentalist tries to derive his principles"—p. 3). Logical empiricists are criticized for focusing their critique upon the looseness and ambiguity of natural language. Implicit within their critique is the *a priori* assumption that "the real must accord with exact description." Rather than exact descriptions, Craik maintains one must be content to work with analogies which through successive refinements converge on the descriptions of a real world. Thus Craik writes:

> . . . This perhaps is the root of the matter: scientists and philosophers alike are distressed that inexact definitions should work well, both for practical and theoretical purposes. Whenever a paradox does arise, they attribute it to this inexactness, which is partially correct; but they fail to see that their remedy of exact definition may be impossible and unattainable by the very nature of the physical world and of human perception, and that their definition should be corrected in the way of greater extensiveness and denotative power, rather than greater analytical, intensive or connotative exactitude. For instance, when the perception or the description of reality meets with difficulties such as the paradoxes of error and illusion the philosopher should not retire within his own fortress, withdraw his brave claims to be knowing reality, and defend bitterly a few strongholds such as the self and sense-data. Rather he should launch out and try to gain widespread support for his theory of perception by linking it with physiological and physical processes, and making vague but general alliances with the great world of facts outside him. (1943, pp. 4–5)

But neither is Humean skepticism to be countenanced. Hume, like the later phenomenalists, was committed to exact descriptions of sensory experience. Hence material object assertions and those of causal relation were rejected on philosophical grounds even though naive observation and a correspondence theory of truth might dictate otherwise. Craik argues that our experience of causality is genuine. At the macroscopic level it emerges from the principle of "the inability of two similar objects to occupy the same space at the same time" and principles of the transfer and distribution of energy. Although the principle of causality is conceptual and is expressed symbolically, we learn through experience that our causal concepts do indeed provide alternative causal hypotheses among which experience will decide. Thus Craik writes:

> Now I am not arguing that the existence of an interactive factor in our concepts of objects puts a causal principle into reality, but the exact reverse—that our concepts of objects are derived from, and constructed to fit, reality, and therefore that they, and all the features they include when they 'fit the facts,' are indicative of the nature of the preexisting objective reality. (1943, p. 46)

In light of the backlog of empiricistic criticism of the principle of causality, this might appear to be a mere dogmatic rephrasing of a discarded naive realism. There is, however, a subtle defense of this realism not to be found among Craik's philosophical predecessors, and at the same time an *a priori* assumption that is not explicitly drawn. Thus Craik puts forth the suggestion that the mind, or the nervous system, models the causally related physical world. Rather than the abstract categories and schemata characteristic of Kant's conception of the mind, it is the very nature of the perceptual mechanism to determine the structure of experiences. Perceptual ordering and structuring are to be identified with the mechanics of the object world. But at this point, Craik asks more than our tacit approval. He proposes his realism as a guiding perspective in our scientific work.

By suggesting that the perceptual mechanism determines the mechanical nature of the object world, Craik does not imply that somehow the mechanical mind exudes or intuitively projects a mechanical world. Rather in processing information and mediating response by its own unique properties, the mind proceeds along mechanical lines conformal with those of physical processes. If we ask what kind of mind is this that is both mechanical and generative of causal mechanical constructions of experience, we must first ask not what the mind as a special organ or a special stuff contributes to this construction but what kind of physical system itself would generate such constructions. The theoretical-experimental tactic, therefore, is not to look at the mind as a unique functional entity upon which experience is contingent, but to look for physical models which will simulate in detail all those functions which we can describe for the mind. Indeed, rather than relying on the ontological doctrine that the physical process mind generates behavior and experience, we look outside the mind for its appropriate models in physical systems. Thus Craik would have been inclined to agree with the precept of later cyberneticists (see following sections): if a behavioral function can be fully described in causal terms, then a physical model (at least in the schematic sense) can be found to simulate that function.

Thus the significance of Craik's argument in behalf of the cybernetic hypothesis: one physical process models another. Knowing what we do of the mind and its functions, we seek hypotheses and explanations through the medium of cybernetic models. But what is a model? Craik details an answer. A model of some system is another physical system "which has a similar relation-structure to that of the process it imitates." And by "relation-structure" he means that the physical model "works in the same way as the process it parallels."

As a prospectus this is all very well, but how do we know that we are entertaining and constructing models with this desirable relation-structure? Here Craik adopts what we must acknowledge to be a metaphysical assumption. There is limited variety in physical systems and physical process. The tactic of modeling is that of pursuing constructions with a maximum amount of positive analogy. Models which display negative analogy are misleading as heuristic devices to the extent of that negative analogy. Hence the development of a scientific theory of mind and behavior proceeds hand in hand with the refurbishment and modification of our models. But since we are dealing *prima facie* with a physical process mind, the enduring pursuit of better and better models converges upon the primary physical system itself.

> . . . the point of interest for our present enquiry is that physical reality is built up, apparently, from a few fundamental types of units whose properties determine many of the properties of the most complicated phenomena, and this seems to afford a sufficient explanation of the emergence of analogies between mechanisms and similarities of relation-structure among these combinations without the necessity of any theory of objective universals. (1943, p. 55)

Craik then asks what kind of nervous system is capable of processing the multifarious flux of experience into the limited variety of conceptualizations we come to know and utilize. Since one sees in the physical world processes which appear to simulate nonphysical cognition, the cognitive system itself is taken to be physical and capable of implementing generalization, perceptual invariance, causal relation. Here, it should be emphasized, Craik is making a novel argument in behalf of reductionism. We require a theory of mind which can account for the mind's processing the complexity of input from the physical world in the efficient and parsimonious way that it does. We need to explain what Kant and other intuitionists take to be the *a priori* base of cognitive function. And we look to the physical system itself to achieve these cognitive functions. If we perceive and conceptualize order in the physical world, then it is fitting that the instrumentality for such ordering is itself an orderly physical process.

Thus there are instances of symbolization in nature; we use such instances as an aid to thinking; there is evidence of similar mechanisms at work in our own sensory and central nervous systems; and the function of such symbolization is plain. If the organism carries a 'small-scale model' of external reality and of its own possible actions within its head, it is able to try out various alternatives, conclude which is the best of them, react to future situations before they arise, utilize the knowledge of past events in dealing with the present and future, and in every way to react in a much fuller, safer, and more competent manner to the emergencies which face it. Most of the greatest advances of modern technology have been instruments which extended the scope of our sense organs, our brains or our limbs. Such are telescopes and microscopes, wireless, calculating machines, typewriters, motor cars, ships and aeroplanes. Is it not possible, therefore, that our brains themselves utilize comparable mechanisms to achieve the same ends and that these mechanisms can parallel phenomena in the external world as a calculating machine can parallel the development of strains in a bridge? (1943, pp. 60–61)

Since publication of his essay, other psychologists have followed Craik in conceptualizing psychology along cybernetic lines (cf. Note 3.3). We look for mechanical systems to simulate organic processes on the grounds that limited possibilities of explanation will point to the positive analogy between organismic and mechanical function.

THEORY OF AUTOMATA

The reader will note that in the preceding discussion of the cybernetic hypothesis little or no attention was paid to the detail of the black boxes implementing the cybernetic model. The model provides a heuristic for the development of a theory of behavior only if we can experimentally point up the positive analogy between the functional detail of the black-box component and the components of the nervous system. Indeed, for Craik, one looks for a kind of convergence in the details of two physical systems—the one, the physical model and the other, the physical system modeled. In the general theory of automata we set aside the issues of physical or structural analogy and restrict ourselves to functional analogy in the more abstract computational sense. Thus if we can stipulate the logical structure of our automata in schematic form, we need not be concerned (in the theory of automata) with the actual structural detail as to how each black-box component carries out its operations. Therefore among the set of all conceivable automata there will be many which are inappropriate as cybernetic models of the nervous system. This is because of their substantial negative analogy. But within this set of automata we will also find those which do serve as useful heuristic models of the nervous system. If the general theory of automata reveals certain inherent limitations of automata of a given kind, and the general theory can be shown to cover our useful cybernetic models, then obviously statements about those inherent limitations of automata apply to our models.

In his popular essay on the theory of automata, John von Neumann (1951) alludes to this difference in treatments between physical models and more abstract automata in the following way. In the former case we are concerned with the structural and functional details of the elements of system as concrete realizable entities; in the latter case we are interested in formal properties of those elements functioning as an integrated totality. The one is subject to concrete descriptions; the other to formal, axiomatic analysis. Since the theoretician need not and most often cannot attend to the structural detail of the elements, he is content to treat them axiomatically. Thus his entire theory is developed in a purely formal manner.

> Axiomatizing the behavior of the elements means this: We assume that the elements have certain well-defined, outside, functional characteristics; that is, they are to be treated as "black boxes." They are viewed as automatisms, the inner structure of which need not be disclosed, but which are assumed to react to certain unambiguously defined stimuli, by certain unambiguously defined responses.
> This being understood, we may then investigate the larger organisms that can be built up from these elements, their structure, their functioning, the connections between the elements, and the general theoretical regularities that may be detectable in the complex syntheses of the organisms in question. (von Neumann, in J. R. Newman (editor), *The World of Mathematics*, 1956, p. 2071)

Crude "black boxes" are obviously not enough. We require something more than place holders intermediating input and output. We need explicit statements concerning the functional detail of our mediators if we are to lend formal integrity to our automata. Important developments in the theory of automata emphasize this need for explicit functional (i.e., computational) descriptions.

McCulloch-Pitts Theorem

In their early work McCulloch and Pitts (1943) established what has become one of the most significant theorems in all of the theory of automata. Making certain assumptions as to the functions of neurons, for any input-output behavior of a finite automata, there is a possible construction of a nerve-net which will simulate that behavior. Emphasis is to be placed initially on the behavior of a finite automata, for if any phenomenon can be "completely and unambiguously" described in terms of a concatenation of occurrences, then it is subject to simulation by the finite automata. Thus in a clear exposition of the significance of this result von Neumann writes:

> It has often been claimed that the activities and functions of the human nervous system are so complicated that no ordinary mechanism could possibly perform them. It has also been attempted to name specific functions which by their nature exhibit this limitation. It has been attempted

to show that such specific functions, logically, completely described, are per se unable of mechanical, neural realization. The McCulloch-Pitts result puts an end to this. It proves that anything that can be exhaustively and unambiguously described, anything that can be completely and unambiguously put into words, is ipso facto realizable by a suitable finite neural network. Since the converse statement is obvious, we can therefore say that there is no difference between the possibility of describing a real or imagined mode of behavior completely and unambiguously in words, and the possibility of realizing it by a finite formal neural network. The two concepts are coextensive. A difficulty of principle embodying any mode of behavior in such a network can exist only if we are also unable to describe that behavior completely. (1956, p. 2090)

The relevance of this important result for the argument of reduction is obvious. Since some finite automata and some ideal nervous system (a system of McCulloch-Pitts nerve networks) both can be regarded as interpretations of a formal system, then any limitations of the formal system must be shared with interpretive systems. Let us assume three systems: the formal system L, the finite automata A, and the ideal modular nervous system N. By virtue of the fact that L is a formalization of A, and A and N are isomorphic, both A and N are interpretations of L. Hence any limitations of L will be shared by virtue of its interpretations in A and N. Should this not be the case, i.e. should the limitations not be shared, then L could not be regarded a formalization of A or correspondingly of N.

The question may, of course, arise as to whether the logicomathematical rubric utilized by McCulloch and Pitts (the Carnap and Russell-Whitehead logistic) constitutes an adequate vehicle for the formal mapping of *all* cognitive and intellective functions of which we find the human organism capable (cf. Note 3.4). But even granting possible restrictions on the realizability of cognitive functions by nerve networks, then to the extent that human acts of computation can be fully described within the logical calculus, we can realize that computation by a nerve network. Should deficient properties of the calculus show up as, for example, in Gödel's theorems, these very properties would be assignable to the neural network which is a realization of the formal system.

We should observe that McCulloch-Pitts' treatment is a restricted one (see Papert's introduction to McCulloch's *Embodiments of Mind*, 1965). Only those behaviors describable in relatively simple finite descriptions and subject to formalization within the Russell-Whitehead logic are dealt with (e.g., digital systems). The formal means for describing human understanding, *per se*, even the understanding of the concept of numbers, may be wanting. However, for those acts of computation and understanding which are in fact describable in terms of propositional logic, one may realize the act of computation by a suitable nerve network. For more extensive acts of computation and more generalized automata we turn to the analysis of Turing machines.

Turing Machines

Of all the machines that are of interest to the reductionist doubtless the most important are those pencil and paper machines that enable us to analyze the nature and range of computability and to evaluate the capacities of any conceivable machine. There are, as we have seen, different types of machines. Actual hardware machines may, of course, be of interest to the reductionist as structural models, but they are somewhat limited in conception and the negative analogy that permeates all of the engineer's efforts to simulate organic process tends to mislead the behavioral scientist. Schematic black-box machines may serve as heuristic devices for generating theoretical constructs, but even these are to be regarded as tentative, ready to be replaced by neurophysiological theories when their experimental support is well established. Pencil and paper machines, i.e., logical machines, are yet again different. Being concerned only with the logical implementation of acts of computation, these machines may tell us very little at all about the human computer system. Yet it is true all the same that they are informative for the issue of reductionism. In the matter of computation, the analyses of these logical machines will inform us as to what machines can and cannot do. If the nervous system as conceived by the neurophysiologist is indeed a computer, then it is subject to the limitations established by the logical analysis of machines. On the other hand, if there is something unique about the human computer that renders it non-reducible, then the logical analysis of machines should give some indication as to where the uniqueness of human computation rests.

The pencil and paper machines here to be discussed are those stemming from the work of the English logician A. M. Turing. A so-called Turing machine concerns the states, vocabularies, operations, and programs necessary for computation rather than any machinery as to how the actual states and operations of computation are to be materialized. Any computational procedure that can be spelled out in detail, any algorithm, can be realized as a Turing machine. Since the theory of Turing machines deals with logical systems in general, theorems can be derived from it that are of interest to the theory of any kind of computational machinery which simulates systematic logical computation.

Very generally a machine or computer is any system which computes by systematically moving from one determinate state to another. From the initial input and the program for producing a succession of logical states (configurations) the machine continues to compute until a solution to the problem is reached, in which case the machine stops, or in the event no solution is achievable, the machine goes on computing forever. It is obvious then that computation is a step-by-step process in which the machine moves from one state to another according to an explicit finite set of operations. Any deterministic machine is just such a computer wherein its operations can be conceived as a program for producing a succession of states.

A Turing machine is simply conceived. Its "material" components consist of a tape, a scanner, a driver, and a writing mechanism. In addition there is a program. The tape is of any length subject to infinite splicing should that be required. It is divided into squares upon which symbols in the machine alphabet can be printed. The scanner is able to inspect any given square of the tape at a given time, and passes the information to the executive componentry of the machine. The driver mechanism, upon instruction, can exercise one of three options. It may drive the tape such that the scanner will scan (a) the square to the left of the one presently scanned; (b) the square to the right of the one presently scanned; or (c) the square that is presently scanned (i.e. leave the tape stationary). Finally, the writing mechanism is such that it can print any symbol in the machine alphabet (including the "blank symbol") on the scanned square, it can erase any symbol already there on the scanned square, or it can substitute any other symbol for the one printed on the scanned square (i.e., erase and print).

Such is the machinery. We need no actual driver, no hardware, although it would be easy to construct such a machine. We can visualize the machine and its operations in purely conceptual terms. And interestingly this machinery of scanning, printing, and so on, is not the Turing machine as such. It is simply the vehicle for conceiving the operations of the actual machine.

The actual Turing machine consists of a program of instructions as to what the mechanical components should do when the input from the scanner and the internal logical state or configuration is known. As we shall see such a machine can be presented purely in symbolic terms, in which each complete instruction specifies what the machine is to write and what state it is to move into in the next step of a set of operations.

We now require the following: Let

$$S_0, S_1, \ldots, S_j, \ldots, S_n$$

be members of the finite machine alphabet,

$$q_1, q_2, \ldots, q_i, \ldots, q_m$$

be possible internal configurations in the finite set of all possible configurations, and

$$R, L$$

be the symbols instructing the driver to move the tape such that the square next to be scanned is either to the right or to the left of the one presently scanned. Then any quadruple such as $\langle q_i S_j R q_l \rangle$ represents an instruction to the machine, wherein we may read the instruction as "when in internal state q_i scanning symbols S_j scan the square next on the right and move into state q_l." Thus any machine with a finite program can be represented by a set of quadruples each of which is constructible from the set of all possible instruction types:

$$\langle q_i S_j S_k q_l \rangle \tag{1}$$

$$\langle q_i S_j R q_l \rangle \tag{2}$$

$$\langle q_i S_j L q_l \rangle \tag{3}$$

$$\langle q_i S_j q_k q_l \rangle \tag{4}$$

Here quadruple (1) indicates that when the machine is in state q_i inspecting symbol S_j, it is to replace S_j with S_k and move into state q_l; (2) indicates that when the machine is in state q_i inspecting symbol S_j it is to scan the square next on the right and move into state q_l; (3) indicates that when the machine is in state q_i inspecting symbol S_j it should scan the symbol next on the left and move into state q_l; (4) is required of more complex machines capable of self-interrogation and indicates that when the machine is in state q_i inspecting S_j it is to move into state q_k or q_l contingent upon the answer to some interrogation.

Now note that any computational act can be represented by a set of instantaneous descriptions any one of which is composed of the state of the entire tape, an internal state, and the inspection of a given square.

Thus $\qquad S_1 S_2, \ldots, S_i q_i S_j, S_k, \ldots, S_R \tag{5}$

would represent the sequence of symbols on the tape at the instant the machine is in state q_i inspecting the square with the printed symbol S_j. Since letters of the machine alphabet can be repeated, (5) above can be misleading. Letting P be the sequence of symbols in squares left of the square presently scanned and Q the sequence of symbols to the right of the square presently scanned, we write (5) simply as

$$P q_i S_j Q \tag{6}$$

Thus any instruction from our set of instructions indicates that the machine is to move consecutively from one instantaneous state to another. Thus, for example, quadruple (1) indicates that the machine is to move from instantaneous state α to instantaneous state β, where

$$\alpha: \quad P q_i S_j Q$$

$$\beta: \quad P q_l S_k Q$$

Quadruple (2) is the instruction for the succession

$$\alpha: \quad P q_i S_j Q$$

$$\beta: \quad P S_j q_l Q$$

where the scanner in instantaneous state β now scans the first symbol in the sequence Q. Additional successions can be provided for quadruples (3) and (4). Finally we note that any computational act can be represented as a succession of instantaneous states. Thus if $a_1 \rightarrow a_2$ represents a succession, then $a_1 \rightarrow a_2 \rightarrow \ldots \rightarrow a_\beta$ represents a solution of a computational problem, where a_β is the terminal instantaneous state. That is to say, $a_\beta \rightarrow a_\beta$ . . . .

Let us now visualize a Turing machine that can carry out all problems in the addition of positive integers. Here we require an alphabet of only two symbols:

$$S_1 = 1$$

$$S_0 = 0$$

And the set of quadruples constituting the appropriate Turing machine for simple addition is

$$\langle q_1 S_1 S_0 q_1 \rangle$$
$$\langle q_1 S_0 R q_2 \rangle$$
$$\langle q_2 S_1 R q_2 \rangle$$
$$\langle q_2 S_0 R q_3 \rangle$$
$$\langle q_3 S_1 S_0 q_3 \rangle$$

This same machine can also be presented in alternative matrix form

	q_1	q_2	q_3
S_1	$S_0 q_1$	$R q_2$	$S_0 q_3$
S_0	$R q_2$	$R q_3$	$S_0 q_3$

where the given marginal couplet $q_i S_j$ yields the appropriate instruction. This table, then, taken in conjunction with the tape instructs us as to the progression of instantaneous states.

To show how this machine will compute the sum of any two integers, we first introduce the conventions for tape coding of numbers and for tape readout. Let S_1 be the stroke symbol 1. Then for any integer n we associate an expression on the tape as $n+1$ consecutive stroke symbols. Thus the number n is entered

$$\overbrace{1 \ 1 \ \ldots \ 1}^{n+1}$$

(Since zero is a numerical expression different from S_0, the blank symbol, it is represented by one stroke.) However, the answer is read out of the tape at the conclusion of its computations simply as the total number of strokes on the tape. These apparently arbitrary conventions need not perturb us, for so long as we know how to enter or encode our numbers on the tape and then in turn decode the tape at the termination of computation, the machine will fulfill its purpose of computing arithmetic sums. (For another Turing machine designed for addition see Note 3.5.)

Suppose now we wish to compute the sum of 2 and 3. We first enter our numbers on the machine tape with the expression

$$\ldots \ S_1 S_1 S_1 S_0 S_1 S_1 S_1 S_1 \ \ldots$$

All other expressions over the ellipses can be regarded a blank (i.e., S_0).

We begin the computation with our Turing machine in state q_1 scanning the first S_1 on the left. Utilizing Table 1, the computation now follows sequentially with the following progression of instantaneous states:

$$(q_1)\underline{S_1}S_1S_1S_0S_1S_1S_1S_1$$
$$(q_1)\overline{S_0}S_1S_1S_0S_1S_1S_1S_1$$
$$S_0(q_2)\underline{S_1}S_1S_0S_1S_1S_1S_1$$
$$S_0S_1(q_2)\underline{S_1}S_0S_1S_1S_1S_1$$
$$S_0S_1S_1(q_2)\ \underline{S_0}S_1S_1S_1S_1$$
$$S_0S_1S_1S_0(q_3)\ \underline{S_1}S_1S_1S_1S_1$$
$$S_0S_1S_1S_0(q_3)\ \overline{S_0}S_1S_1S_1$$

Note that "(q_i)" indicates the logical state of the machine at any given instant and that the symbol immediately to the right of the position of q_i is an indication of the symbol scanned. The parentheses and underlining are included merely to point this out. Also observe that a stopping state is reached when the machine is in logical state q_3 scanning S_0. No further computation is dictated. According to our rule for decoding, our answer is then read out as the number of S_1 symbols on the tape (cf. Note 3.5). Other machines for subtraction, the identity function, the successor function and multiplication can be readily designed (cf. Davis, 1958, Chapter 1) such that the whole of the arithmetic of natural numbers is readily accommodated by such machines.

It is apparent that such machines are not intended as hardware designs. No one would propose that an adding machine designed with explicit componentry of a Turing machine would ever be a mechanically efficient one.

Universal Turing machines. Let us visualize a set of possible Turing machines Z_1, Z_2, . . ., Z_n such that each machine is designed to compute functions of given kinds (addition, subtraction, and so on). A theorem in the theory of Turing machines then states that there is a universal Turing machine U such that it can compute any function computable by any possible Turing machine. This important theorem can be established by means of arithmetizing any possible Turing machine Z_i by translating it into a Gödel number (cf. Note 3.6) and following it by the function to be computed (Davis, 1958, p. 64). However, the means for realizing this is a technical matter beyond the present purview. Fortunately, there is a simple demonstration of a universal Turing machine (Arbib, 1964). From the set of all possible symbols of machine alphabets and all possible internal states then all possible machine quadruples are constructible. Hence all possible Turing machines are enumerable in order of their complexity. Since all possible Turing machines are "effectively enumerable" we proceed to enumerate a sequence of machines $Z_1, Z_2, Z_3, \ldots$ until we find a machine that can compute the function in question.

COMPUTABILITY

Throughout our discussions we have made reference to computable functions, acts of computation, and so on. We need now to define what we mean by computability without getting into the technical literature on recursiveness (Kleene), λ-definability (Church), and computability. The equivalence of these expressions has been established, and in general they relate to the property of the solvability of a numerical function. Therefore we may say that a numerical function $f(x_1 x_2 \ldots x_n)$ is computable if there exists an effective procedure for computing it. Obviously the concept of an algorithm applies to computable functions, for an algorithm stipulates an effective procedure for computing functions of a given kind. For example, the formula $\binom{n}{r} p^r q^{n-r}$ presents an algorithm for computing the $(n-r+1)$th term in the familiar binomial expansion for whatever n, r.

Ideally, of course, we would like to find algorithms for all meaningful functions no matter how complex. The so-called Entscheidungs problem of the mathematical formalists sets up the quest. Is there an effective procedure for deciding whether a meaningful formula, not an axiom, in a formal system is a provable theorem of the system? If so, every provable theorem would, of course, be computable. However, since 1930 several dramatic results in metalogic have been established which have demonstrated the impossibility of our ever achieving this ideal. Though we have means certainly for defining computability and means, in certain limited systems, for deciding which formulae are computable, no effective procedure can be established, in a system such as number-theory, for deciding which formulae in the theory can be derived within its defined operations. Gödel's theorem of incompleteness, to be discussed in a following chapter, demonstrates conclusively that there can be a true formula in the formal theory not provable in the theory itself. And Church (1936) has shown that there is no algorithm for deciding whether any given formula is provable within the formal number theory. Even though Turing was to show that a Turing machine could carry out the computations for any computable function, he was also to reveal that no Turing machine could compute, i.e. decide, which formulae in the set of all formulae are computable and which are not. That is to say, a Turing machine cannot solve its own stopping problem. One cannot thereby determine whether the machine will ever reach a stopping state in its effort to compute some problematic function (cf. Note 5.3).

Significance for Reductionism

As in most work in metamathematics, automata, and logical machines, the logical mechanics of computation may be remote from the actual human computer which we must visualize in biophysical terms. Digitalization of the human computer system, of course, simplifies things for us as in the case of the McCulloch-Pitts nerve nets. However, the significance of these results does not rest in any effort to map in isomorphic fashion the functioning of the nervous system. What the person computes, the nervous system implements. And the theory of Turing machines reveals that what can be precisely described in the way of a computational act can be effectively simulated by a Turing machine. Thus if we can describe in deterministic terms the step-by-step procedures of our computation, then it is possible to conceive a Turing machine which can compute the same result. If the nervous system is the instrument of human computation, then to the extent we can fully describe the progression of states in the act of computation, there is a possible Turing machine, a possible finite automata, to serve as a model of the nervous system.

Such a sanguine promise should be sufficient to support the credo of the programmatic reductionist. However, the question of logical barriers to complete reduction remains. Any act of computation as explicitly described serves as the prospectus for a Turing machine. But can we simulate in this sense all acts of computation? Can we, as human computers, compute a formula noncomputable by any "extant" computer? We are led to believe from the theory of Turing machines that we can build a computer, a Turing machine, to compute the result of any well-defined act of computation. Yet for any computer we can show something to be "computably true" which the machine cannot compute. For example, we can show that a universal Turing machine cannot solve its own stopping problem, which is to say that if we were to feed that problem to the machine it would go on computing forever without reaching a decision. Historically, however, the confrontation of this problem of incompleteness and noncomputability is to be found initially in the remarkable work of Gödel.

NOTES

NOTE 3.1

I have taken a somewhat more general purview of the cybernetic hypothesis than will be found in much of the literature (e.g., Wiener, 1948; Wisdom, 1951; George, 1961). As initially conceived, cybernetics was the study of self-steering, control mechanisms in which mechanical communication plays a large part. Strong emphasis was placed on the concept of feedback. Information of output is fed back into the machine to control (either to amplify or to dampen) the continuing output of the machine. However, since it is obvious that in our studies of the behavior of organisms we are dealing with self-guidance systems, any machine which can be said to simulate these behaviors would satisfy Wiener's conception of the cybernetic hypothesis. Indeed W. Ross Ashby (1956) subscribes to this extension of the cybernetic hypothesis in his own distinguished text on the subject. And J. Z. Young (1964) adopts Ashby's notion of the homeostat as a model for brain function.

NOTE 3.2

The issues of simulation, *per se,* are somewhat tangential to the main discussion of the cybernetic hypothesis and the theory of automata. Thus we take occasion in this note to amplify on certain implications that simulation may have for a realization of a psychoneurological theory of behavior.

In our emphasis on extension of positive analogy, we are saying that the cybernetic hypothesis is programmatically useful to the extent that it generates functional hypotheses which possess structural significance. The machine, the simulator, whether it be material or logical, should afford us some suggestion as to how the organismic system works. Phenomenological analogy, as it were, is not enough. In the same way the behavioristic emphasis upon pure behavioral criteria for simulation is apt to be misleading. Hence we read and hear much pretentious stuff on the purposiveness of machines. (See, for example, Rosenblueth, Wiener, and Bigelow, 1943; Taylor, 1950, a,b; and Rosenblueth and Wiener, 1950, for an edifying exchange on purpose in machines.) A machine, it is argued, is purposive if it behaves to all appearances like a purposive entity. Hence self-guiding mechanisms and homing vehicles are putative purposive mechanisms. One might argue as Richard Taylor (*Action and Purpose,* 1966) does that this is an unwarranted suppression of the discriminative implications of intentional terms. A homing torpedo, for example, can be designed to behave in an apparently purposive manner. But it is a machine all the same, *sans* any purpose of the kind which is embodied in the intentions of its designer. The machine may act as if it has a goal, but it is not goal oriented in the same sense that the machine's designer is. Skinner's pigeons, trained to guide a free-gliding missile (Skinner, 1960), may simulate the renowned Kamikaze pilots of World War II but their intentions are clearly not the same. Perhaps there is good reason for behavioral translations of intention and purpose (see Chapter 6), but the critique clearly rests in the concept of purpose. Edification, I am inclined to feel, does not come by ignoring the significance of that debate in favor of the gambit that machines satisfy certain behavioral criteria of purpose.

Finally, in the present context, we should point out that the cybernetic hypothesis stands somewhat apart from black-box schematizing. It is the more explicit heuristic. The difference is clearly drawn in Ashby's discussion of black-box theory.

> The problem of the black box arose in electrical engineering. The engineer is given a sealed box that has terminals for input, to which he may bring any voltages, shocks, or other disturbances he pleases, and terminals for output, from which he may observe what he can. He is to deduce what he can of its contents. (Ashby, 1956, p. 86)

The difference between the black-box hypothesis and the cybernetic hypothesis is clear. Applying the former hypothesis, a person is to "deduce," hypothesize, as it were, what kind of extant entity the box might contain. The state of machine knowledge is presumed complete. Our task is to infer what kind of entity, in the set of known entities, inhabits the box. Applying the latter hypothesis, a person is to construct a model of the organismic system whereby the assumed analogy will enable him to make inferences concerning the actual componentry of that system. The one case calls for detective work, as it were, a systematic approach of varying input and observing output, in a manner akin to trouble shooting. The other is a matter of explicit description and design.

The indiscriminate use of black-box schemata in psychology and physiology often fails to make this distinction between substitution and construction, or between an expository device and theoretic heuristic. Another way to look at the distinction is to consider the black-box approach as the more phenomenological. The method of the black-box specialist is to establish a set of input-output states over a given time period and then to find a machine that embodies the formal properties of its representation. Although these phenomenological descriptions may afford some basis for inference concerning the components of the system, they do not enable us to specify a "unique diagram of internal connections" (Ashby, 1956). Apropos of this point, Mario Bunge (1963, 1964) contributes a "general black-box theory" which is both abstract and phenomenological: abstract in that it proposes a set of mathematical equations for various input-output relations; phenomenological, because the allowable interpretations of the equations are only in terms of extraorganismic observational variables. And as Bunge implies, a theory which formalizes the behavior of perfectly transmitting, damping, or amplifying boxes under various stimulus conditions does not relieve us of the need for making inferences as to the mechanics of the box itself.

Argument as to the distinction between the cybernetic hypothesis and the black-box hypothesis is developed fully in an excellent essay by Gregory (1961).

NOTE 3.3

Among his contemporaries, Craik was legendary both for his mechanical skills and for his ability to conceptualize organic systems in mechanical terms. He was a master-builder of cybernetic models. Much of his published work, including a long chapter in *The Nature of Explanation,* is occupied with ingenious cybernetic designs for cognitive and behavioral functions. For an appreciation of Craik's gifts, see Sir Frederick Bartlett's obituary note to be found in the recent collection *The Nature of Psychology* (a selection of papers, essays, and other writings by Kenneth J. W. Craik).

For additional treatments of the cybernetic hypothesis we consider briefly two works: Miller, Galanter, and Pribram: *Plans and the Structure of Behavior* and J. A. Deutsch: *The Structural Basis of Behavior.* The former work takes a point of view favorable to reductionism; the latter the point of view that one can conceive the structure of a behavioral system without recourse to its physical embodiment.

Miller, Galanter, and Pribram: *Plans and the Structure of Behavior* is an unusual book. One gets the impression from the authors' remarks that it was conceived somewhat fortuitously, only to emerge as a crisp plan taking form in their informal discussions. The authors, a psycholinguist, a psychophysicist, and a psychoneurologist, respectively, all came to visualize the need for a cognitive theory of behavior to be conceptualized in cybernetic terms.

Miller, Galanter, and Pribram initially assert that it is the task of the behavioral scientist to "proceed with caution," that is, to report and analyze what can be observed with as little recourse to postulation as possible. But postulation is necessary because of the cognitive-purposive implications of our behavioral acts. Traditionally psychologists have been divided into "pessimists" and "optimists." The pessimists are those who believe that man's cognitive activities and his purposve action are too complex ever to be deciphered in the formal systems of science. The optimists on the other hand tend to oversimplify complex behaviors within paradigms. Neither point of view will suffice if we are to turn psychology into a science of meaningful units of behavior. We need a systematic analysis by which we can translate purely cognitive activity and purely cognitive representation into behavioral activity. There must be some link between the perceiving and thinking and the action. A purely conceptual analysis of such a system (e.g., that of Tolman) will not suffice. Either the subject becomes lost in thought and inaction, or there is no need for thought. On the other hand, physiological representations would turn the trick, but only if we have some means of conceptualizing structures of thought and intention as these are manifest in behavior. The authors seek to conceptualize such structures by means of a cybernetic model.

But first, the dichotomy of molar-molecular representation must be resolved. The total meaningful act is molar and it must have systemic representation. On the other hand, the problem of cognition and action can be resolved only by reducing the molar unit of analysis into its molecular constituents. However, the molecular units cannot be reduced to mere reflexes; a concatenation of reflexes, or even a concert, does not generate a cognitive theory of behavior. For the authors, both the molar and the molecular units have a common systemic structure.

Before turning to these structures it is necessary to take a broader purview of an organism in action. In a cognitive-behavioral representation of action we conceptualize the organism as having a *Plan*. "*A Plan is any hierarchical process in the organism that can control the order in which a sequence of operations is to be performed.*" (Miller, Galanter and Pribram, 1960, p. 16) Thus a Plan, a determinate sequence of operations, can be visualized as the program of the organismic computer. The overall, response pattern, the hierarchical organization, is to be considered the behavioral *strategy;* the molecular units implementing that strategy, the behavioral *tactics*. Finally, the cognitive component of the behavioral system is to be known as the *Image* (i.e., "all the accumulated, organized knowledge that the organism has about itself and its world"). Note that no reference is made to consciousness or mental entities. These have always been problematical for the cognitive implementation of behavior. As the authors see their work, their problem is "to explore the relation between the Image and the Plan." (p. 18)

This problem, which we might call the physicalistic reduction of the mind-body problem, is to be resolved now by incorporating the concept of the Image into that of the Plan. To do this we must establish what might be called the cybernetic rubric of the analysis, the TOTE unit. TOTE is short for Test-Operate-Test-Exit. Its distinctive character is cognitive feedback. Its physiological representation, as in most cybernetic models, is not detailed. The phases of the unit are just those phases we find sequentialized in our conception of the Plan. Schematically, the TOTE unit is represented as follows:

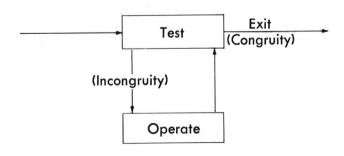

FIGURE 3.1. A diagram of a TOTE unit.

Galanter (1966) describes its functioning as follows:

> The unit functions as follows. The test phase is construed as a sensitive device capable of detecting incongruity between some internal state of its own, which we shall call an *image,* and the external environment, or the behavior. Just as the thermostat detects an incongruity between the surrounding temperature and the temperature for which it is set, the test phase of the TOTE contains a representation of what 'should' be the case. We shall call this template contained in the test phase of a single TOTE element an *atomic image.* All incoming information to the organism enters one or another of the test phases of some TOTE or other. That information is compared with the atomic image of the test. If the comparison is successful, then the test phase transfers its control of behavior along through the exit arrow to some other TOTE. If, on the other hand, there is an incongruity between the image and the input, then the test phase transfers control to the operate phase of the TOTE through the other arrow that leaves it. The operate phase continues to function, reporting back to the test phase in a more or less continuous fashion, until the incoming information from the operate phase matches or agrees with the image of the test phase. Control of the organism's behavior is then transferred out of that particular TOTE unit via the exit arrow. (1966, p. 323)

Note that the TOTE unit is to represent both the strategy and the tactics of behavior, both the molar and the molecular units. Thus the operate phase of some larger TOTE unit (the strategy) itself may be composed of a set of smaller units, all having the TOTE structure. Visualize yourself driving your car from home to work. The whole act can be described as a molar TOTE unit. But the operate phase of this molar unit can be represented by a sequence of smaller TOTE units constituting the implementation of a Plan through the sequence of the tactical acts involved in stopping, starting, passing, turning, and so on. One can further and further subdivide, but never, in behavioral analysis, below the TOTE unit.

But how are we to conceptualize the medium of the TOTE unit? What is it that we conceptualize as being transmitted along the directional arrows of the TOTE sequence? The authors propose three possibilities (levels of abstraction): (1) energy or neural impulse; (2) information; (3) control. For the first alternative, energy is to be represented in neural activity; for the second, information is analyzed according to the theoretic notion of correlation (controlled variance); for the third, control, the highest level of abstraction, takes the form of instruction at the operative cognitive level. Control is embodied in the generic language for expressing the executive relations between phases of the TOTE unit, or, more palpably, between units in the information-schematic of the behavioral system. The generic language thus enables us to describe these systemic relations between processes themselves expressible in the energetic or the information languages.

In their remarks on simulation it is clear that the authors are concerned only with functional analogy (see page 82). Hence if we visualize an automaton capable of implementing TOTE units we are not to be concerned with the simulation of "behavior *per se*" but only the psychologist's record of behavior. Moreover, the authors are not concerned with simulating mere molecular details of the nervous system. Hence, they reject the McCulloch-Pitts theory of nerve nets, not because it may fail to simulate well-described computer acts, but because it is an alternative which does not conceptualize the fundamental unit as being a cognitive-behavioral one. The fundamental unit of analysis is the TOTE unit, not the nerve net, even though systems of nerve nets may very well represent a possible realization of TOTE units. Their own plan conceptually is to integrate the components Plan and Image into a functional whole.

This being the case, then, integration of Plan and Image into the TOTE unit is to be visualized in either energetic or informational terms. One language does not preclude the other. But how is this integration to be achieved? The obvious area of application is in problem solving. It should be apparent now that Plan and Image are the conceptual units of their analysis, whereas the TOTE unit itself is to be regarded as the structural unit. Since science and the tactics of research are conceptual matters, it is incumbent upon us to determine how we are to utilize our conceptual frames in implementing the TOTE unit. Here the authors are confident that Plans rather than Images instrument the search for a problem solution and for the resolution of incongruity. Although, for some, it is conceived that problem solution is contingent upon the clarification of the Image (i.e., a clear Image of the problem leads directly to a mechanical solution of the problem), the Image alone will not translate into the functional details of Testing. It is only in the Plan of attack that we visualize the efficacy of feedback. Each operate phase in the larger TOTE unit represents the effective testing of a hypothesis (i.e., a Plan). Hence problem solving incorporates a Plan implementing the molar TOTE unit. However, the succession of trial hypotheses and their testing are to be represented as sub-TOTE units reflecting subplans. Thus in the tactics of problem solving there is a hierarchy of plans, where for each higher order Plan there is a set of lower order tactical Plans. In principle there is no restriction upon this ordering, from classes of Plans to classes of classes of Plans and so on, with the level of logical type presumably reflecting the intelligence of the organism in its problem solving task.

This in substance provides an outline of the authors' treatment of the cybernetic hypothesis. It is the outline of a conceptual machine, if you will, by which we analyze behavior. Yet what is the status of reduction through all this? Miller, Galanter, and Pribram conclude their essay with speculations concerning the heuristic value of their analysis. "When behavioral phenomena are carved at their joints, there will be some sense in which the analysis will correspond to the way the brain is put together" (p. 196). The conceptual system provides the theoretical spectacles for looking at the nervous system.

The authors' speculations are indeed tentative. It is clear, however, that they favor a systemic analysis along the lines of the TOTE unit over "the notions of a reflex telephone system with an enigmatic switchboard, or inhibitions and excitations rippling majestically over the surface of the brain . . ." (p. 209). In brief, they find evidence that the inner core of the brain (the limbic system) is instrumental in executing plans. It appears to be the processing unit carrying out the instructions of a program. The outer core, the association areas, appears to embody the memory unit storing the operations to be utilized in the Plan. Emphasis, however, is on the Plan and the programming of sequential acts. The Miller-Galanter-Pribram paradigm is well suited for handling both instinctive acts as described by the ethologists (e.g., Thorpe, 1963) and complex acts of human problem solving.

Deutsch: As a second example of the application of the cybernetic hypothesis to psychology, let us consider J. A. Deutsch's introductory remarks for his book *The Structural Basis of Behavior.* Deutsch espouses a case for cybernetic modeling, but without the assumption that the hypothesis be reductive in nature. Whereas for Miller, Galanter, and Pribram the TOTE unit can be presented as a neurological as well as a purely conceptual hypothesis, for Deutsch the model or the "structure" of the cybernetic model need have only conceptual significance. Indeed it is better that our explanatory structures be free of any pretentions to physiological embodiments. Thus Deutsch emphasizes the difference between a structural system, as such, and its putative embodiment. But first let us pick up Deutsch's argument in favor of structural explanations of behavior.

Deutsch begins by distinguishing between explanations by description and by generalization (that is, by instantiation) and those which are structural in character. Although the former may involve hypothetical constructs which extend the generalizability of basic phenomenological laws, it is the latter type in which hypothetical constructs play a predominant role. The development of structural explanations proceed in two stages: one, the formulation of a system "whose properties tally with our observations of behavior"; two, identification of the elements of the system with neurological entities. Stage two thus represents the embodiment of the structures in stage one. Though Deutsch does not demean the endeavors of stage two when there is legitimate maturity of the reducing science, he is emphatic that theoretical psychology need only be a stage one endeavor.

It is well to note that explanation by instantiation is not causal in character. Such explanations are classificatory. So-called causal explanations are structural in nature, for these involve hypotheses that enable us to deduce descriptions of lawful behavior. Regarding the distinction, Deutsch points to a simple adding machine: we may derive purely phenomenological laws of its operations, but also we may adduce structural explanations of those operations in terms of its mechanical components.

Deutsch then enunciates his nonreductive defense of what we have called the "cybernetic hypothesis." One could deduce behavioral propositions from a complete physiological theory, were there one; however, the psychologist can only infer possibilities of structure from his observations of behavior. The distinction between "deduce" and "infer" is to be emphasized. To deduce is to engage in straightforward logical inference; but to "infer" is to engage in conjecture, the intention of which is to devise structures whose logical ramifications permit the deduction of behavior. Conjecture, however, may be of only one or of several possibilities, or of perhaps an unlimited number of such possibilities. And this conjectural basis of structural explanation does not constitute argument against reductionism. Our conjectures, after all, can be of physiological structures. But to this, Deutsch responds:

> To this type of procedure the objection can be made that it involves the creation of physiological mythology; for to suggest physiological mechanisms without direct observational warrant for their existence is fanciful. There is a great deal of substance in this objection but it cannot be treated as an objection to all kinds of attempts to arrive at a structural explanation. It applies only to a particular type of speculation—that which cannot in principle be checked by observations undertaken on the behavior of the animal as a whole or, in other words, the type of observations normally made by psychologists. These speculations concern the embodiment of the system employed. For instance, to attempt to guess at the particular change which occurs in the central nervous system during learning in the framework of a theory purporting to explain behavior is not only unnecessary but also purely speculative. . . . (Deutsch, 1960, pp. 11–12)

At one point Deutsch suggests that physiological speculation, or the seeking of embodiments, is fruitless, if not misleading, because the access to neural structure is technologically limited. But he later writes:

> We do not need to know the physical identity of the elements of the calculus in order to be able to design systems to perform a set of operations or to display a certain type of behavior. . . . There has been no clear distinction between that part of an explanation of behavior which can be expressed as an abstract system and the identification of the elements of this system in terms of actual physical counterparts. The foregoing analysis has tried to make it clear that it is possible to separate these two steps. Once the distinction is clear it becomes fairly obvious that a psychologist need only speculate about the system and not its embodiment. It is not incumbent upon a theorist to suggest what is the embodiment of his hypothesis; a complete specification of its embodiment would add very little to the explanatory power of his system. (1960, p. 14)

It is well to point out that Deutsch's persistent rejection of reductionism is made on methodological grounds alone. He does not assert that reductions are in principle impossible. He follows in the tradition of mechanism and cybernetics, and differs from other partisans of cybernetics only in counseling that the proper role of the psychologist is to construct structural theories of behavior without respect to neurophysiological hypotheses.

This is very defensible methodology. However, one should be cautious about misconstruing the theoretical tactics as genuine antireductionist bias. For the most part the cybernetic hypothesis has been supportive of reduction. Certainly that was the case in Craik's early writings on the subject. When Deutsch writes "It becomes fairly obvious that the psychologist need only speculate about the system not its embodiment," he is emphasizing the logical rather than the epistemological aspects of structure. It is the logical structure of behavioral theory that counts initially. The issues of inventiveness and analogy belong to the psychology of discovery.

These, however, are not issues that we can ignore. A discussion of modeling and the role of analogy (e.g., Braithwaite, 1962; Hesse, 1963) would take us too far afield, but it is not amiss for us to insist that structures that serve as mediators in behavioral descriptions should be interpretable as other than abstract constructs. Analogy is bidirectional from the primary to the secondary sciences. Analogues between well-formalized systems are implemented by appearances common to two domains of experience. In this sense, all modeling, all structural theories are based on embodiments. Doubtless Deutsch is correct in insisting that the constructs of behavioral theory need not be physiological. That is not to say, however, that they will or should be composed of abstract structures divorced of any embodiment. It is perhaps a moot point whether the abstract calculus of a theory needs to have embodiment at all, i.e., an interpretation. However, Deutsch's analysis is based on analogy as to structure and function between behavioral and mechanical systems. Schematic functions are, in a sense, interpretable, as in the case of the "abstract" layout of an information or a communication system. Although mediating functions can be conceived in relatively abstract terms, questions of the medium in which the process function is to be "embodied" are always relevant. We are reminded by Craik's argument: the pervasiveness of mechanical structure implies that cybernetic modeling is a defensible heuristic for visualizing possibilities of physiological embodiment.

Another point to be considered concerns the nature of structure itself and its possible relation to material embodiment. By a structural system Deutsch means a system of entities in which the appropriate calculus for the system permits the deduction of behavioral propositions. Such entities may be material analogues, existential hypotheses, or purely abstract terms. It is clear, however, that Deutsch is not concerned with purely abstract constructs. So far as structure is concerned there is a point at which we can describe a process or a function without worrying about structural detail. That is, we purportedly bridge the input-output continuum with a schematic description of a process occurring over time, and without the embodiment of structural components being specified. Let us suppose, for example, a structural system composed of a simple reflex chain involving input-feedback-output. Association is not ruled out. Let us visualize a conceptual nerve net involving a feedback circle. The logical properties we assign to this net permit the deduction (and explanation) of the reflex behavior. Admittedly we utilize this conceptual network only to the extent it affords us the explanatory rubric for the simple reflex behavior. Deutsch would argue that we need not be concerned with the embodiment of the components of the nerve net. And on this he would be correct so long as the structural system permits a comprehensively precise explanation of the behavior. This being the case, however, he does require grounds for judging the positive analogy between the structural system and the thing represented to be more or less complete. To be sure he has no need for the embodiments we might expect from a molecular biologist. But the more detailed the descriptions and representations by the psychologist, the more relevant they should be for the neurophysiologist. If analogy is to mean anything to us, it is that alternative representations have a common structure. Thus a structural system at one level of description should be compatible with a structural system at another level of description.

Were we to become convinced that at no point in our inquiries is reductionism a significant directive to the psychologist, then all psychologists could join the uncritical instrumentalists. But then, we could surely count on there being two sciences of behavior; one following the lead of Craik and the other appealing to a coterie of systems inventors playing picture games of representation. To some extent this is the case, especially when great emphasis is being placed on predictive models. However, in choosing between a conceptual system that is interpretable in the language of a reducing science and one that is not, there is little question where the choice should rest. So long as neurophysiological reduction is a logical possibility, it will be relevant as a criterion for the evaluation of psychological theory.

NOTE 3.4

Although the argument of the McCulloch-Pitts paper ("A Logical Calculus of Ideas Immanent in Nervous Activity") is complicated by an unfortunate mixture of symbolisms, its assumptions and results are readily stated. Noting that the "all or none" properties of the neuron reveal a kinship to two-valued logic and that the spatio-temporal character of neuronal activity follows the consequential pattern of a propositional argument, the authors visualize the functional properties of neurons as being subject to treatment by means of propositional logic. Focusing upon synaptic inhibition and facilitation, and the temporal chaining of neuronal events, they adopt the following set of assumptions:

1. The activity of the neuron is an "all-or-none" process.
2. A certain fixed number of synapses must be excited within the period of latent addition in order to excite a neuron at any time, and this number is independent of previous activity and position on the neuron.
3. The only significant delay within the nervous system is synaptic delay.
4. The activity of any inhibitory synapse absolutely prevents excitation of the neuron at that time.
5. The structure of the net does not change with time. (1943, p. 22)

Assume now a system of neurons with the above properties. A "solution" of a nerve network will then be one in which the complex state of the inner neurons of the system is made an explicit function of the states (activation) of a set of peripheral neurons (those not activated from within the system). Then for any automata with a set of inputs, outputs, internal states and a set of next state transformations, there is a "realization" of that automata if one can construct a nerve network which will simulate the computations or input-output behavior of the automata. Now every finite automata is definable as a temporal propositional expression (TPE). The proofs of the argument then establish in general that for every describable finite automata, every TPE, there is a possible realization in terms of a nerve network.

Bibliographic note:

The argument in the original paper of McCulloch and Pitts is cumbersome. A sophisticated but simplified discussion can be found in Arbib: *Brain, Machines and Mathematics* (1964). An elementary discussion of McCulloch-Pitts nerve nets can be found in George: *The Brain as a Computer* (1961), but without reference to the theorems of realizability. An excellent and comprehensive discussion of neural network theory is to be found in Minsky: *Computation, Finite and Infinite Machines* (1967).

NOTE 3.5

Alternative forms of adding machines are possible. For example, we may consider adding the plus sign to the vocabulary of the machine. We may then devise a machine with the machine table

	q_1	q_2	q_3
S_1	Rq_1	Lq_1	S_0q_3
S_+	S_1q_2	S_+q_2	S_+q_3
S_0	Lq_3	S_0q_2	S_0q_3

A feature to note about this machine is the clear indication of the condition producing a stopping state. A stopping state is reached if for any $\langle q_j S_i \rangle$ couplet no change is dictated in progressing from one instantaneous state to another. Thus whenever the machine input state combinations are q_2S_+, q_3S_+, q_2S_0, q_3S_0 the machine reaches a stopping state and a solution. Now consider the addition $11+111$ $(2+3)$, where no convention of $m+1$ strokes is required for entering any integer m. We start the machine scanning the first stroke on the left in state q_1.

Note now the progression of computation. The machine inspects the first S_1 and proceeds to the next leaving the tape unchanged. On reaching the sign S_+ in state q_1, it replaces S_+ with S_1 and goes into state q_2. It then backtracks to the left and goes into state q_1. Hence it continues to inspect the series of S_1's on the tape until it reaches the first blank S_0 to the right. Being in state q_1 inspecting S_0 it moves to the left and goes into state q_3. At this point the machine replaces S_1 which it is now scanning with S_0 and then proceeds to its stopping state. In effect this machine replaces S_+ with S_1 and then proceeds to erase the last stroke symbol S_1.

A simple Turing machine for generating the successor function of any number n, and hence any positive integer, gives the table

	q_1	q_2
S_1	Rq_1	
S_0	S_1q_2	S_0q_2

Note this machine can compute the successor of any number n if upon computing $n+1$ it then terminates its operations. This is the case for the above machine. For example, write $n=4$ as . . . 011110 . . . on the tape. Start the machine in state q_1 inspecting the first stroke on the left. It then proceeds to inspect but to leave unchanged all stroke symbols, and on the occurrence of the first 0, i.e., S_0, it replaces S_0 with the stroke S_1. It then goes into a stopping state. Note for any machine table such as the above two, we can specify those instantaneous states which if reached will result in a terminal state and hence in the computable solution to the problem. Thus for any prior combination q_jS_i, as indicated in the marginal variates of our table, the next state dictated entails no change, i.e., if $q_jS_i \rightarrow S_iq_j$ then that state is a terminal state.

NOTE 3.6

The technique of mapping a symbolic argument by Gödel numbers is given in some detail in Chapter 5. Here we note simply that any symbol which is a constitutent of a symbolic expression can be assigned a number arbitrarily selected from a sequence of digits, say the sequence of odd digits beginning with 3 (Davis, 1958). Then any quadruple which is an expression in the argument of Turing machines can be mapped by using these symbol numbers as the exponents assigned to the sequence of primes which maps the order in which the symbols appear. Thus suppose it is the case that we have the following symbols and their corresponding Gödel numbers:

Symbol:	q_1	q_2	S_1	R
	↓	↓	↓	↓
Gödel numbers:	3	5	7	9

Then for the ordered quadruple $\langle q_1S_1Rq_2 \rangle$ we would have

$$2^3 \cdot 3^7 \cdot 5^9 \cdot 7^5$$

This is a Gödel number of the expression and translates uniquely into that expression. Furthermore, any set of quadruples of Turing machine Z will yield a Gödel number which is the product of the Gödel numbers of all quadruples. Hence any machine Z can be expressed as a Gödel number which is the product of the Gödel numbers of its ordered quadruples. In effect, if the Gödel number of the machine Z is written on the tape of the universal machine, U, and if it is followed by X_0 the number to be computed, then U will compute that number (Davis, 1954).

CHAPTER 4

Simulation

CAN A machine think? Can a machine be conscious? Are machines purposive? These are questions frequently posed in computer circles. They attest to our ingenuity in devising machines and machine programs which simulate man-like behaviors. Yet it can be argued that the issue of simulation is tangential to the discussion of reductionism and the cybernetic hypothesis. One may formulate an elaborate cybernetic hypothesis concerning the nervous system without having in mind a particular simulator. And one may build a simulator without intending to simulate precisely a particular behavioral process. Simulation is germane to the discussion of reductionism only as it reflects upon our capabilities of representing, modeling, or realizing behavioral systems in mechanical terms. If we can build machines to simulate complex behaviors, then at least we have realized the possibility of describing such behavioral "computations" in mechanical terms. The existence of some ingenious simulator makes all the more poignant the mechanical assumptions along which the psychoneurologist proceeds. And since the mechanical system is a realization of a system of logical rubrics, we are assured there is no logical barrier to success in our proceeding in accordance with these assumptions. The mystery is removed from problem solving, creativity, and thinking wherever we can build simulators to simulate these complex acts.

To simulate is to produce a machine capable of performing functions similar to those performed by the thing simulated. It is clear, however, that a simulator may prove to be more a curiosity than a heuristic to understanding the organismic mechanisms of behavior. It may prove itself computationally without establishing itself as any kind of surrogate for the nervous system. For example, there is that familiar spring-driven toy car or beetle (Sluckin, 1954) which runs randomly over a tabletop, but which always turns abruptly about and toward the center of the table whenever its front wheels protrude beyond the edge. This machine behaves very much like a young, naive laboratory rat set free to explore the top of just such a table. But it is obvious that the positive analogy is limited. The lateral wheel suspended beneath the chassis of the toy is nothing like the intricate mechanisms which implement the rat's behavior. Or, to take a more imposing example, our splendid planetariums and their projectors simulate to an astonishing degree the apparent movements of our planetary system. Yet even here the analogy is limited. In fact, were we, as naive observers, to study the projector as a heuristic for theorizing about the heavens, we would incline more toward Ptolemy than Copernicus.

A number of highly ingenious mechanisms have been devised for simulating simple behaviors of organisms. From lowly sow bugs (Tolman, 1939, 1941) to the homeostat (Ashby, 1952), we find remarkable simulators of certain types of behavior. But in every case, the analogy is limited so far as concerns the embodiment of circuitry of the nervous system. We are impressed with these mechanisms but only because we find that relatively simple machines can display behaviors remarkably like those of complex adaptive organisms. Grey Walter (1953), for example, has designed an electronic conditioned reflex machine (Cora) and a motivated searching-seeking mechanism (*Machina Speculatrix*) that conjointly simulate adaptive behavior. Yet machines that learn and machines that search out a source to charge their own batteries are not models of the nervous system. Photoelectric cells, vacuum tubes, neon tubes, and batteries are not necessarily components which provide rich analogy for the neurophysiologist— even when the combining of diverse components generates unpredicted behaviors similar to some in the organismic repertory. Ashby's well-known homeostat displays purposive, equilibrium-seeking behavior of a kind that appears to pervade organismic adjustment. Still, a system of magnets controlling the flow of electricity over feedback circuits suggests only that equilibrium seeking and internal balance are not unique to protoplasmic systems.

ANALOGY

"Simulation" like "reduction" requires a certain amount of semantic clarification if it is to be of use in the philosophy of science. To simulate of course means to imitate, but more explicitly simulation is a matter of accomplishing well-described behavioral results, the dimensions of which are arbitrarily selected. Thus, if we are concerned only with the description of molar acts and achievements, and subsequently the simulation of these acts, we may say of this simulator that it possesses *functional* or phenomenological analogy. On the other hand, if we are concerned with the molecular constitutents of these molar acts and wish to simulate in detail the constituent processes underlying these molar acts, then an appropriate simulator can be said to demonstrate *structural* analogy. Finally, if our simulator with structural analogy were in its material realization to be like the object simulated, it would possess *existential* analogy as well. Of these types of analogy it is clear that simulation of organismic behavior involves either functional or structural analogy or both, but seldom if ever existential analogy. Yet it is well for us to keep in mind the idea of existential analogy. In so doing we may be spared some of the more exorbitant claims of robotology.

Let us now formulate the idea of simulation in somewhat general terms sufficient to distinguish between positive and negative analogy existing between an object (behavioral system) and its analogue.

Let O and M designate the organism and simulator respectively. Then for O there is a set of possible input variables $\{s_i\}$ sufficient for the description of any molar input S in the language of O, and a set of possible output variables $\{r_j\}$ sufficient for the description of any molar output R. Likewise for M there are sets $\{s_i'\}$ and $\{r_j'\}$ for the description of S' and R' in the language of M. Then O is said to be simulated by M if the following conditions obtain:

(1) for every S constructible from the elements in $\{s_i\}$ there is an S' constructible from the elements in $\{s_i'\}$;

(2) for every R constructible from the elements of $\{r_j\}$ there is a substitutable R' constructible from the elements in $\{r_j'\}$;

(3) for any $S \rightarrow R$ formulating lawful relation in O there is a substitutable $S' \rightarrow R'$ formulating a lawful relation in M, and such that in their respective languages the formulations represent interpretations of the same logical calculus.

If these conditions hold without exception over the entire domain of O's behavior then M can be considered a complete or total simulator of O. Thus for any S–R sequence in O there is a substitutable S'–R' sequence in M such that O's behavior is computable by the simulator M. If these conditions hold only over a subdomain of O's behavior then M can be considered only a partial simulator of O.

As yet, nothing has been said of analogy. Let us distinguish between *functional* analogy and *structural* analogy. If M is a complete or total simulator of O, the functional analogy is total; that is to say, there is positive analogy without negative analogy and M is functionally analogous to O. Visualizing O and M as computers it is really immaterial which computer we should use for an act of computation over the domain of events in O for which the analogy holds. Input and output would have equipollent translations in the languages of both. If M only partially simulates O, the functional analogy is incomplete. There will be negative analogy (incomplete simulation) between M and O to the extent that subsets of events representable as $S \rightarrow R$ functions in O are not in the domain of events simulatable in M. In other words, the negative analogy pertains to those events in O nonsimulatable by events in M. It is apparent that in functional analogy we are concerned neither with the material substances in which O and M are realized nor with the structures that implement those functions. Our analogy is therefore phenomenological in the sense that we are concerned only with specifying environmental (input) and behavioral (output) states that are expressible in terms of molar propositions appropriate to O. A simulation then entails that behavioral propositions, with suitable translations, be derivable in the language of M. Thus, as examples of such behavioral propositions, we would have: "O chooses alternative A over alternative B"; "O adds two and two to get four"; "O engages in vicarious trial and error before turning right." Propositions such as "O's blood pressure increases x millibars" and "Muscle fibre Y contracts" would not be propositions in the phenomenological language of O.

On the other hand, with structural analogy we move from the molar aspects of functional analogy to the simulation of molecular structure and mediating process. That is to say, if every conceptually relevant molecular component of the event S and every molecular component of the event R are representable by elements in $\{s_i'\}$ and $\{r_j'\}$ respectively and if the domain of $S \rightarrow R$ events covers mediating as well as peripheral events then our analogy will be structural as well as functional. The degree of positive structural analogy in the simulation of a function will itself be a function of the fineness of the molecular grain imposed upon the entities and events that fall under the general purview of functional analogy. Conceivably, we may have a high degree of positive functional analogy with minimum structural analogy (as for example in some types of automatic pilots), or we may have a high degree of structural analogy with minimum functional analogy (as, for example, a meticulous plastic model of a jet engine). However, in most of our efforts and programs in simulation we are concerned with functional analogy. Our primary goal is to simulate molar output. We tend to be concerned with structural models and structural analogy only in those cases where the simulator possesses the initial prerequisite of functional analogy.

This, of course, does not preclude the tactic of developing simulators with functional analogy by initially attempting a design that manifests structural analogy with the object simulated. Indeed, the kinship between functional and structural analogy is the salient aspect of Craik's formulation of the cybernetic hypothesis. It is well to emphasize the kinship of functional-structural and molar-molecular distinctions. If we simply simulate the results of a problem- or goal-defined computational act, we are exploiting the functional analogy between, say, M and O. We are concerned with the simulation of molar acts, by whatever means. If, in addition, we are occupied in mapping in one-to-one detail all of the mediating or transitional states which produce that molar result, we are concerned with designing a simulator M which displays structural analogy with O as well. But by structural analogy we mean the simulation of intraorganismic molecular functions, not the duplication or even the modeling of particular physical or biophysical structures. As for this latter modeling, that is, the modeling of material structure *per se,* we require an additional type of analogy.

By *existential* analogy we mean structural analogy in a medium identical with that of the object simulated. Thus the existential analogue for an O with optimal positive analogy would be his identical twin. Between a human computer and an electronic computer, there would be almost no existential analogy. Of course, should we be able to build electronic computers with components of organic plasma, we would be able to introduce existential analogy; but the metallic as against the colloidal structures set M and O apart. It should be remembered that any mechanical computer can be represented as a Turing machine. However, a Turing machine is logical rather than material machinery. Thus, between a mechanical computer and its corresponding Turing machine, there will be at most only limited existential analogy.

As we shall see later, a great deal of the "romance of robotology" can be dispelled when we make clear the distinctions between these types of analogy. Moreover, we should observe that many useful simulators carry little pretense to analogy. Many computers falling under the class of artificial intelligences are designed for computational acts, the pattern of which bears little resemblance to human acts of computation. By any conceivable means, such computers are designed to compute results of which a human computer is capable. To that extent there may be limited functional analogy between the simulator and the human computer. However, the means or tactics of computation for the two are quite dissimilar. Conceivably the human computer is digital-like in its computation of continuous functions. On the other hand, an analogue computer may simulate the results of such computations, without displaying significant analogy as to how the human computer operates. To simulate is not to say unqualifiedly that the simulator computes or behaves analogously to the object simulated. It may be that for the simulator only the end result counts. For example, we may add with an abacus, a Babbage machine, a desk calculator, a digital computer, or an analogue computer. They are functionally analogous in that they compute identical results, but they perform their functions with different mechanisms.

SIMULATORS

A review of the many kinds of simulators would constitute a compendium in itself. We take note only of a limited number, sufficient to adumbrate the variety of psychological functions which are simulatable (cf. Note 4.1). Since we have distinguished between functional and structural analogy, we shall adopt a similar classification for the description of simulators. A simulator is a functional simulator if it imitates or simulates the molar properties of the object behavior. Thus it is the very character of a simulator to be a functional simulator. A simulator is a structural simulator if, in addition, it simulates certain well-defined molecular properties of organismic response as well. Thus an ideal structural simulator would be one which simulates the mediating processes and functions implemented by the central nervous system.

Functional Simulators

We take it as precept that if a psychological function can be well described strictly in behavioral terms, then it is possible, in principle, to conceive a mechanical simulator which will simulate that function. There is no proof of such a general proposition, but its credibility is supported by the results of McCulloch and Pitts (1943) and of Turing (1937); namely, if an act of computation can be well described then it is possible to conceive a machine which will carry out those computations, at least in coded form. Implicit within the precept is the surmise that behavior is a form of mechanical computation. Even where behavior displays trial and error or stochastic properties, its conception is mechanical in nature. Simply defined, learning is the enhancement of response over a period of time. This "enhancement" is in general contingent upon a modification of the internal state of the organism as either structurally or cognitively defined. Thus classical conditioning presents learning at its simplest structural level; perceptual learning presents learning in its cognitive complexity. Both types of learning have been simulated.

In a 1946 paper, Boring lists a number of early attempts to simulate simple conditioning phenomena. Of these, practically all incorporate simple circuitry and relays which effect the transference of response from an initial adequate stimulus to a substitute one. Stevens (1929), for example, designed a machine which simulated conditioning as a function of change (decrease) in resistance at critical connections. For the most part, the system was a relatively crude one involving electromagnets and levers. But despite its cumbersome structure, Stevens designed it with a particular conceptual nervous system in mind. Watson (1930) and Ellson (1935) were also able to produce conditioning "toys" by utilizing systems of magnetically modified relays. Clark Hull was involved in the designing of two different simulators (Baernstein and Hull, 1929, 1931; Krueger and Hull, 1931), both of which proved more versatile than mere learning toys. One simulator involved toluene mercury thermal relays which simulated memory decay as well as learning. The other simulated similar functions by means of a series of polarizing cells chargeable from a power source during active conditioning. What is especially interesting is that both machines were successful in simulating generalization (irradiation), extinction, and inhibition. Bradner (1937) also utilized mercury toluene cells in the design of a machine whereby learning was effected as a function of variable resistance.

Thus, even in psychology's age of pretechnology there appears to have been little difficulty in the simulation of simple conditioning phenomena. Although for the most part there was no intention of simulating the structural detail of such concepts as neurobiotaxis and the reflex-arc, the reliance upon circuitry and variable resistance generated a specious analogy to synaptic function. If nothing else, such toys served to emphasize that learning could be understood in purely mechanical terms devoid of any mystique concerning the uniqueness of viable organic substance.

Mechanical simulators need hardly be constructed at all. Schematic artifacts realizable in several material forms might serve the purpose. Thus Block (1965) is able to conceive a simple learning machine with paper cups, chips, and counters and an appropriate set of instructions. This machine learns to play a variant of the game of Nims ("Last One Loses") with a record of winning against an opponent which exceeds chance. It learns by the simple expedient of self-instruction to alter its internal structure as a function of losing a game. In time it develops a structure constituting the optimal set of instructions as to how many chips should be drawn when the number of chips remaining in the pile is specified. Such a machine is clearly a curiosity. But since one soon discovers that the machine mechanically implements the strategy that the perceptive human player arrives at by ratiocination, he is tempted to attribute to it a certain degree of structural analogy (cf. Note 4.2).

Perceptual learning presents much more complicated phenomena, for here recognition and discrimination, as well as large memory storage, are required. Machines of the complexity of present day electronic computers are required. A digital computer programmed to play checkers (Samuel, 1959) selects moves on the basis of the input state of the game at any time and the storage of past records, thereby recognizing the situation and playing according to "experience." Thus, this machine simulates perceptual learning over a very limited task. The EPAM computer program (Feigenbaum, 1959; Feigenbaum and Simon, 1961) constitutes a machine which can simulate various recognition and verbal learning tasks. Any processable stimulus input is sifted through a discrimination net, such that at the terminal node a comparison can be made between the input and the "image" of the terminal node in the discrimination net. Thus the machine effects a systematic procedure for classifying stimulus objects. Learning takes place, either as a function of the machine's "growing" the discrimination net or as a matter of developing the "images" of the terminal nodes effectively serving as responses to stimuli.

In the EPAM program we approach structural as well as functional analogy. Not only does the machine simulate certain verbal learning tasks (verbal recognition, paired associate learning, and so on), but it presents a description as to what processes occur in the achievement of recognition and classification. We are not sure, of course, how the human computer effects recognition and discrimination, but it is reasonable to conjecture that it is done by some procedure of systematic matching and testing such as is simulated in a discrimination net.

Structural Simulators

As we turn to more and more complex functions, the molar achievement, so to speak, needs to be broken down into its molecular processes and means-ends subsystems. Therefore, on a reflective analysis of adaptive or problem-solving behavior we conceptualize means-ends processes essential to the task of reaching a terminal solution. And in the simulation of molar achievement we seek to build machines which simulate these means-ends processes. Logic machines (Newell, Shaw, and Simon, 1957), chess-playing machines (Newell, Shaw, and Simon, 1958), geometry solvers (Gerlernter, Hansen, and Loveland, 1960), and symbolic automatic integrators (Slagle, 1961) all seek to simulate molar behavior by implementing means-ends processes analogous to those effected by the human problem-solver. The strategy of simulation is straightforward. If we can describe a problem-solving task in terms of a continuum of process steps (i.e., deterministically), it should be possible to devise a machine program to simulate those steps. Even personality, if it is fully describable in terms of affect, memory, thinking, perception, and action, ought to be simulatable (Tomkins, 1963). (cf. Note 4.3)

Since building the versatile "humanomaton" (Tomkins, 1963) is doubtless beyond our present computer resources, let us confine the discussion to relatively simple cognitive machines. By virtue of an analysis of human strategies for the identification of stimulus objects, Hunt and Hovland (1961) devised a digital computer program which generates hypotheses for stimulus classification and which then implements a test procedure for each hypothesis. Inputs are thereby conceptualized according to conjunction, disjunction, and relation. Indeed, such a machine should be able to discriminate between the coded inputs of healthy and pathological tissue cells.

Most problem-solving machines are designed for specific types of problems such as chess, checkers, double acrostics, or even composing music (Reitman, 1961); and, in general, each machine is realized in terms of a large scale computer program. These machines are limited-purpose machines. Obviously a digital computer program for solving checkers problems is not adaptable directly to solving problems in geometry. A human problem-solver is, of course, more versatile. Here the "computer" which solves a problem in chess is organically the same computer that may solve a problem in geometry or may compose a melody. In general the human problem-solver proceeds by setting up a goal, by detecting differences between its present situational state and the goal state and by adopting means-ends strategies that will reduce the discrepancies between the present state and the desired goal (Bartlett, 1932; Duncker, 1945; Wertheimer, 1945). The General Problem Solver, GPS (Newell, Shaw, and Simon, 1959; Newell and Simon, 1961, a, b, 1963) is a programmed digital computer which is designed to simulate just such a problem-solving process. In general, the program seeks to reduce the difference between some prior state, a, and a terminal goal state, b. In achieving this end it may transform the original a and b discrepancy into a more abstract or recognizable difference. It may set up subgoal strategies, and it may operate upon the initial state a in order to transform the goal discrepancy into a more manageable form.

In mapping human problem-solving, the GPS has been able to solve the transport problem of the missionaries and cannibals (Newell and Simon, 1963). Three cannibals and three missionaries are to get from one bank of a stream to the other. The means of transport is a boat capable of carrying one or two persons, but no more. The essential restriction is that at no time and place in the transport procedure are the cannibals to outnumber the missionaries. Thus visualize

$$MMMCCCB|$$

as the prior or initial state, a, and

$$|MMMCCCB$$

as the terminal state, b, with the vertical bar symbolizing the stream. The differences to be resolved are always differences between the prevailing distribution of personnel and boat and some more desirable state. The solution thus proceeds to the terminal goal by means of achieving a set of subgoals. Indeed, as one plays the game with pencil and paper, he observes that this solution follows just such a process (cf. Note 4.4).

Problem-solving machines are for the most part functional simulators. Perhaps only occasionally do they incorporate processes bearing close structural analogy to the object simulated. More striking structural analogy is found in those simulators which are explicitly designed to realize systems patterned after conceptions of the nervous system. Thus Clark and Farley (1955) and Rochester, et al. (1956) have sought to program computers to simulate the cell assembly of Hebb's conceptual nervous system (Hebb, 1949). Milner (1957) has attempted to represent schematically an improved cell assembly system in terms that lend themselves to simulation. Similarly, Rosenblatt (1958) has been able to utilize the statistical properties of such assemblies in the design of the perceptron, a simulator capable of cognitive learning.

Doubtless the most venerable but by no means the most complex simulators are those that simulate adaptive, purposive behavior. Various self-guidance and homing systems are relatively complex. However, *Machina Speculatrix* (Walter, 1953) and the homeostat (Ashby, 1952) simulate simple adaptive behaviors, so simple that we are tempted to attribute structural analogy to them. *Machina Speculatrix* is an "electromechanical species" which senses and seeks power sources for reconstituting its own energy supply. Its system of photocells, motors, amplifiers, and feedback circuits enable it to explore the environment, avoid noxious stimuli and obstacles, and approach goal situations where its batteries are recharged. Indeed, the machine displays adaptive behaviors not conceived in the original design (cf. Note 4.5). Ashby's well-publicized homeostat simulates simple homeostatic goal-seeking behavior. Assume an organism which lives in a constantly varying environment, yet which is always seeking a state of equilibrium. Every adaptation and adjustment may in turn create a critical disbalance, yet the organism continually responds in such a way as to reestablish a state of equilibrium. The homeostat simulates an organism in just such a milieu. It is constructed of magnets, potentiometers, and commutators in which adjustment is effected by four functional units that are interconnected by feedback circuits. Thus any field which deflects four magnetic needles from a state of equilibrium results in a complex response restoring the equilibrium. If environmental parameters are introduced to disturb the system, it responds by concerted equilibrium seeking. If the inputs (values of the parameters) are controlled by a randomizing device, the system becomes continuously adaptive and simulates behavior in keeping with the principle of ultrastability; namely, the principle of continuous equilibrium seeking.

Our sample of simulators covers only a few of the more publicized ones. None of the machines portends emergence of a robot age. Even the Newell and Simon General Problem Solver is adaptable only to fairly simple problems. What is important, however, is not that some particular computer is versatile, but that any behavioral function, well described in step-by-step computational terms, appears to be realizable in machine componentry. The human computer is not a machine in the strict sense of the term. Yet if its functions are realizable in machine terminology, indeed, if our understanding of organismic functioning is determined in large part by that language, then speculations concerning the extent and limits of simulation are germane to questions concerning the extent and limits of our understanding of organisms (Bibliographic note, cf. Note 4.6).

SIMULATION AND ROBOTOLOGY

The foregoing survey of simulators, brief and cryptic as it has been, reveals the achievements in the area to be impressive. Little wonder then, that we have succumbed to the romance of robotology. All that is missing is the sigh and the wistful glance. Machines can solve problems, play chess, learn, choose, and create. They can recognize, translate after a fashion, make decisions in the face of uncertainty. Why not then go all the way, endow them with consciousness, and yield to them their reflective moments, even their soulful wrestlings with the meaning of existence. Indeed why not? Many romancers have accepted the challenge. May we not judge machines to be thoughtful and conscious in the same way we judge our fellow men to be thoughtful and conscious?

Positivistic candor inclines us to answer affirmatively. But only in a sense, yes. No one claims to have built a machine with a tender mind. Behaviorally, man and machine display striking analogy. But man and machine differ all the same. It is hard for us, comfortable perhaps in our cradle of plasma, to give up our sense of special apprehending privilege, hard for us to think of the question, "Can a machine be conscious?" as being little more than a joke. Is the argument in behalf of simulation not a bit presumptuous? Let us have a look.

By robotology I mean simply that man is presumed to be machine-like and that in principle man and all his distinguishable functions can be faithfully represented or simulated by a machine. Hence, in carrying simulation to more esoteric functions, we find ourselves attributing thought, intelligence, purposiveness, and even feeling and consciousness to a machine. This attribution of the softer cognitive and appetitive functions to hardware machines is made possible by our exploitation of functional analogy. We formulate criteria as the basis for analogy. Hence if we find machines satisfying more or less some explicit behavioral criteria, we assign to them the attribute of organisms from which we have extrapolated these criteria. Thus Michael Scriven (1960) finds that the "compleat robot," satisfies a budget of "performatory" criteria over a range of complex human functions. He argues that there are at least no behavioral grounds for not attributing such functions as creating, choosing, learning, understanding, perceiving, and feeling to the compleat robot. No behavioral grounds *per se* can be offered for distinguishing between M and O in terms of what can and cannot be simulated.

One of the most poignant statements of the "performatory" test for simulation can be found in a paper by A. M. Turing (1950). (Scriven, in fact, relies on such a test.) Suppose the machine, $M,$ and the organism, $O,$ are being teletypically interrogated in any way an interrogator chooses. The responses of M and O are, of course, their respective computations, the results of which are teletypically encoded. The question of attributing properties of organismic behavioral function to the machine then rests upon how well M plays the "imitation game"; that is to say, how well M can conceal his identity when the interrogator is forced to identify the source of every teletyped response. It may, of course, be that present machines are as yet incapable of playing the imitation game effectively. However, it is not a question of extant machinery, but of machines in principle. Turing, like Scriven, finds no convincing grounds why, at least in principle, a machine could not pass the performatory tests of imitation in such a way as to restrict the interrogator's accuracy to chance. Given machinery and battalions of programmers, there are neither logical nor technological barriers to simulating in every important detail those functions which we presumptuously reserve for man.

On the grounds of performatory tests in general and imitation games in principle, several writers have inclined to attribute human-like behavioral functions to machines. For example, MacKay (1951, 1952) finds that machine artifacts are capable of intelligent, goal-directed activity. They can receive, select, store, and send information. They can modify their computations in terms of changes in their own internal states. They can learn, reason, and modify their tactics in the pursuit of goals. As probabilistic reasoning machines they can even simulate the essential indeterminism of man. (MacKay, a machinist, is also an indeterminist concerning self-determination, cf. MacKay, 1966.) In response to the question, "Can we produce artifacts which would provide evidence of mentality comparable with that acceptable from a human being?" (1952, p. 61), MacKay argues that there is no barrier in principle which would prevent a possible artifact from passing the appropriate tests. Mentality, as manifested in learning, perception, attending, and hallucinating, can in each case be simulated. All that is required is that the artifact perform in certain prescribed ways.

Scriven (1960) has reviewed a similar list of achievements for machines and finds no behavioral tests that would enable us clearly to distinguish between man and machine. "Could an artifact be a person?" Conceive any list of behavioral criteria you can and if the artifact passes them, including a positive response to the above question, then there would be no behavioral grounds, Scriven asserts, for denying that artifact "being." Wisdom (1952) in an early symposium on the subject of mentality and machines, concurs that machines display "mentality" on all behavioral tests, although there may be some difficulties for stipulating the behavioral conditions for insight and emotive expression. However, as to the matter of assigning consciousness to machines, Wisdom demurs. If epiphenomenalism is true, namely, that consciousness is nonparticipative in behavioral process, then consciousness is trivial. If epiphenomenalism is false then technological limitations are such that consciousness can not be reproduced in machines. But as to consciousness, Thompson (1965) goes all the way in behalf of "machine theory." If present behavioral tests for assigning consciousness to organismic beings can, in principle, be passed by machines, then refusal to acknowledge the possibility of conscious machines is philosophically indefensible.

Consciousness and Machines

Since Thompson's argument forces the issue beyond mere performatory tests of methodological behaviorism, let us follow it in greater detail. To rely upon behavioral descriptions of consciousness would simply decide the issue for "machine theory" *ex hypothesi*. Thus, simply to stipulate a few behaviors for the machine to simulate would weight the argument in favor of machine theory. We need to approach consciousness in terms of what it is in the context of human behavior *and* inner experience. But if, in the difficulty of describing "inner life," we agree that behavioral criteria are sufficient grounds for ascribing consciousness to human organisms, they also become sufficient grounds for ascribing consciousness to machines. All that is required is a technology sufficient for us to simulate certain well-described behaviors. Suppose, however, we now consider the suggestion that in spite of a machine's passing performatory tests, it is still a machine, and it is the very nature of a machine not to be conscious. Such a tactic obviously begs the question. We set up a test procedure for ascribing consciousness to objects, in fact, a test procedure that is applicable in ascribing consciousness to human beings; but if a machine were to pass it, we would declare the test invalid. If we initially agree as to the relevance of performatory tests, then it is inappropriate to resort to *ex cathedra* pronouncements on the logical incompatibility of machine and mental languages. As a final point, Thompson considers what impact the ascription of consciousness to machines might have on the mind-body problem. He concludes that the possibility of conscious machines neither complicates nor resolves any of the issues of the traditional arguments. At most, for the machine theorist the possibility of parallelism or epiphenomenalism would force technological developments in the direction of structural as well as functional analogy.

The arguments for ascribing or not ascribing consciousness to machines can be directed to either one of two questions: (1) Is there a possibility that machines in fact possess consciousness? and, (2) What is the nature of our inductive grounds for attributing consciousness to objects other than ourselves? The two questions are in some respects quite different. We need to consider them separately, although, as we shall see, both converge on the issue of analogy.

Can a machine in fact be conscious? Let us suppose that a machine simulates a specified set of problem-solving cogitative behaviors, and that upon interrogation it types out answers indicating that it is aware of its internal states. Furthermore, the machine responds in a seemingly knowing way to questions of how it feels, what it sees, and so on. Since there seems no barrier in principle to constructing such a machine (cf. Putnam, 1960), why should we not be convinced that in fact such a machine is conscious, or has states of self-consciousness? We may still demur. Behaviorally we do have grounds for ascribing consciousness to this machine, but the question of fact is another matter.

Now we are impressed with the immanent presence of our own consciousness, and we find that immanence to be something quite different from behavior. There is a suspicion here that in the argument for attributing consciousness to machines we are exploiting analogy at the expense of sincerity. Consciousness just *is* something that machines do not possess. Functional and even structural analogy between man and machine are not enough; we require existential analogy as well. Thus Clack (1966) points to the obvious weakness of Thompson's argument, and to all arguments that would ascribe consciousness to machines on the grounds of functional analogy. An artifact may pass the performatory tests, may write a printout, or speak that it is aware, is seeing blue, feeling pain, and so on, and yet fall short of the principal analogy we look for in human organisms; i.e., structural *and* existential analogy. Ascribing consciousness to machines is not quite like ascribing it to another person, or even to a subhuman primate.

The cyberneticist, Satosi Watanabe, clearly, succinctly and, we might add, impatiently states the case against the robotologists.

> The behavioristic method may or may not be able to detect the difference between presence and absence of consciousness. If not, it simply demonstrates that the behavioristic method is inadequate in discovering and describing the whole reality, since the existence of my consciousness is an undeniable *fact* to me.
> If a machine is made out of protein, then it may have consciousness, but a machine made out of vacuum tubes, diodes, and transistors cannot be expected to have consciousness. I do not here offer a proof for this statement, except that it is obvious according to well-disciplined common sense. A "conscious" machine made out of protein is no longer a machine, it is a man-made animal. I do not deny this possibility. On the other hand, let us not be carried away by a mechanical romanticism which takes a hidden animistic satisfaction in imagining a "soul" in electric robots, even if this romanticism is cloaked in cold logical arguments, and even if it is phrased as if it were trying to refute the concept of consciousness in general. (1960, p. 145)

But then let us consider the second question. What is the nature of our inductive grounds for attributing consciousness to objects other than ourselves? In addressing ourselves to the question, "Can a machine be conscious?" are we not really engaging in a bit of philosophical exegesis? Doubtless many of the essays (e.g., Putnam, 1960; Scriven, 1960; Thompson, 1965) are just that—efforts to define philosophical muddles over the subject of consciousness in terms of machines and simulation. Thus one is recalled to the earlier philosophical discussions of "other minds" (J. T. W. Wisdom, 1952; Ayer, 1959; Austin, 1946; Ryle, 1949). Ascribing consciousness to another person or object is different from ascribing it to myself. In the latter case, I have direct evidence which is both sufficient and necessary for ascribing it to myself. But in the former case, my evidence is hearsay and analogical. Since the other object may misconstrue the interrogation or lie, its behavior is neither sufficient nor necessary for my attributing consciousness to it. What then are my grounds for ascribing consciousness to other persons? They remain analogical. I give an affirmative answer by faulting the question. In one sense the question implies that no answer is possible. There are no possible grounds for my attributing consciousness to other persons (the analyst's version of the solipsistic predicament). But in another sense, that of how we may possibly give a defensible answer, the answer is in terms of analogy. Thus, I may think that I have no good reason for denying consciousness to another person even though my evidence for ascribing it to him is different from the evidence I have for ascribing it to myself. I observe that the person under the circumstance of interrogation, or collective judgment, utilizes similar language, behaves in a similar way, displays similar structure and is constructed of similar material. That is to say, my ascription of consciousness to the other person is contingent upon my observing functional, structural, *and* existential analogy. Doubtless it is the absence of existential analogy that weakens the argument of the machine theorists.

Still, just as one is not happy with the prospect of attributing what we know as consciousness to metallic machines, so we are not altogether happy with the argument that properties are assignable only if a criterion of existential analogy is met. Machines do display a purposive-type behavior and so do organisms. Machines do solve problems and so do organisms. And so on. Why, we may ask, are behavioral criteria not adequate to the task of assigning properties to functional objects?

Again we ask, "Are behavioral criteria sufficient for the ascription of consciousness to machines?" We begin by stipulating a finite set of behavioral criteria. If a machine passes the corresponding tests then we ascribe consciousness to it. But only on the grounds that such criteria and such tests provide a sufficient demonstration of the presence of conscious phenomena. Suppose, however, that one were not to accept these particular criteria. Suppose the tests were judged insufficient for establishing the presence of consciousness. Being restricted to behavioral tests, a person may prescribe an augmented set of criteria. He may design additional tests, say as to cogitative processes, verbal behavior, and so on. But obviously we can never satisfy the intransigent skeptic. What constitutes the sufficient set of behavioral criteria is never a question of logic, it is always a matter of convention. And consciousness, according to our skeptic, is always a question of what *is*; it is a matter of ontology. Furthermore, ontological questions are never resolvable by convention. To be sure, they may be laid aside by conventional agreements, but they are not answerable by them.

So what of all this argument? We may only answer that the argument of the skeptic is a permissible one. Granting this, we may then wonder what role consciousness can play in the understanding either of man or of machine. Even granting consciousness to the local observer, what systemic defense has he for attributing consciousness to objects other than himself? Treating consciousness ontologically, as the given what-is, is scientifically not defensible. Treating consciousness as a conceptual convention to be translated into terms of behavioral disposition, renders consciousness, *per se,* dispensable. As a conceptual convention we might well begin by defining consciousness in terms of functions a machine can indeed perform, and then proceed to discover that we can attribute such functions to man and organism as well. For the skeptic, then, it is just possible that we go about analogy and the attribution of properties in just the reverse direction that we ought. The point remains, however, that at best, consciousness is a problematical matter for any science (cf. Note 4.7).

The intentional argument. Related areas, where behavioral criteria for simulation are assumed problematic, involve notions of cogitation and intention. The argument of intentionality is of such importance in a discussion of reductionism that it warrants a special chapter. However, it is to the point that we preview the issue of intentional descriptions in this discussion of simulation.

Some of the earliest work on simulation (Rosenblueth, Wiener, and Bigelow, 1943; Ashby, 1952; Walter, 1953) drew attention to the remarkable analogy between purposive behavior of organisms and the behavior of artifacts incorporating servomechanisms and negative feedback. If we visualize the performatory criteria of purposive behavior to be on-going self-corrective behavior culminating in a terminal goal state, then, to be sure, machines, actual and conceptual, can pass the performatory tests. Self-guiding missiles constantly correct their course until they reach their destination. Mechanical governors and thermostatic control systems simulate elementary homeostatic systems. And so on. The complexity of such systems is fairly limited, but at least the functional analogy between machine and organism is impressive. However, here too the critic raises the question whether behavioral criteria are sufficient indications of purposive behavior. In behalf of the intentionalistic argument several writers (e.g., R. Taylor, 1966; C. Taylor, 1964) have observed that the *sine qua non* of intentional behavior is intention itself, held presumably in the focus of consciousness. Richard Taylor (1966), for example, assesses purposive behavior in terms of a self-guiding torpedo and its designer. The machine does what, in a sense, it is programmed to do. Its purpose is pseudopurpose, and only in that it fulfills certain superficial behavioral criteria. On the other hand, it is the intention of the designer to design a machine which will achieve a certain goal, namely, the destruction of a target. A properly functioning machine may perform faultlessly and yet by chance, for example, by the adventitious distraction of its sensing apparatus, fail its mission. However, the machine cannot be said to have failed its purpose, since it is designed only to respond to its sensing apparatus. Clearly the case is different for the designer. A distractible machine may fail to serve *his* purpose.

One might argue at this point that both machine and designer are purposive but at different levels. The machine is a low-level simulator; the designer is functioning at a higher level of purpose. Doubtless we could build a tracking machine at the launching site which would function to compensate for the local distractions of the projectile machine. Together the two subsystems would join in simulating a higher level of purposive behavior. So long as the criteria for self-corrective goal-seeking are behavioral ones, our machines pass the test.

Or take a somewhat more teleologically complex but less efficient system, the guided missile system of Professor Skinner (1960). Skinner designed a gliding missile to be launched from a plane, but which was to be guided by a pigeon performing a simple instrumental task. The pigeon was trained to peck at a target on a projected display surface in order to receive reinforcement. The projection of the target surface itself varied with the attitude of the gliding missile. Thus, as the pigeon pecked the continually displaced target, he introduced corrections in flight attitude by virtue of linkage to the tamboured target surface.

Now here is an interesting mixture of organism and machine. How are we to judge this self-correcting system, even from Taylor's own criteria of what is purposive? Should we say the pigeon is purposive but the machine is not; i.e., we have a purposive subsystem in a nonpurposive machine? But then suppose we were not to know that a pigeon rather than a machine was at the controls? Behaviorally it makes no difference. By the performatory test the machine-pigeon system and the machine-machine system function analogously. By Taylor's criterion we are driven back to the notion that purposive behavior is characterized alone by "having an intention." And if "having an intention" is nonbehavioral, we are caught up again with the mental accompaniment of organismic behavior. But as we have seen, so far as simulation is concerned, "having an intention" can only be translated as behavioral disposition. If "having an intention" is something else than behavior and if, at the same time, it has no consequences in behavior, then having an intention is irrelevant to the simulation of intentional behavior.

Another "mentalistic" objection to simulation is raised by Gauld (1966). According to him, knowledge or the comprehension of a concept or its meaning implies more than a set of behavioral specifications and precepts. For example, we may visualize the idea of sportsmanship as entailing a set of behavioral patterns, each pattern of which is appropriate in a given setting. This however, implies an exhaustive set of behavioral specifications under all conceivable circumstances. Hence, Gauld's argument continues, in emphasizing behavioral criteria and behavioral dispositions we are precluded from ever simulating a particularly novel sportsmanlike response.

This argument is but another twist on that familiar adage of the machine age: A machine can only do what it is programmed to do. So, what does this tell us of the "ideation" of machines? It tells us only that present instructions are incomplete concerning some novel situation. It is no more reasonable to assert that the lack of an appropriate behavioral protocol represents a fundamental deficiency in a simulator than it is to attribute a fundamental deficiency to a machine-like human computer because he does not know the correct ritual responses to make when, say, he has an audience with the Pope. That the human being is a more complex computer than is a machine in matters of sportsmanship is hardly to be denied, but that fact in itself does not impose a fundamental deficiency or limitation upon the machine when it confronts novel situations calling for sportsmanlike behaviors. All that is now required is a machine with a more comprehensive set of instructions. Gauld suggests that we have concepts of a game and of sportsmanship which are not reducible to sets of explicit responses. Perhaps so, but behaviorally we may be able to account for the emergence of new-situation behavior in terms of generalization. At least we are not informed by Gauld or by others what the extrabehavioral ramifications of ideas and concepts are.

Doubtless, as Gauld suggests, individuals may invent games on the basis of some nascent concept and then proceed to build the rules as the game develops. This, however, does not constitute a serious hindrance to simulation. Until the rules have been spelled out, the putative game has not been formalized into a true game. Illumination of an idea and then reification of possible structures may tell us something of how games are invented, but not eventually of how they are to be played. Were it otherwise we could dispense with rule-books, which are as necessary to man as they are to machines.

SIMULATION AND EXPLANATION

Having provisionally adopted the cybernetic hypothesis, it might appear that successful simulation would represent a physical realization of a scientific explanation. There is some plausibility to this argument, but on assessment we must reject the notion that the simulation of behavior is in any substantial sense equivalent to its explanation. To explain an event is to render its description a logical consequence of the application of a formal theory. The theory is a deductive system containing postulates and rules of inference, but it is also anchored to observational variables in the phenomenology of the science. Hence, the deductive system will possess both a syntax and a semantic. Now the most we can claim for a successful simulation is that it represents a possible interpretation of our theoretical calculus, but with a semantic different from that of our initial theory. At best the simulator offers us a model of a theory, but a model bearing the prospects of negative analogy. Indeed the simulator may display substantial structural as well as functional analogy yet remain a simulator. The existential analogy is missing. The function of a theoretic explanation is after all to provide explanations in a language appropriate to the media in which both implicit and explicit processes are materialized.

This of course does not preclude our adopting simulation as a heuristic tactic, or of our expositing it as an interpretation of the cybernetic hypothesis. The question of how akin simulation is to explanation is a question of the extent of structural analogy. On one hand, machines with substantial functional analogy may provide hypotheses as to structural processes; the machine realizes one system sufficient for simulation. This is the tactic that comes under Craik's conception of psychological explanation; that is, to formulate a possible rubric for a psychological explanation is to construct a mechanical process of which the organism may be a realization.

On the other hand, a simulator may be constructed to compute a significant class of functions or to perform a given class of tasks with or without pretensions to structural analogy. Let us visualize our simulator as representable by a Turing machine which computes by moving from one instantaneous state to another until some terminal state is reached. Any given transition among its states can be visualized according to an input-output schema, $S_i \rightarrow S_m \rightarrow S_o$, in which S_m designates the set of mediating processes. In the event our simulator presents a heuristic vehicle for understanding the human computer, S_m is a process mappable in the organismic domain by virtue of some formal calculus. In the event no such isomorphic mapping is possible, at best our simulator is a functional simulator over some specified class of behaviors.

To the extent that a simulator and the deductive system of the theory are both interpretations of the same calculus, coextensive mapping is possible. Thus the coextensive simulator would present a faithful analogue of theoretic explanation. Quite generally, however, we may expect the mapping *not* to be coextensive. It is on this basis that we may clearly differentiate between simulator and theory as means for understanding.

Let us now visualize a computer M than can play the Turing game against O over a certain class of behaviors. Assuming structural analogy we may expect that M may serve as a vehicle for generating behavioral consequences analogous to those that can be generated in the theory of O. However, we observe that the postulates incorporated in the guts of M are complete in the sense that they are represented by explicit programs, whereas in the theory of O, the postulates, if hypothetical constructs, have an open-texture of meaning. Thus not only does a theory of O seek to provide explanations over generalizations of past performance, but also it seeks expressions of postulates (laws) sufficient to generate as yet untested hypotheses. That is to say, a theory of O becomes meaningful in use; postulated processes become articulated only as we systematically seek ramifications of the theory. Comparing the two, M and the theory of O, M has obsolescence built into it in a sense that the theory of O does not. As a consequence, the two domains of deductive consequences cannot be properly regarded as coextensive.

Now if our theory of O were to be regarded complete in that no hypothetical construct remained uninterpreted, then indeed we might visualize a simulator M whose output is isomorphic to that of O. And if the theory of O were constricted to a specifiable domain of behavior, we might extend this domain by augmenting the postulates of the basic theory. In this way we might circumvent the predicament of the open-textured construct. The theoretical constructs of the expanded theory would always satisfy the requirements of intervening variables. But also in this way we might augment the extant simulator M so as, in effect, to move toward more and more inclusive machines. Then every theory of O, no matter how extensive, would be representable by a simulator, by virtue of the inclusive feature of the universal Turing machine.

Unfortunately this tactic will not do. We do not initially construct psychological theories with explicit reductions of the theoretical terms. What is unique to the theory is the open-textured hypothesis. Reduction of the hypothesis takes place, if at all, only through our researches, that is, only as we succeed in converting the hypothesis to a logical construction or a description. But initially it is the open-texture of the hypothesis that renders the theory of O a theory with potential for reification. And it is that hypothesis that cannot be built into a simulator (cf. Note 4.8).

CONCLUSION

The significance of the arguments against simulation of cognitive or intellective processes is not so much the reminder that machine technology is in its formative precognitive state (that is not the case), but that the description of human cognition and intellective process is incomplete. We are constantly reminded of how complex human intellectual functions are, and how little we know of them. In the state of our comparative ignorance, two alternatives are open to us. One is to continue the quest for more complete descriptions satisfactory to science; the other is to surrender the quest either to the mystery of mentation, or to the more explicit idea that the intentionalistic predicament in thinking precludes scientific under-standing in the traditional sense. The difficulties are great, to be sure, but to discourage the quest on the presumptive grounds that these difficulties are insurmountable is to reiterate the familiar but tired cry that human thinking and the human soul are forever beyond the pale of scientific under-standing. It is one thing to assert that simulation now falls short of giving us comprehensive insight into cognitive behavioral processes; it is quite another to imply that the desired understanding is forever beyond our reach. It is one thing to suggest that the romancers of simulation are pre-maturely presumptuous; quite another to pronounce that there are logical barriers to the understanding of human functions through the tactics of simulation.

The student new to the literature doubtless finds the issues hanging. He need not think that simulation has carried development of the robot to such refinements that he finds himself in the presence of near-familial mechanical cousins. On the other hand, he need not remain convinced that the unique and complex faculties of the human soul are forever beyond understanding. Simulation must be accepted for what it is—the successful attempt of utilizing purely mechanical systems to imitate certain behavioral functions. Simulation has shown us at least that there need be no mystery as concerns thinking, perceiving, evaluating, being aware, and so on. Description is essential. Those behavioral functions we can describe in detail and can understand are the very functions we find it possible to simulate. Understanding itself comes to us in seeing that a positive analogy exists between the functional descriptions of mechanical and of organic systems.

As for robotology and the ascription of consciousness to machines, well, that bit of entertaining lore should not distract us from what the cybernetic hypothesis has to offer as the base for understanding. And if indeed there is something inexpressible about purposiveness and the inten-tional predicament, which, of course, is subject to doubt, then we may as well let it go at that. That which cannot be described cannot be understood in the conventional scientific sense.

In brief, then, the cybernetic hypothesis is a useful heuristic to the understanding of organismic function. It offers both the language and the tactic for our researcher. Simulation is a corollary endeavor. Its successes reveal that the mechanical rubric is sufficient for understanding behavior. Failures in simulating complex cognitive processes may reflect deficiencies in understanding. But then what is it to understand consciousness, aware-ness, the personal involvement in intention? Which is the greater error? To criticize machines because they are not conscious? Or to attribute conscious-ness to machines because they satisfy certain performatory tests? After all, if we do not make sense of the concepts of consciousness and awareness in our understanding of perceptive, viable organisms, why should we be requested to make sense of consciousness in the context of perceptive, reflective machines?

The question then should not be whether machines are purposive, whether they think, possess consciousness, solve problems, or make decisions in lifelike manner; but rather it should be whether these behavioral processes can be simulated by mechanical models. For the purpose of drawing out the significance of machine analogy, let us assume for a given class of behaviors that we have a comprehensive description of a computational details of the nervous system. Moreover, assume that we can formalize this description in terms of a calculus. Then for machine analogy in terms of simulation we require that the machine description and the neurophysiological description, in their respective nomenclatures, are both interpretations of that same calculus. But to say this is not to say the neuro-organic system is really a machine, nor that the functions of that system are no more than mechanical phenomena describable in the machine language.

Nor are we saying that machines are for all appearances lifelike. A machine is not a human computer and a human computer is not a machine. The sooner we dispel the myth of robotology the better. If the biomechanist sets out to build a machine he might begin his construction with colloidal rather than metallic substances. And he would be constructing a machine unique in its material substance. However, so long as he should undertake his construction in the rubrics of cybernetic systems, he would still be constructing a machine. Should he, from the vantage of systematic knowledge, succeed in synthesizing a living organism, the question of understanding through simulation would become irrelevant. His understanding, as it were, would be relatively complete.

As for the significance of analogy, assume a possible systematic set of descriptions S_o, and a second systematic set of descriptions S_m, and a formal calculus T such that S_o and S_m are both interpretations of T in the sense that basic statements in S_o are isomorphic with basic statements in S_m through the medium of T. In developing the set of statements S_o we may exploit the analogy that exists in their presumed conformality with S_m. Analogy thus becomes the heuristic for our understanding the functions of the science whose set of descriptions is S_o. As is usually the case in our building models for psychology and biology, we formulate our mechanical analogue by virtue of such shared processes as inupt-output, feedback, mediation, damping, amplification, and so on. We clearly see in psychological function an analogy with mechanical function. Indeed, the language of psychology may appropriate terms from the language of mechanics. Still, a rigorous description requires an incisive language. Thus, for every statement in S_m and correspondingly in S_o we seek a translation in the formal language of the calculus T. Ideally, we seek to formalize the theoretical language of our science in order to escape the inconsistencies and the ambiguities implicit within natural language. Hence the development of a systematic language in psychology by means of the analogy with mechanical systems may result in restrictions as to theoretical concept and vocabulary. But such restrictions are only provisional. We are not saying that psychology is nothing but a kind of mechanics. We can have machine simulation of human behavior without the behaving man being nothing but a machine. We can have reductionism in psychology without thinking, feeling, and knowing being nothing but neurophysiological process. In each case the reduction is methodological, so to speak, rather than ontological.

The issue becomes one of the adequacy of descriptions, of understanding, rather than one of inexpressible ontology. If the languages of psychology and cybernetics point to the possibility of their both being realizations of a formal calculus, then the analogy serves as the vehicle of description and understanding. As we know, the language of mechanics is more readily axiomatized than that of psychology. Not only must we ask if there is analogy between psychology and mechanics, but also if the S_m-T paradigm is really sufficient to permit interpretation or mapping of all the meaningful statements in S_o.

This question of interpretation points directly to the significance of certain theorems on the incompleteness of formal systems. If T, through the S_m-T paradigm, is an incomplete system, then is it possible that certain well-described functions in the set S_o are not interpretable in the S_m-T paradigm? Is it the case that Gödel's theorem of incompleteness implies that the ideal of complete simulation is unrealizable? Such an argument has been made, and to that argument we turn in the next chapter.

NOTES

NOTE 4.1

It is not necessary to go into the technical details of various simulators. It is sufficient for our purposes to indicate what machines can in fact or in principle compute or simulate. Thus, for example, MacKay (1951) sketches schematically (i.e., black-box details) a machine whose stochastic properties render its functions not strictly determinate. Even though we may remark on the indeterminateness of human behavior; e.g., as in creativity, originality, preference, transitional response probability, and so on, we may yet conceive a stochastic machine with variable thresholds and transitional response matrices capable in principle of simulating these organismic behaviors. The mere possibility of simulation according to a cybernetic schema offers the possibility of representing these indeterminate organismic functions in mechanical terms. Consequently, most of the philosophical argument, even by people highly skilled in computer technology, is of a nontechnical nature so far as concerns the actual circuitry and hardware of computers and simulators. One notes that much of digital computer design takes place initially in terms purely of logical rubrics. Then, and only then, does it become the task of the engineer to contrive material realizations of these designs.

NOTE 4.2

Block's machine G.1 (Block, 1965) is constituted of a set of numbered cups, each of which contains three counters numbered 1, 2, and 3. The number of the cup selected for instruction corresponds to the number of chips on the pile from which draws are to be made. Random selection of a counter from the cup instructs the machine player as to the number of chips to be drawn from the pile. The opponent begins by throwing a pair of dice to determine the number of chips in the initial pile. And the machine player draws first with option of taking 1, 2, or 3 chips, with the opponent following and exercising the same option. The purpose of the game is to force the other player to draw the last chip. As we analyze the game, it soon becomes apparent that a player can force a win whenever he can force his opponent to draw to a pile of 5 or 9 chips. Since the perceptive player drawing initially can always win when he draws to 2, 3, or 4, and since he can always force a draw to 5 or 9 when the dice determine an initial pile of 6, 7, 8, 10, 11, or 12, he can expect to win in every case except when the initial pile is either 5 or 9. And since the probability of the dice turning up 5 or 9 is 8/36, the expectancy of winning for the perfectly rational player is the complementary probability 28/36. The machine player soon reaches this asymptote of expectancy.

The question of structural analogy centers upon whether the machine player plays the game analogously to the rational human player. There is functional analogy between the two players in that both machine and rational human player (each given the option of drawing first) will each achieve the asymptote of winning. However, it is clear that the strategies are different. The rational player reaches the asymptote by means of insight into the 5–9 draw. That is, cognitively, there are pivotal insights that instrument his game. The machine is a mechanical player; and though it behaves as if it had insight, it really becomes a deterministic machine with a set of instructions for each input but without its incorporating or simulating anything like insight. Here the problem of accepting purely behavioral criteria of human function is clearly defined for us: Does this simple machine display insight?

NOTE 4.3

Problems which complicate the ideal of simulation are not restricted to those of consciousness and intention. Tomkins (1963), for example, lists the following items among the problems confronting us in our efforts to simulate personality:

(1) A humanoid automaton should be motivated, be capable of energy storage and replenishment, be capable of self-reproduction, and be a pain-sensitive system.

(2) The automaton must reflect the postulated relationship between the drive and affect systems.

(3) The automaton must simulate feedback on the motor or effector system.

(4) The automaton must incorporate feedback into the perceptual-control system.

By and large, Tomkins thus insists that the automaton must faithfully simulate a system describable in terms of an affect theory of motivation. The problems here are difficult to say the least, but they are not such as to preclude the possibility of simulation. The focal issue for Tomkins is affect, but affect in terms of central activation rather than raw feels as such. Complex as the issue may be—as pictured, for example, in the architecture and mechanics of the reticular arousal system—it seems clearly to be resolved through the mechanics of feedback. Any internal state of the system itself becomes a source of informational input into the ongoing process of the system. Thus we may visualize the processing function of the reticular and limbic systems as well schematized in an overall cybernetically conceived system (Pribram, 1960). Pain, on the other hand, seems to be a rather unique affect; but it, too, becomes problematical only if we insist on its special status as a raw feel. However, pains, as separable from the affect-behavioral complex, are, if anything, inarticulable (Turner, 1967). Pain can be incorporated into a reliable semantic only if we treat it in terms of reaction, control, or, generally, behavioral disposition. Thus pain, too, is simulatable in terms of the mechanics of feedback systems.

As we look at Tomkins' list, we can point to no extant robot which incorporates all of the behavioral features we must simulate. The cybernetic challenge, however, is not to build robots. We need only show that each and all of the well-described behavioral features which distinguish the human organism can in principle be simulated by a mechanical system whose principles are well understood. There has been ample demonstration of our capacity to build complex feedback systems. Indeed, the term "feedback" which now permeates both descriptive and reductive behaviorism, is borrowed from cybernetics. Energy seeking, storage, replenishment, have all been ingeniously simulated by *M. Speculatrix* (Walter, 1953). We may even visualize a self-reproducing Turing machine (von Neumann, 1951) which by no means does injustice to recent insights into genetic coding. At least, Tomkins' catalogue of humanoid functions turns up no logical nor, for that matter, technological barrier to the simulation of human personality as conceived in behavioral terms.

Although Tomkins' paper ("Simulation of Personality: The Interrelationships Between Affect, Memory, Thinking, Perception, and Action") was prepared for a symposium on the computer simulation of personality, he follows rather the inverted strategy. Conceptualizing how one must describe the complex phenomena of personality in machine-like terms, he then proceeds to develop a theory of personality whose structure necessarily is subject to simulation. This is certainly an allowable procedure. Any theoretical treatment of personality is selective. Its definition of phenomena, as well as its theoretical framework, is conceptually restricted. A theory of personality quite obviously is not a theory of the totality of all behavior, all response, but only of phenomena both conceptually and contextually defined. This being the case, then personality according to a particular theory indeed becomes simulatable if the conceptual corpus of that theory is generated from within a kind of information processing language. This at least is Tomkins' tactic. And what is especially interesting is that this information processing vantage provides insightful and innovative methods for describing personality. Tomkins first develops an affect theory of motivation, and then proceeds to develop the cognitive functions of concept formation, memory, and thinking primarily in informational, classificatory terms. Memory functions to minimize class membership, concept formation functions to maximize class membership, and thinking functions to minimize the maximum membership classes. Personality, in these terms, represents an efficient information processing system. It is also interesting to note that Tomkins' description of personality is in terms that make it possible to distinguish conscious from unconscious functions and to localize the systems of "transmutation" which implement the person's intentions.

Like Turing (1950) before, Tomkins records a budget of objections to simulation: (1) Simulation entails an invidious comparison of man and machine and hence results in the alienation of man; (2) machines are clearly inferior to man as ambulant adjustive systems (hence the idea of simulation also contributes to the alienation of man from his image as sentient being); (3) simulation generates a fear of man's domination by machines; (4) modest success in simulation breeds arrogance and "pretentious aspirations" on the part of machine builders. Such objections, we may observe, are easily met. Conceptual orientations, as such, do nothing to demean the status of man. Theories of genetics, evolution, physiology, psychodynamics have all been similarly accused. The objections in terms of man's alienation are simply misconceived. To simulate complex human functions is to understand. Indeed, simulation is made possible by our understanding. "Machine" and "machine-like" are doubtless terms bearing unpleasant connotation. But why should they? If a machine-like organism is revealed to have value structure and make judgments, has it any the less distinguished itself than historical man who had to prove his humanity in the age of pretechnology?

We should not leave this brief discussion of the simulation of personality with the impression that successful computer programs for the simulation of personality are close at hand. They are not. What is asked for is an objectification of personality theory in language which offers logical grounds for simulation (Reitman, 1963). However, there are obstacles in the way of objectification. Energy concepts (transformation and replenishment) are not readily duplicated by machines. Machine programs are serially constructed, whereas human problem-solving (thinking—insight) appears to be "parallel" (Reitman, 1963; Hovland, 1960). Moreover, the vagueness of these parallel processes makes it difficult to conceive explicit sets of descriptions which would render their simulation possible. Doubtless energy concepts, parallel structures, and vagueness are problems for the computer technologist to work out. Reitman, at least, believes we will succeed in these tasks if we succeed in the task of objectification.

We should not however be lulled into some false assurance that the task of objectification will be merely a matter of better vocabularies, better programs, and time. To describe simple problem-solving in terms of a series of logical consequences is one thing; to describe human creativity in the nebulous language of illumination, incubation, insight is yet another.

Consider the following passage of Bertrand Russell:

> Everyone who has done any kind of creative work has experienced, in a greater or less degree, the state of mind in which, after long labour, truth or beauty appears, or seems to appear, in a sudden glory—it may be only about some small matter, or it may be about the universe. The experience is, at the moment, very convincing; doubt may come later, but at the time there is utter certainty. I think most of the best creative work, in art, in science, in literature, and in philosophy, has been the result of such a moment. Whether it comes to others as to me, I cannot say. For my part, I have found that, when I wish to write a book on some subject, I must first soak myself in detail, until all the separate parts of the subject-matter are familiar; then, some day, if I am fortunate, I perceive the whole, with all its parts duly interrelated. After that, I only have to write down what I have seen. The nearest analogy is first walking all over a mountain in a mist, until every path and ridge and valley is separately familiar, and then, from a distance, seeing the mountain whole and clear in bright sunshine. (1946, pp. 144–145)

Doubtless many of us will recognize the beautiful and succinct aptness of this description. But is it in any way the kind of description, or does it in any way presage the description that a machine theorist's idea of objectification calls for?

And finally, what of the observation:

> We are all aware that many scholars and artists tend to consider the main drift in American psychology to be a kind of barbarous reductionism; a narrow model that denies those "higher" attributes and "emergent" qualities upon which man's distinctiveness in nature, and his *worth* in essence, are said to depend. (Rosenberg, 1963, p. 120.)

Unfortunately, the language of the skeptical humanist is not always helpful in our understanding of the higher attributes. If these processes, these emergent properties, are not to be described objectively, then what will be the basis of our understanding? Reference here to forms of unobjectifiable understanding may appeal to a coterie of intuitionists, but unfortunately these forms are not very helpful. As in the case of purpose and intention (see Chapter 6), we must seek the description of higher attributes in reducibly objective terms.

NOTE 4.4

It is a relatively simple matter to conceive a pencil-paper machine which will carry the required solution of the missionary-cannibal puzzle.

$$\text{Let} \qquad x_i = \begin{cases} M_1, M_2, M_3 \\ C_1, C_2, C_3 \end{cases}$$

Let B be the transmitter operator (i.e., the boat) such that it transports one or two x_i in whatever combination is allowable. And let the vertical stroke | symbolize the river, dividing its banks. Then, for any transportation of X's, B must be on the bank from which the transportation of one or two X's is to take place.

We begin the game in the state

$$MMM\ CCC\ B|$$

and are to achieve the goal or terminal state

$$|MMM\ CCC\ B$$

The order of M's and C's is immaterial but at no time is the number of C's on either bank to exceed the number of M's on the same bank.

The rules or instructions by which our machine attacks the puzzle are as follows: Each instruction is visualized in terms of the operation to be carried out by the operator B, as B inspects the particular situation (the personnel) existing on the opposite bank. For each such allowable situation, B follows one of two alternative instructions, the fundamental rule being if rule 1 is followed on the first occasion that B inspects any definite situation K, then 1′ is followed on the next occasion B inspects the same definite situation K. And so on, alternately, 1 and 1′ in the successive occurrences of K. The set of alternate rules are as follows:

(1) if B inspects the null situation, then
      (1) *BMC*
      (1′) *BCC*   alternately
(2) if B inspects C, then
      (2) *BCC*
      (2′) *BC*   alternately
(3) if B inspects CC, then
      (3) *BMM*
      (3′) *BC*   alternately
(4) if B inspects MC, then
      (4) *BMC*
      (4′) *BMM*   alternately
(5) if B inspects $MMCC$, then
      (5) *BM*
      (5′) *BMC*   alternately

(6) if B inspects MMM, then
     (6) BC
     (6') BCC alternately
(7) if B inspects $MMMC$, then
     (7) BCC
     (7') BC alternately

The rules stipulate what operation B is to carry out contingent upon the situation which B inspects as existing on the opposite bank. Thus, for example, the first operation B carries out is BMC, namely, B transports one M and one C to the opposite bank. And if, for another example, B inspects CC for the first time during the solution, B transports two M's to the opposite bank. Should this be the second occasion upon which B, from whatever bank, inspects CC, then B transports one C to the opposite bank. The machine rules are set up initially to solve the missionary-cannibal puzzle in a minimum number of transportations. The solution now readily proceeds as follows. (Note that the rule given is for the particular situation presently inspected. The next step follows upon implementation of the rule in effect at the preceding stage.)

Situation	Rule
$MMMCCCB$|	(1)
$MMCC$|MCB	(5)
$MMMCCB$|C	(2)
MMM|$CCCB$	(6)
$MMMCB$|CC	(3)
MC|$MMCCB$	(4)
$MMCCB$|MC	(4')
CC|$MMMCB$	(3')
$CCCB$|MMM	(6')
C|$MMMCCB$	(2')
CCB|$MMMC$	(7)
|$MMMCCCB$	Stop

We introduce the stopping rule when the desired solution is reached (i.e., null on the left bank).

The above set of instructions yields the optimal solution. Note, however, that whether we start with the nonprime rule or the prime rule, makes no difference so long as the fundamental rule of systematic alternation between the two is followed. Suppose, for example, we interchange the prime and nonprime rules so that on the first occurrence of a situation K, we first follow the prime rule and then the alternate nonprime rule. The reader may verify that a solution is then reached in 39 transportations. The reader may verify that other interchange between prime and nonprime alternatives will also lead to solutions so long as the fundamental rule of alternation is followed.

Obviously, this pencil-paper machine is not a material simulator. It does, however, represent a computer which solves our puzzle in systematic mechanical fashion. And since its design reflects a systematic description of how the human computer proceeds, it does possess substantial functional analogy with the human problem-solver confronted with the logistics of transporting missionaries and cannibals without the decimation of the former.

NOTE 4.5

W. Grey Walter (1953) happily records a taxonomy of electromechanical species. Besides *Machina Speculatrix,* there are *Machina Docilis,* a teachable conditioned reflex analogue; *Machina Labyrinthea,* a digital computerized maze-solving analogue (R. A. Wallace); *Machina Sopora,* Ashby's homeostat. By combining components of these several species, one is able to beget mutations among the species. Thus *Machina Speculatrix Berkeleye* is an object-incentive seeking variant of *M. Speculatrix.*

NOTE 4.6

Bibliographic note:

Titles on automata and computer simulation now number in the thousands.

For general treatments and symposia the reader is referred to: H. Borko (Editor), *Computer Applications in the Behavioral Sciences* (1962); E. A. Feigenbaum and J. Feldman (Editors), *Computers and Thought* (1963); F. H. George, *The Brain as a Computer* (1961); B. F. Green, Jr., *Digital Computers in Research* (1963); W. F. Reitman, *Cognition and Thought* (1965); and K. M. Sayre and F. J. Crosson, *The Modeling of Mind* (1963).

For shorter treatments on simulation of behavioral processes see E. R. Hilgard and G. H. Bower, *Theories of Learning,* 3rd Edition (1966), Chapter 12; G. A. Miller, E. Galanter and K. H. Pribram, *Plans and the Structure of Behavior* (1960), Chapter 3; A. Newell and H. A. Simon, Computers in Psychology, in R. D. Luce, R. R. Bush, and E. Galanter (Editors), *Handbook of Mathematical Psychology,* Vol. 1 (1963).

For the general theory of automata see J. von Neumann, The General Theory of Logical Automata, in L. A. Jeffress (Editor), *Cerebral Mechanisms of Behavior* (1951), reprinted in J. R. Newman (Editor), *The World of Mathematics* (1956); J. von Neumann, *The Computer and the Brain* (1958).

For an important area of simulation not reviewed in the text, see the following references on pattern recognition: G. P. Dinneen, Programming Pattern Recognition, *Proc. 1955 Western Joint Computer Conference* (1955); O. G. Selfridge, Pattern Recognition and Modern Computers, *Proc. 1955 Western Joint Computer Conference* (1955).

For work done in Russia, the following are available in translation:

A. G. Arkadev and E. M. Braverman, *Computers and Pattern Recognition,* translated by W. Turski and J. I. Cowan (1967); N. M. Amaxov, *Modeling of Thinking and the Mind,* translated by L. Feingold (1967).

NOTE 4.7

In brief, the writer has argued that the language of consciousness is not germane to the development either of psychology or neurophysiology, and certainly not to the development of the science and technology of simulation. He would further contend that within the explanatory rubrics of science, consciousness, *per se,* has little meaning at all. We cannot reduce consciousness to neurophysiology, nor can we suggest that such a proposal would be meaningful. Therefore, to introduce mentalism into machinery is needlessly to befuddle the issue. If consciousness is to be regarded as merely a dispositional term replaceable in every instance by behavioral terms, it is obfuscating and disruptive to interpolate a language which historically has been philosophically problematical, and especially in contexts where explicit operational terms can be utilized. If consciousness is to be regarded as that special mental stuff that has plagued the science of psychology, then to introduce it into robotology is needlessly to regress the science of cybernetics and machines to those prescientific preoccupations that obscured the science of behavior. In such a case, it ought then be suggested that cybernetics has methodologically more to learn from a psychology that eschews mentalism than psychology has to learn from cybernetics.

It is not the writer's intention to deny consciousness or whatever is the mental stuff that characterizes awareness. Rather, as he shall argue later in Chapter 6, consciousness is taken to fulfill a symbolic function. Its proper function is a semantic one, to symbolize an object on one hand, and to symbolize that viable neurophysiological process is occurring, on the other. Still, these symbolic functions remove consciousness from the class of describable entities. They remove consciousness from the roles of cause and effect. Debates over whether machines are conscious may elucidate the philosophical problems of verifying consciousness in other human beings; or even of the meaning of consciousness, but they are irrelevant for problems of simulation. A machine that is conscious would behave in a way no different from an unconscious machine. We program behavior into machines, not consciousness. Indeed, if as the behavior criterialists wish to argue: "There is no difference between consciousness and behavioral descriptions," we can let it go at that. "What a machine and man share is the common property of behavior." That is all we need to say.

NOTE 4.8

A somewhat similar point is made by J. A. Fodor (1968) in his own discussion of simulation. Not only must a good theory be compatible with observation, but it must prove amenable to inference in the counterfactual situation; it must distinguish between laws of nature and generalizations; and it must project its inductions according to "reasonable simplicity restraints." A good simulator may also satisfy these requirements, but we are assured of this only if the simulator is both *strongly* and *weakly* equivalent to the organism, that is only if it possesses structural as well as functional analogy with O. The difficulty in establishing equivalence between simulation and theoretic explanation rests in our inability to give strict interpretations of those mediating processes for which we have only the hypothesis.

CHAPTER 5

The Argument From Gödel

ASK YOURSELF, "Can I do something my nervous system can't?" This in brief, expresses what to many is the significance of Gödel's proof of undecidability for psychology. To put it in terms of this question requires our visualizing the nervous system as an ideal computer whose operations can be fully described and thereby axiomatized along the lines of arithmetic and symbolic logic.

The argument proceeds as follows: Assume a logic, a formal system L, as sophisticated and comprehensive as you wish to make it. Then I can produce a statement, meaningful in L, which I can show to be true, but which remains undecidable, i.e., neither provable nor disprovable, within L itself. Since my nervous system is functionally mappable now in terms of this ideal L, the implication of Gödel's proof seems to be that I can demonstrate the truth of a theorem of L which is undecidable within L itself, and hence within the describable operations of my nervous system. If you counter that this system L clearly does not map the operations of my nervous system, then substitute any other augmented system L' and this implication of Gödel's theorem will hold all the same.

But first, some background is needed—in order to visualize the significance of Gödel's theorem for metamathematics, we need briefly to touch upon certain developments in the foundations of mathematics. And, in order to appreciate the significance of the theorem for issues of reductionism and scientific explanation, we need to review some important results in the theory of automata.

REMARKS ON THE FOUNDATION OF MATHEMATICS

The nineteenth century was one of great productivity in mathematical thinking, both in the development of new subject matters and in critique.

113

Yet what distinguished it most from preceding years was the emergence of a critical discipline, the purpose of which was to examine the logical foundations of mathematics. The timeliness of this new discipline was occasioned in part by the development of mathematical logic (Boole, Peirce, Jevons, and others), and in part by problems concerning infinitesimals (Weierstrass), the continuum (Cantor), and especially alternative geometries (Bolyai, Riemann, Lobachevski). Traditionally, mathematical reasoning had been regarded a reliable, if not idealized, instrument of inference, regardless of whether a nominalist or realist view was held concerning mathematical entities and relations. But with an increasing number of problems arising concerning these entities and relations and with emergence of alternative axiom systems in geometry, it became imperative to establish mathematics as a unified discipline that is free of any inherent contradiction.

In order to systematize all of mathematics, one begins with the basic discipline, arithmetic. Here the fundamental entity is number; and if the entire domain of number can be established by means of fundamental notions and operations, then, as that domain of number is incorporated into algebra, geometry, and analysis, the whole of mathematics will become a unified discipline as reliable as arithmetic itself. Two questions then become salient. What is the nature of our entities? And, can we establish that the fundamental discipline enables us to say all that is to be said in the mathematical language, and to say it without contradiction?

Three schools of thinking, so to speak, have emerged concerning these foundations of mathematics: the *logistic* one which would reduce all mathematics to logic; the *intuitionist* one which would construct by finitist methods all of mathematics from intuited entities; and the *formalist* one which, operating within the formal system itself, with its own unique nonintuited, nonlogically constructed entities, would establish the consistency and completeness of the basic system. The issues are complex and often highly technical (cf. Note 5.1), but we may avoid much of the continuing argument by focusing upon a point of common concern, namely, that mathematics, whatever its foundations, should be established as a reliable system of inference.

Now the question of the "reliability" of mathematics itself becomes a technical matter revolving, as we shall see, about the issues of consistency and completeness. Should we opt for these properties of a reliable mathematical system, then to be sure a mathematized scientific theory would share in those properties of reliable inference insofar as the theory incorporates that mathematical system into its logical calculus. But whereas the scientist himself may take comfort in a theory elaborated by mathematical argument, the foundations of mathematics themselves are not altogether secure. Although the logicists were able to reduce mathematical entities to logical entities such as classes of classes, paradoxes arose which challenged pretentions to consistency in the overall mathematical argument. Furthermore, the abstract entities, the classes, needed to be constructed through procedures of selection; constructions requiring an infinite possibility of selection become problematical in themselves. Thus the logicists had to follow Russell in meeting these difficulties. They resorted either to Procrustean fiats which precluded certain types of paradoxical argument (the theory of types) or they adopted postulational tactics (the axioms of choice and infinity) to overcome difficulties in the construction of sets.

However, if mathematics is not strictly reducible to logic, if the mathematical entities are intuitively given, and if the convincing character of mathematical proof carries with it some intrinsic appeal to our intuitive endowments, as both intuitionists and formalists argued, then mathematics should offer a theory of proof not strictly reducible to the paradigms of logical proof. If mathematics, of itself, is reliable then its theory of proof should reveal that mathematics to be consistent. Moreover, mathematics should be complete in the sense that all true, meaningful statements in the mathematical system should be provable within the system.

In these opening remarks we have considered mathematics in general terms. We will do well now to concentrate on arithmetic and the theory of numbers. Also, we will need to speak of mathematics as a formal system, such that in the metamathematical language we may speak of mathematical theory as being formalizable within a logical rubric. Arithmetic so treated becomes a formal system. Therefore, if arithmetic is to be a reliable system of inference, we must demonstrate that the formal system possesses the properties of consistency and completeness.

Let us assume that the quest for establishing the reliability of our formalized system is realizable. We must then show, in the context of the present work, that it is a meaningful one as well for the logics of behavioral science. The pattern of the argument is easily stated. If a scientific theory is to be reliable, its formal structure of systematic inference must satisfy the ideal properties we associate with systems such as arithmetic. Thus, for any scientific theory presented as a deductive system, we visualize a formal system which is the calculus of the theory (Braithwaite, 1953). The scientific theory is itself an interpretation of that calculus. However, the reliability of theory is reflected, as it were, in the reliability of the formal system. If the formal system were inconsistent or incomplete, then so would be the scientific theory. There is, however, an important assumption: that the scientific theory and its formal system are comprehensive descriptions and representations of the subject matter of our science. Thus, the surmise of a theory presumes descriptions and constructions which are "complete" in the sense of providing causal or deductive mediations in the chain of scientific inference. A scientific theory provides explanation in the sense that a deduction of the event to be explained is forthcoming upon application of the theory. The question then of the reliability, or even of the possibility of a theory, rests on the possibility of complete descriptions.[1] If now we visualize the possibility of complete descriptions for behavioral science, as well we might for input-mediator-output functions of the nervous system, we may compose our prospectus for a science on the possibility and the promise of complete descriptions over the subject matter of the science. Any weakness in the formal rubrics of the theory will, of course, be reflected as a weakness of that scientific theory itself.

The object of formalism in metamathematics is to establish the self-sufficiency of formal deductive systems; that is to say, it should be demonstrable that the system is free of contradiction and that it can implement the deduction of every meaningful true proposition in the system. To fulfill this objective, two conditions must be satisfied; one, that of *consistency,* and two, that of *completeness.* A formal system is *consistent* if it is the case that contradictions cannot be derived within the system. That is to say, it is never the case that both P and not-P can be derived as theorems of the system. A formal system is *complete* if for every meaningful proposition in the system and not an axiom of the system (i.e., one that is a possible theorem), either its assertion or its negation can be proven within the system. That is to say, either P or not-P must be provable. Thus, either P or not-P must be provable for the system to be complete, and not both, if the system is to be consistent. In the event that neither P nor not-P is provable, and yet P is a meaningful proposition in the system, then that proposition is undecidable in the formal system, and the system is said to be incomplete, at least insofar as it concerns P.

Let us pick up the story at a point where problematical paradoxes arose to complicate the task of formalizing arithmetic. It is known that certain finite systems, such as that of a sentential calculus without quantifiers, are consistent. However, such systems are not sufficient to cover all of the operations of arithmetic. In an early effort to formalize a broader base for formal systems, Gottlob Frege (1844, 1903) undertook the analysis of arithmetic in terms of set theoretic entities, only to be apprised by Bertrand Russell that his argument contained the rudiments of a paradox. Russell's paradox is akin to that of Epimenides, the Cretan, who asserted that all Cretans are liars. However, as we shall see, this paradox of self-reference is much more general than that we use to tantalize the beginning student of logic.

[1]Note that "complete description" here implies a complete inference chain whether this includes statements of purely deterministic or probabilistic relations. By reliability of a theory or a formal system I mean that it satisfies the criteria of logical consistency and logical completeness.

One needs also to distinguish between syntactical and semantical completeness of a theory. A formal theory is syntactically complete if all true statements that are not taken as axioms, are derivable within the formal calculus of the theory. On the other hand, a formal theory is semantically complete only if all true statements appropriate to the interpretation of the theory (i.e., all lawlike statements not introduced as axioms) are derivable within the theory.

Let us confine ourselves to the abstract language of classes. We define a *normal* class as a class of things that does not include itself. For example, the class of human beings, the class of sailboats, the class of correct responses, and the class of fundamental particles in physics are all normal classes. In no case does the class contain itself as a member. A class which does contain itself as a member is designated a *nonnormal* class. For example, the class of all logical entities, the class of verbalizable things, and the class of all abstract ideas are *nonnormal* classes. In each of these cases the "class" itself is a member of the defined class. Symbolically, now, let

n be a normal class
$\bar{n}$ be a nonnormal class

and let

N stand for the class of all normal classes
    i.e., $N = \{n_i\}$
$\overline{N}$ stand for the class of all nonnormal classes
    i.e., $\overline{N} = \{\bar{n}_j\}$

Now N and $\overline{N}$ are themselves both classes and are thereby subject to classification in our schema. That is to say, N and $\overline{N}$ each belong either to $\{n_i\}$ or to $\{\bar{n}_j\}$ as the case may be. A paradox arises when we attempt to classify N.

(a) Assume N is a member of $\{n_i\}$ the class of all normal classes. Then $\overline{N}$ is a member of itself, since $N = \{n_i\}$. Hence N is nonnormal by definition, and therefore N belongs to $\{\bar{n}_j\}$. Thus if we assume N to be normal, we must conclude that it is nonnormal. Now if a proposition implies its own negation, we must affirm that negation. We must conclude that N is nonnormal.

(b) But assume now that N is nonnormal. N is now a member of $\{\bar{n}_j\}$ the class of all nonnormal classes. Since N is initially defined as the class of all normal classes, i.e., $N = \{n_i\}$, it does not include itself. Hence it is a normal class. Thus if we assume N is nonnormal we must conclude that N is normal. Hence we have proved contradictory theorems yielding the paradox of the class of all normal classes; namely, N is normal if and only if it is nonnormal.

This paradox has many ramifications. In order to counter it within the logistic framework (Russell and Whitehead, *Principia Mathematica*), Russell developed his theory of logical types. In effect this theory proscribes all arguments of the above type on the grounds that the properties or predicates we utilize in defining class inclusion are of a different, or lower, logical type than those we utilize in classifying classes. Thus we have the class of things, say, then the class of classes, then the class of classes of classes, and so on, in which case the defining property for class inclusion represents, in serial order, a higher logical type. If, by this theory of types, we are prohibited from mixing levels of logical types, we can, by fiat as it were, avoid apparent contradictions.

More specifically, let us represent any proposition by $P(x)$ in which x is the particular and P is the property or characteristic which we assign to x, as yet undesignated. Now consider the argument

$$P(x)$$
$$x = P(x) \quad \text{as a value of } x$$

and by substitution we have

$$P[P(x)]$$

This then is an argument which leads to the kinds of contradictions we find implicit within Russell's paradox. And it is the kind of argument that the theory of types disallows. In brief, this argument from the theory of types stipulates that a proposition, $P(x)$, cannot be used as a value of its own argument.

For example, suppose I say

P.1: Ideas that occur to one on the spur of the moment invariably turn out false.

P.2: Proposition P.1 occurred to me on the spur of the moment.

Together P.1 and P.2 entail that if P.1 is true, it is false. Therefore, by the theory of types we should not assign the property "occurring on the spur of the moment" to proposition P.1.

Keep in mind now that this proscription from Russell's theory of types has become an allowable refinement in efforts to establish consistency of formal systems. Any argument that violates the proscription becomes exceptionable on formal grounds. At first glance Gödel's argument appears to violate this proscription; but, as we shall see, the ingenious tactic of mapping the argument onto arithmetic itself enables Gödel to circumvent the difficulty.

GÖDEL'S ARGUMENT

In general terms, Gödel's theorem of undecidability states that, assuming a formal system L, such as arithmetic, to be consistent, there is a possible theorem in L which can be demonstrated to be true in a metasystem, but which is undecidable within L itself. The argument in outline is as follows:

(1) Let $W_q(q)$ be a proposition in a formal system L.

(2) Then $W_q(q)$ is either provably true or provably false if L is complete; and not both, if L is consistent.

(3) As a possible theorem we take

(a) $T: W_q(q)$

Now the property of unprovability is well-defined within the formal system L. Therefore as the interpretation of (3a) we take

(b) $W_q(q) \equiv W_q(q)$ is unprovable in L

namely, a proposition which asserts that it is itself unprovable. Granting the legitimacy of this expression (3b), the proof of Gödel's theorem readily follows.

If L is consistent then either $W_q(q)$ is true or it is false. Assume that $W_q(q)$ is true; then, of course, what it asserts is true. Hence, if $W_q(q)$ is true, it is unprovable in L. But if we assume L to be complete and $W_q(q)$ is true, then $W_q(q)$ is provable in L. Thus assuming completeness of L involves us in a contradiction.

Does taking the other tack rid us of the contradiction? The answer is, "No!" Assume that $W_q(q)$ is false. Then what it asserts is false. Hence $W_q(q)$ is provable in L. But again, if $W_q(q)$ is provable in L we must conclude by virtue of (3b) that $W_q(q)$ is unprovable in L. We are back at the point of assuming $W_q(q)$ to be true. There is no escaping the contradiction.

We see then that regardless of whether we initially assume $W_q(q)$ to be true or false we are led to the proposition "if $W_q(q)$ is provable then it is unprovable." Now this is an apparent contradiction. We could account for the contradiction if the formal system L were inconsistent. But an inconsistent formal system is not an allowable base for deductive inference, since from an inconsistent system any proposition can be deduced. The defensible tactic at this point is to assume L to be consistent. Now, if within a consistent system L, a proposition implies its own negation, we negate the proposition. Hence we have indeed established that "$W_q(q)$ is unprovable in L." Moreover, what $W_q(q)$ asserts is true.

As presented here, the proof looks very much like those examples of self-reflexive argument which the theory of types disallows. But note we prefaced the argument granting the legitimacy of the expression

$$W_q(q) \equiv W_q(q) \text{ is unprovable in } L.$$

In order to show that this expression is a legitimate one, even within the Russell logic, we must turn to Gödel's ingenious arithmetic mapping of his argument.

Gödel Numbers and Arithmetic Mapping

An argument in the formal system L can be mapped onto an argument in the formal system G if for every symbol and operation in L there is an isomorphic, one-to-one transformation in G, and thus every statement in L has a unique transformation in G. The ingenuity of Gödel's mapping rests in his taking as the medium of G a subset of entities in L itself. The argument about the formal system L is mapped onto arithmetic which is part of the system L. As Gödel indicates, the argument in G is to be the "isomorphic image" of the argument in L (where L is to be the system of PM, *Principia Mathematica*).

We now give in abbreviated form the mechanics of the Gödel mapping.

Logical constants and variables.   To each logical sign and variable we assign an odd number. The set of logical constants is somewhat arbitrary, but they must be sufficient to accommodate the argument of PM. Thus for

Constant	Gödel Number
0 (nought)	1
f (successor)	3
~ (negation)	5
V (or)	7
Π (for all)	9
((left bracket)	11
) (right bracket)	13

The list can be extended to include the familiar symbols of implication (⊃), the existential quantifier (∃), conjunction, punctuation marks, and so on, to facilitate symbolic expression.

To variables of the first type, i.e., individual variables, we assign the ordered series of prime numbers beginning with the prime number greater than the highest prime assigned to the logical constants. Thus, were the above list to exhaust the set of logical constants, we would have:

Individual variable	x	y	z . . .
Gödel number	17	19	23 . . .

For variables of the second type (classes of individuals) we have:

Classes of individuals	p	q	r . . .
Gödel number	17^2	19^2	23^2 . . .

For variables of the third type (classes of classes of individuals) we have:

Classes of classes	P	Q	R . . .
Gödel number	17^3	19^3	23^3 . . .

And generally for variables of the n-th type we assign as Gödel numbers the powers of primes in the series 17^n, 19^n, 23^n, . . ., p^n, ... Note that all of the symbols of the sentential and functional calculi can be mapped by such numbers and all of the symbols of arithmetic. We now need a device for ordering these symbols into well-formed formulae.

Formulation.   We order the symbols in a well-formed formula by the series of prime numbers 2, 3, 5, 7, 11, 13, . . ., and we identify the symbol at each place in the series by raising the appropriate prime to the power of the Gödel number identifying the symbol. Thus, for $p \supset q$ we may write $\sim (p \sim q)$. And utilizing the code above, for $\sim (p \sim q)$ we write the Gödel number as the product: $2^5 \cdot 3^{11} \cdot 5^{17^2} \cdot 7^5 \cdot 11^{19^2} \cdot 13^{13}$.

Let the number of a formula be the number $n(i)$, where $n(i)$ is now the Gödel number of the ith formula in a series of formulae. Note now that the Gödel number $n(i)$, that is, the Gödel number of a given formula, is unambiguous. In the example above, we are assured that $n(i)$ decodes into $\sim (p \sim q)$ and only $\sim (p \sim q)$ by a fundamental theorem proved by Euclid: *Every integer greater than 1 can be factored into a unique product of primes.*

An argument in a formal system is represented by a string of formulae. For example, for *modus ponens* we have

$$p \supset q$$
$$\underline{p \qquad}$$
$$\therefore q$$

in its familiar form. For each formula in the spring $p \supset q$, p, q we can assign a Gödel number. Thus, in order, these numbers are $n(1)$, $n(2)$, $n(3)$ and the order of the string itself is mapped according to a product of ordered primes. Thus, the Gödel number of our string of formulae is

$$2^{n(1)} \cdot 3^{n(2)} \cdot 5^{n(3)}$$

and for a k formulae string we have generally

$$2^{n(1)} \cdot 3^{n(2)} \cdots p_k^{n(k)}$$

where p_k is the kth prime in the ordered series of primes.

Proof Schema.   Much of Gödel's memorable paper is occupied in the definition and clarification of terms such as "immediate consequence of," "formula," "axiom," "recursive function," "consistency," "provability." The preliminary discussion implements the rigor of his argument. For the purposes of our own informal presentation we need only introduce the important concept of a proof schema.

Observe that any argument on the formal system L can be represented by a string of formulae beginning with the axioms and ending with the formula of the proposition to be proved or deduced. Hence every theorem of the system L has a Gödel number such that that number is the exponent of the largest prime factor (i.e., $n(k)$ of $p_k^{n(k)}$) in the Gödel number of the string. In brief, then, we may write xBy to designate the property: the string with the Gödel number x is proof of the formula with the Gödel number y. And by virtue of our proof schema y is the power to which the largest prime factor, in the Gödel string of factors, is raised. Expressions such as xBy are used only informally in the argument to follow, but it should be emphasized that they are integral with our understanding of the concept of provability. If for any formula with Gödel number y there is no string such that y becomes the exponent of the terminal prime factor in the Gödel number of the string, then indeed that formula is unprovable in the formal system. What is important to emphasize is that we can be explicit about the property of unprovability within the formal system.

GÖDEL'S PROOF, AN INFORMAL SKETCH

We are now prepared to undertake a sketch of Gödel's proof of the theorem of undecidability.[2] Let us visualize a formal system L sufficient to include arithmetic. Within L we define a denumerable sequence of properties which we can assign to the integers

$$W_1 \quad W_2 \ldots W_n \ldots$$

The definitions of such properties are akin to sentence forms except that no specification is made as to which integers or set of integers has a given property. Hence the sentence forms utilizing W_1, W_2, . . ., W_n . . . contain one or more free variables. More explicitly we may write

$$W_1(p), W_2(p), \ldots, W_n(p), \ldots$$

in which p is the free variable taking the value of some integer. Thus $W_n(p)$ reads, "the integer p has the property W_n." The assignment of properties to integers is, of course, provisional. Either the assignment is axiomatic (such as the successor function) or it is subject to proof contingent upon the axioms of the system. Hence "the sentence $W_n(p)$ is provable" is a meaningful proposition; and so is "$W_n(p)$ is unprovable," when we assign some value to p.

Since the set of W_i are properties of integers and the set of values over p are themselves the integers, then it is possible to express any given sentence form, $W_n(p)$ as a Gödel number. Let $G(n,p)$ then be the Gödel number of the sentence $W_n(p)$.

Suppose now we wish to stipulate that assignment of the property W_n to the integer p results in an unprovable proposition. We then write

The sentence $W_n(p)$ is unprovable in L.   (1)

Note that expression (1) is a sentence form and it expresses a property of $W_n(p)$ which is also a sentence form.

But now we observe that the property of unprovability is subject to definition in terms of Gödel numbers. Recall that a statement in the formal language L is a theorem (i.e., provable) in L if its Gödel number occurs as

---

[2] The present sketch follows the argument as presented by Mostowski (1942), and as simplified by Schlegel (1967).

the exponent of the largest prime in the Gödel number of a proof. Hence, in place of that theorem we may substitute a statement of the form xBy ("x is the Gödel number of the proof of the formula whose Gödel number is y"). Thus an alternative and equivalent expression of (1) is

$G(n,p)$ is not among the set of Gödel numbers for which we can find an expression $xBG(n,p)$.

Here $G(n,p)$ is a substitution for y. In briefer form we write

$G(n,p)$ is not among the Gödel numbers of provable theorems in L.

(2)

Now expression (2) is a sentence form, and $G(n,p)$ is some integer to which we are assigning a property, unprovability in the Gödel formulation of proof. This being the case let us write this sentence form as $W_q(p)$. In a sense then $W_q(p)$ is a sentence form defining unprovability. That is, it asserts that the formula with Gödel number p is not among the set of Gödel numbers of statements for which there are proofs in L. And such statement serves to state the meaning of unprovability in Gödel terms.

Now note that $W_q(p)$ is one of the sentence forms in the denumerable set of all sentence forms in L. Thus it is a formula in L for which we can compute a Gödel number. We assign the Gödel number q to the statement $W_q(p)$. Since q, a Gödel number, is an integer, one in the set of all integers, we may assign some property or set of properties to it. For this assignment we select the property of unprovability, namely W_q. And we have the statement $W_q(q)$.

Reflect now on the construction of $W_q(q)$. In this statement we have assigned the property of unprovability to the Gödel number of the formula which itself stipulates the conditions of unprovability. Thus $W_q(p)$ defines unprovability for the formula with the Gödel number p. And for p we substitute q which is the Gödel number of the formula $W_q(p)$.

We are now ready to set up the proof of the theorem of undecidability. Recall that

The sentence $W_n(p)$ is unprovable in L.

(1)

and

$G(n,p)$ is not among the Gödel numbers of provable theorems in L. (2)

are equivalent expressions. Statement (2) differs from statement (1) only in that it is expressed in a self-reflective metalanguage; i.e., a language that enables us to speak about L in the language of L. Note also that (a) $W_q(p)$ is an expression of statement (2), (b) q is the Gödel number of $W_q(p)$, and (c) $W_q(q)$ is an instance of $W_q(p)$ with q replacing the free variable p. Since $W_q(p)$ is an expression of (2), $W_q(q)$ expresses the statement

$G(q,p)$ is not among the Gödel numbers of provable theorems in L.

(2')

This follows because q is just the Gödel number $G(q,p)$ and W_q expresses the predicate assigning unprovability within the Gödel schema.

But we have already considered q to be a possible value for the free variable p. Making that substitution, we have $G(q,q)$, and

$G(q,q)$ is not among the Gödel numbers of provable theorems in L. $\quad$ (2″)

We observe that (2), (2′), and (2″) are all statements of the same kind. They differ only as Gödel numbers encoding the formulae to which we assign unprovability.

Since (1) and (2) are extensionally equivalent expressions, we now ask what is the linguistic expression equivalent to (2″). It is the statement

The sentence $W_q(q)$ is unprovable in L. $\quad$ (1″)

Now we recall that $W_q(q)$ is an expression of statement (2′), and since q is a substitution instance for p in $G(q,p)$, $W_q(q)$ is also an expression of (2″). Hence we find by the equivalence of (1″) and (2″)

$$W_q(q) \equiv W_q(q) \text{ is unprovable in } L \qquad (4)$$

(i.e., $W_q(q)$ is equivalent to 2″ and 2″ is equivalent to 1″). The proof of Gödel's theorem now follows the argument detailed at the beginning of the exposition.

We take $W_q(q)$ as a putative theorem in L. If L is consistent then $W_q(q)$ is either true or false, but not both. Assume that $W_q(q)$ is true. Then by virtue of (4) we may certainly conclude that $W_q(q)$ is unprovable in L. But now assume that $W_q(q)$ is false. By virtue of (4) we then conclude that it is false that $W_q(q)$ is unprovable in L; hence, $W_q(q)$ must be provable. Assuming $W_q(q)$ to be false now enables us to construct the following proposition: "If $W_q(q)$ is provable in L, then $W_q(q)$ is unprovable in L." This, of course, is a contradiction. And since $[(p \supset \sim p) \supset \sim p]$, we conclude that $W_q(q)$ is indeed unprovable in L. Moreover, $W_q(q)$ as seen in (4) is a true proposition. Thus, there is at least one proposition in L, namely, $W_q(q)$, that we have demonstrated to be true by our metalogical considerations but which remains unprovable in L.[3]

There are two important aspects of this argument which we must emphasize in order to point up the significance of the theorem. One, we must assume that the formal system is consistent. Although any statement asserting the consistency of L is equally undecidable in L (a second

[3] Or, to phrase the argument somewhat differently, assume that L is complete with respect to $W_q(q)$. That is, we assume $W_q(a)$ to be provable in L. Then if L is consistent we conclude by virtue of (4) that $W_q(q)$ is unprovable. Hence if L is complete for $W_q(q)$ we must conclude that it is incomplete. But if the completeness of L implies its incompleteness, and if L is consistent, we must conclude that L is incomplete. That is to say $W_q(q)$ is indeed unprovable in L. And we have shown that $W_q(q)$ is true, since $W_q(q)$ itself tokens that $W_q(q)$ is unprovable in L.

important theorem of Gödel), the consequences of not assuming consistency would be cataclysmic. And two, granting that L is consistent, we have shown by virtue of the Gödel schema in the metalanguage that $W_q(q)$ is indeed unprovable. Thus we have shown that at least one putative theorem is true, namely the theorem of the undecidability of $W_q(q)$; a theorem, therefore, which cannot be proven in the formal system L.

Gödel's theorem on consistency. Another equally important theorem proved in Gödel's paper establishes the unprovability of consistency within the system even for consistent systems. We have intimated that the consequences are dire for inconsistent formal systems. From an inconsistent set of axioms any proposition can be proven. Suppose both A and its contradictory not-A to be axioms of a system. Then it follows that we can derive both B and not-B for whatever proposition B.

Initially we assert A; hence:

$$A \qquad (1)$$

$$(A \cup B) \cap (A \cup \bar{B}) \qquad (2)$$

where (1) and (2) are easily shown to be equivalent expressions. Now we assert our contradictory axiom:

$$\bar{A} \qquad (3)$$

But

$$\bar{A} \cap (A \cup B) = B \qquad (4)$$

and

$$\bar{A} \cap (A \cup \bar{B}) = \bar{B} \qquad (5)$$

Hence (2) and (3) entail

$$B \cap \bar{B} \qquad (6)$$

Within the context of his paper, Gödel at no point speculates that our formal systems are inconsistent. Rather, he proves that any statement in L which asserts the consistency of L is not provable in L, assuming that consistency. Thus, assuming the consistency of L, that consistency is not provable in L (cf. Note 5.2).

THE ARGUMENT FROM GÖDEL

The implications of Gödel's proof would appear clearcut. In a system as basic as arithmetic or the symbolic logic of *Principia Mathematica,* there are meaningful statements which are demonstrably true, yet which cannot be proved within the axiomatic development of the system itself. Hence, such systems are incomplete. Now a computer and the well-described nervous system (McCulloch and Pitts, 1943) are the realizations of just such logical systems. Hence the human computer demonstrates the truth of a proposition which is undecidable by any prospective realizations of our computer systems. We are indeed faced with the possibility that a human computer can prove something that its mechanical guts cannot.

This has been called "The Argument from Gödel" (Smart, 1963). Since it receives explicit, and perhaps its most popular, expression in the essay of Nagel and Newman (1958), I give their account of it in detail:

> Gödel's conclusions bear on the question whether a calculating machine can be constructed that would match the human brain in mathematical intelligence. Today's calculating machines have a fixed set of directives built into them; these directives correspond to the fixed rules of inference of formalized axiomatic procedure. The machines thus supply answers to problems by operating in a step-by-step manner, each step being controlled by the built-in directives. But, as Gödel showed in his incompleteness theorem, there are innumerable problems in elementary number theory that fall outside the scope of a fixed axiomatic method, and that such engines are incapable of answering, however intricate and ingenious their built-in mechanisms may be and however rapid their operations. Given a definite problem, a machine of this type might be built for solving it; but no one such machine can be built for solving every problem. The human brain may, to be sure, have built-in limitations of its own, and there may be mathematical problems it is incapable of solving. But, even so, the brain appears to embody a structure of rules of operation which is far more powerful than the structure of currently conceived artificial machines. There is no immediate prospect of replacing the human mind by robots.
>
> Gödel's proof should not be construed as an invitation to despair or as an excuse for mystery-mongering. The discovery that there are arithmetical truths which cannot be demonstrated formally does not mean that there are truths which are forever incapable of becoming known, or that a "mystic" intuition (radically different in kind and authority from what is generally operative in intellectual advances) must replace cogent proof. It does not mean, as a recent writer claims, that there are "ineluctable limits to human reason." It does mean that the resources of the human intellect have not been, and cannot be, fully formalized, and that new principles of demonstration forever await invention and discovery. We have seen that mathematical propositions which cannot be established by formal deduction from a given set of axioms may, nevertheless, be established by "informal" metamathematical reasoning. It would be irresponsible to claim that these formally indemonstrable truths established by metamathematical arguments are based on nothing better than bare appeals to intuition.
>
> Nor do the inherent limitations of calculating machines imply that we cannot hope to explain living matter and human reason in physical and chemical terms. The possibility of such explanations is neither precluded nor affirmed by Gödel's incompleteness theorem. The theorem does indicate that the structure and power of the human mind are far more complex and subtle than any nonliving machine yet envisaged. Gödel's own work is a remarkable example of such complexity and subtlety. It is an occasion, not for dejection, but for a renewed appreciation of the powers of creative reason. (Nagel and Newman, 1958, pp. 100-102)

It is apparent from this view that an objection to computer simulation is to be based upon the impossibility of visualizing extant computer procedures and finite programs sufficient to simulate *all* conceivable acts of human computation. However, it is indeed debatable whether we must of necessity subject ourselves to the constraints of finite programs or to the condition that all conceivable behaviors are to be simulatable by extant computer programs. As the argument develops, there are those who agree substantially with the argument as adumbrated by Nagel and Newman (Bronowski, 1966; Kemeny, 1959; Lucas, 1961; Polanyi, 1958; Schlegel, 1967). And there are those who adopt the counter arguments, either that the significance of Gödel's theorem is misconstrued (Putnam, 1961, 1969; Scriven, 1961), or that our conceptualizations of machines are for the present technologically limited (Arbib, 1964; George, 1961; Smart, 1963).

Let us first consider the arguments that Nagel and Newman simply misconstrue the significance of the theorem of incompleteness. Putnam, for example, writes as follows:

> Let T be a Turing machine which "represents" me in the sense that T can prove just the mathematical statements I can prove. Then the argument (Nagel and Newman give no argument, but I assume they must have this one in mind) is that by using Gödel's technique I can discover a proposition that T cannot prove, and moreover *I* can prove this proposition. This refutes the assumption that T "represents" me, hence I am not a Turing machine. The fallacy is a misapplication of Gödel's theorem, pure and simple. Given an arbitrary machine T, all I can do is find a proposition U such that *I* can prove:
>
> (3) If T is consistent, U is true
>
> where U is undecidable by T if T is in fact consistent. However, T can perfectly well prove (3) too! And the statement U, which T *cannot* prove (assuming consistency), *I* cannot prove either (unless I can prove that T is consistent, which is unlikely if T is very complicated! (1961, p. 142)

This is a restatement, almost word for word, of an earlier statement to be found in his review of the Nagel and Newman book (Putnam, 1960), but in neither case does he elaborate. Let us consider Putnam's proposition U to be equivalent to the proposition $W_q(q)$. Then it is the case that I can demonstrate U to be true, providing I assume the formal system, of which T is a realization, is consistent. This is the significance of one of Gödel's theorems. But from here Putnam's argument appears equivocal. If he means primarily to assert that a Turing machine T can be suitably constructed to prove this proposition (3), then the simulated implication of the Gödel predicament is simply once removed. On the other hand, if he wishes to emphasize the *tu quoque* riposte that the statement U, which T cannot prove, I cannot prove either; that riposte is subject to the charge of dogmatism (Nagel and Newman, 1961). In the writer's opinion the substance of Putnam's argument must rest in the assertion that a Turing machine is capable in principle of proving Gödel's theorem, providing of course, that we give it detailed instructions. But then it is not a question of proving the Gödel-like proposition (3); rather it is a question of T's realizing the consequences of that result in its addressing that result to its own machinery. There is always some proposition, say U', which we, by virtue of our unlimited recourse to the Gödel tactic, can demonstrate to be true but which is undecidable by T.

A perhaps more telling argument is advanced by Scriven (1961). Our formal understanding of computation and proof is purely syntactical, and ultrasystemic. Consequently, we have no assurance that we have given our computers an adequate notion of proof procedures when we commit them to operate within a given formal system.

> As is well known, given any Gödel sentence G which is provably true but undecidable within a system S, it is easy to construct an S' within which it is derivable—the uninteresting way being to add G to the system S. Now, Nagel and Newman are struck by the fact that whatever axioms and rules of inference one might give a computer, there would apparently be mathematical truths, such as G, which it could never "reach" from these axioms by the use of these rules. This is true, but their assumption that we could suppose ourselves to have given the machine an adequate idea of mathematical truth when we gave it the axioms and rules of inference is not true. This would be to suppose the formalists were right, and they were shown by Gödel to be wrong. The Gödel theorem is no more an obstacle to a computer than to ourselves. One can only say that mathematics would have been easier if the formalists had been right, and it would in that case be comparatively easy to construct a mechanical mathematician. They weren't and it isn't. But just as we can recognize the truth of the unprovable formula by comparing what it says with what we know to be the case, so can a computer do the same. (Scriven, 1961, p. 125)

Thus Scriven argues that to give our machine T a set of axioms and procedural rules (such as in Hilbert's formalism or *Principia Mathematica*) is not to give it an adequate idea of mathematical truth seeking. Let us, for example, assume (what we presume to be) a complete neurophysiological description of the human computer O such that a realization of it is the machine T. Granting this possibility, we are not entitled to assume that this neurophysiological description of mathematical reasoning is in fact complete if there are proof procedures, insights, and so on, falling outside its syntactical scope.

But note also Scriven's suggestion that a machine conceivably can recognize the significance and the truth of an unprovable formula; that is to say, it too can recognize its own limitations. Let us grant that somehow we can incorporate into the machine a penchant for transforming the argument concerning Putnam's proposition (3) by virtue of Gödelian techniques. Then not only does the machine prove a theorem of undecidability, but it may be programmed to recognize those computational interrogations which call for applying the theorem of undecidability. However, we must now ask, is recognition all that is called for in the simulation of the human computer? The machine can now print out in explicit terms the general significance of what it has proved, namely, a theorem of undecidability concerning its formal (but not augmented) system L. And, moreover, it can now recognize those computational situations in which the theorem applies; i.e., to any formal system.

In response we must emphasize that whereas the machine recognizes the significance and applicability of Gödel's theorem, it is not capable at the same time of *proving* what it recognizes to be the case. Let us consider our sophisticated Turing machine that is programmed to prove Gödel's theorem. Since this theorem applies to formal systems which are utilized to implement its own programs, we may now in addition instruct the machine to print out in explicit terms the implications of that theorem for all computer programs. Thus the machine is capable of making a general statement on incompleteness which applies to its own computational system and to all others. But what it does not do is prove the specific application of the theorem. It is one thing to recognize the general significance of a theorem; it is another to prove the applicability of the theorem in a specific situation.

Consider now an augmented formal system L' containing a proposition U [i.e., Putnam's proposition, (3)] as an axiom of the system. Consider also a new machine T' which is a realization of L'. Then there is a new proposition U' demonstrably true if L' is consistent, but which cannot be proven in L'. The machine T is presumed to be capable of proving Putnam's proposition (3), and at the same time it is capable of recognizing the significance of that proposition for the new machine T'. Hence we may decode its recognition to assert there is another proposition, say (3'), which is

(3'): If T' is consistent, U' is true,

where U' is a theorem expressing undecidability. But now, although T can work out the proposition (3') as a result of instruction under recognition of the significance of (3), it cannot *prove* that proposition under its present program. Proposition (3) foretells the truth of proposition (3'), but it does not represent a proof. As suggested by Nagel and Newman the advantage of the human computer is as follows: Not only does the human computer "simulate" the machine in recognizing the significance of proposition (3), but if called upon to do so, it can *prove* proposition (3') which it also recognizes to be true by virtue of proposition (3). This the human computer does by his augmented Gödelization of the argument in L', an augmented argument that is denied to the machine T.

Let us recapitulate the argument. We consider T to be a sophisticated machine such that it demonstrates U, $U \equiv W_q(q)$, to be true if L is consistent, where $W_q(q)$ in effect states that U is undecidable in the formal system L. The proof of $W_q(q)$ is recognized by T to have general significance, which by a programmed translation (printout) is intended to apply to a formal system L' and its machine realization T' by virtue of the analogous proposition (3'). Although that printout may very well include a phrasing of proposition (3'), it does not by any means constitute a proof.

It would now seem that we need neither be so pessimistic as Nagel and Newman nor so sanguine as Putnam and Scriven. On one hand, there seems to be no logical barrier to computer simulation of Gödel's proof; on the other hand, the human computer appears to retain a residual advantage in that it displays the flexibility of always being able to prove what, by virtue of its prior knowledge, it recognizes to be the case. So long as we conceive machines to be realizable as Turing machines, then the machine is limited by its finite program. Any given computational act is simulatable by a given Turing machine, but not *all* computational acts of which the human computer is capable. (See Scriven, 1965; Turner, 1967, pp. 361-367). But then, in matters of reductive explanation, we are not asked to explain, that is, to simulate, *all* computational acts—just those specific acts which are in principle amenable to complete descriptions. In this, what I assume to be the proper context of explanation, there appears to be no logical barrier to reductive explanation. To be sure, Gödel's proof suggests a predicament for the simulation of all computational behaviors of the human computer. But any given behavior is in principle simulatable and hence explainable.

There is another response to the argument from Gödel, which is not explicitly stated in the essays of Putnam and Scriven. Scriven's critique of the argument from Gödel is in large part based on the assumption that by confining the machine operations to the syntax of number theory we have not given the machine an adequate idea of mathematical proof and problem solving. But he does not suggest what a more "adequate idea of mathematical truth" might be. However, Smart (1963) and George (1961) have separately suggested that it might be possible to construct inductive machines that would circumvent our presently conceived limitations of machines. Since Smart gives his argument in greater detail, we shall follow him.

Smart first conceives a machine capable of problem-solving ingenuity. In the previous chapter we have been introduced to problem-solving machines (e.g., Newell and Simon, 1959; Minsky, 1961), but Smart's problem-solving machine is more purely conceptual. Problem solving is most systematic when we can provide an algorithm for a given class of problems. However, Church (1936) has established that for the predicate calculus at least there is no possible algorithm which will enable us to decide which propositions are provable theorems of the formal system and which are not. The significance of this result is generalizable to other branches of mathematics as well. In large part, the mathematician's strategies for seeking proofs depend upon ingenuity, trial and error, and rather specifically applied heuristics. Smart conjectures that a machine with practically unlimited time could generate a protracted sequence of symbols some of which possibly might be recognized as legitimate proof strings. Pure random generalization could be circumvented by implementing certain stochastic biases in the generation of symbols. Time saving could thus be implemented through programmed heuristics, but this is not essential to the argument. Such machines would be programmed to recognize a legitimate proof string and in time the stochastic generator might turn up many proofs, say, of number theory, both unknown and known. Who knows, Smart avers, perhaps in time a machine designed for the ingenuity problem might turn up a proof of Fermat's Last Theorem, if such a proof exists.

Smart proposes that if we can mechanize the ingenuity problem, it might be possible to build a problem-solving machine that not only proves and disproves theorems in a formal system L, but also observes its own "linguistic" behavior. Thus by observing its own rules in L, it might convert itself into a higher-order machine utilizing the metalogical considerations of its self-observation. "By ascertaining the rules of its own language L_0 it can convert itself into an L_1 machine, and so it can go up the hierarchy of languages as long as the capacity of its storage units is not exhausted" (Smart, 1963, p. 119). Indeed such a machine would appear to simulate the advantage human problem solvers have over extant computers. The only question then would be whether computer resources are exhaustible as compared with human computers (Turner, 1967, pp. 364-367).

. But of the versatile machine Smart writes: [4]

> At any moment there will be true propositions which it cannot prove, but which it can prove at a later moment when it has converted itself to a machine of greater logical power. Ultimately it will exhaust its storage capacity, but equally the human being will also, literally, become exhausted.
> This method of getting around the argument from Gödel seems to me to be a perfectly plausible one. It depends on the possibility of machines which can learn from experience. It is admittedly beyond our

[4] The idea of an inductive machine was also foreseen by George (1961). As regards the implications of theorems by Gödel, Church, Turing, he writes: "These results have actually led to misinterpretation outside mathematics, in that they were thought to imply that there were some mathematical operations that could not be performed by a *machine,* whereas they could be performed by a human being. This is a mistake, and certainly does not follow from any work done on decision procedures. What does follow is that, in order to deal with certain mathematical operations (for example, those involving the choice of new branches for development), a machine would need to be able to compute probabilities, and to make inductions. It must necessarily be agreed, however, that the machine may make some mistakes in its computations, though we must not overlook the fact that these are exactly the sort of conditions that would apply to a human being performing the same operations." (1961, p. 3)

present technological powers to make a machine of the sort required, but there does not seem to me to be any *a priori* or physical reason why such a machine should not exist. (1963, p. 120)

What may we then conclude? There seems no reason to take exception with Smart's finding the idea of an inductive machine a perfectly plausible one. The one thing he does ask, however, is that we demand almost unlimited resources for the machine. This, of course, is not plausible. A human problem-solver such as Gödel is comparatively a more efficient computer. Insight, intuition, the language of discovery and creativity give a pointedness, a nonrandom character, to human problem-solving not simulated by the inefficient generator of symbolic strings. Even should the inductive machine simulate the Gödelian tactician, it is not at all clear that the computational acts would be anything like helpful replicas of human thought processes.

Be that as it may, we should be reluctant to conclude that Gödel's theorem endows human ingenuity in problem solving with an aura of "ineluctable mystery." The fact remains that scientific explanations are matters of detailed description and rigorous deduction. To that extent, what we can understand and convey of human problem solving comes to us in the way of scientific understanding. And to the extent that we can understand some act of computation and problem solving, it does indeed seem plausible that our understanding of that act can also be realizable in the language of machine simulation (cf. Note 5.3).

Addendum on Incompleteness and Explanation

In the writer's opinion a more telling argument from Gödel involves the inherent incompleteness of any formal system constituting a scientific theory (Schlegel, 1967; Bronowski, 1966). Let us visualize a comprehensive theory of physical phenomena, for example, of mechanics, such that the theory is fully axiomatized in a formal system L. Then Gödel's theorem of undecidability states that some proposition, some theorem, demonstrably true, if the system is consistent, is unprovable in L. Now according to the hypothetico-deductive rubric of explanation, an event or class of events is explainable if the statement which constitutes its description is deducible from the axioms of the system. Let us visualize a set of undecidable theorems $\{P_i\}$ in L. Then by virtue of Gödel (1931) and Church (1936), we have no means of knowing *a priori* whether all statements covering all classes of phenomena, or just which statements, are deducible in L. Thus, it is conceivable that for any theory T there is some class of events expressible as a possible theorem P_j such that P_j is not provable in T, and hence not explainable.

We are, of course, not spared our scientific embarrassment by introducing an augmented theory T', for as we know, the factor of incompleteness now holds for T' and any higher-order augmented theory as well. This being the case, it is possible that some behavioral phenomenon is among the class of unexplainable events. We may, of course, adopt the tactic of incorporating a lawlike statement describing the unexplained event as an axiom of an augmented theory. But this clearly does not satisfy the matter of explaining that behavioral phenomenon. Suppose, for the sake of argument, we are to conjecture that the description of some class of paranormal behaviors is in fact among the undecidable theorems in a formal theory T. It may be that we would then wish to make this theorem, say P_k, part of postulational corpus of the augmented theory T', whereby we could proceed to deduce additional theorems in this new theory. But now our reductive program is clearly rejected, for it is the character of our reductive commitment that all behaviors are to be explained in the formal theory of neurophysiology. The introduction of axioms concerning paranormal behavior puts them beyond the pale of explanation in either T or the augmented T'. Yet paranormal behaviors, if such there be, are just the kind of behaviors we would like to explain. Should the reader wish to demur on the authenticity of paranormal behaviors, as well he might, he may substitute other problematic behaviors of his own choosing. The argument will hold just as well. We are not prone to relegate problems of explanation to the status of postulates; that is to say, it is not helpful to postulate the very thing we set out to explain.

Still the disconcerting possibility, or perhaps even inevitability, of "incomplete theories" should not be treated as fatal to our explanatory quests. We have seen before (Chapter 2) that it is indefensible for us to assume that our theoretic formulations and systems are ever finalized according to invariant concepts and principles. Both our observational and theoretic languages are continually subject to modification in order that we may seek higher syntheses of our scientific disciplines or that we may seek the explanatory rubric for heretofore refractory data. The prospects of logical incompleteness of formal systems should not deter us from our hypothetico-deductive efforts at explanation, for nothing in Gödel's proof tells us that we may not find scientific explanations of *any* conceivable act. At most, we are informed that it is unrealistic for us to assume that we shall ever develop a complete comprehensive theory in a given science, and not that there may be some given phenomenon, some behavior forever outside the pale of scientific understanding.

NOTES

NOTE 5.1

To most of us, schooled as we are in the vagaries of scientific inference, mathematics stands as the quintessence of reason at its unexceptionable best. Doubtless, that is why the mathematician is seen to comport himself with a display of assurance unknown to students of the lesser sciences. Consequently it comes as a moment for reflection that all is not quite right at the foundations of mathematics. As a subject matter, the foundations of mathematics is a highly technical discipline, one for the specialist in mathematical logic. However, enough of it can be adumbrated here to set up the significance of the concepts of consistency and completeness as explicitly dealt with in Gödel's theorems.

(A) *Logicism* (Frege and Russell): This point of view presents the thesis that mathematics is a branch of a logic. Since logic is analytic and hence empty of empirical content (Russell), mathematics itself is an analytic discipline dealing with tautologies, hence empty of empirical content and devoid of any synthetic induction which itself is not reducible to our relatively arbitrary logical constructions.

(1) *Numbers:* Although Frege and Russell apparently do not agree as to the psychogenesis of number concepts they do agree as to procedures for defining numbers, and as to the appropriateness of the basic axioms of the theory of integers (Peano). Number is an abstract entity which we apply to classes. Visualize any two sets, *A* and *B,* which may differ in all properties except that every element in *A* can be paired with an element in *B*. Then their common element is their numerosity. Thus number is defined as "the class of classes similar to a given class." Here the matters of pairing in one-one correspondence and of establishing the equal numerosity between classes are considered to be neither problematical nor circular, although paradoxes arise in the tactics concerning the concept of a class of classes (see, for example, Russell's paradox as discussed in the text). One may then proceed to develop the series of integers by defining 0 as the number assignable to the class of all things not identifiable with themselves, 1 as the number of the unit class, and on through the series of natural numbers by the operation of the successor function. Relying upon the Peano axioms, Russell concurs with Frege in all essentials save that for Russell numbers are concepts which take their meaning only in context, whereas for Frege they have "object" status as logical entities.

(2) *Infinite:* Russell appropriates the Cantorian ideas of denumerable and nondenumerable sets, of infinite and transfinite numbers. The unending series of digits infinitely extended by the successor function is denumerable, digit by digit, whereas the number of points on a line of

any length is not (even though it contains a denumerable infinite set as a proper subset). However, in order to stay within the logical language of classes, Russell requires an axiom of questionable status. Since a class of classes must be populated by elements (propositional functions), there is no logical proscription on the idea that the set assigned the number which is the successor to the number N might be a null set. Hence, N would be the highest possible integer. The *axiom of infinity* excludes this possibility by fiat. Axiomatically we assume an infinite populace for classes, thus there is no integer N such that its successor is a null set. But, as Körner (1960) suggests, the idea of making numbers contingent upon the idea of populated classes conflates empirical and nonempirical concepts.

(3) *Mathematical proof:* Since mathematics is reducible to logic, mathematical proof follows the instrumentalities and paradigms of logical proof. The primary tools of inference are substitution and *modus ponens* (i.e., application of material implication). And proof is carried out on the basis of purely logical propositions. Proof theory is developed under two headings—that of propositions, *per se*, the sentential calculus; and that of propositional functions involving quantification. In the first case, proof is straightforward. All proofs of logical propositions (theorems) are tautological (Wittgenstein), and the truth or falsity of any putative theorem can be unequivocally established by virtue of the algorithm of the truth table. A theorem within the sentential system is true for all arguments of the premises. That is to say, it is true without exception independent of any empirical reference of the sentences. In the second case, that of quantification, proof is more problematical. Although again reliance is placed on substitution and *modus ponens*, completeness of the formal system cannot be assured within the system (a result from Gödel's work).

In general, the theory of proof incorporates the principle of mathematical induction as axiomatic (Peano) and then relies upon substitution and implication as the means for establishing consequential sequences of argument. The logic is a two-valued one. As a consequence, one resorts to argument by *reductio ad absurdum*. If, in assuming the proposition to be proved is false, the argument leads to a contradiction, then we may negate the assumption. That is to say, if we assume $\sim p$, and subsequently show it is the case of $\sim(\sim p)$ then we may conclude p. Straightforward as this argument is in classical logic, we find that it is one which is rejected by the intuitionists.

(4) *Completeness:* Whereas one can readily establish the completeness of the sentential calculus for all tautological arguments based on that calculus (Beth, 1959, Sec. 74); the object of Gödel's proof of undecidability was to show that completeness could not be established for formal systems involving quantification over propositional functions as formalized in *Principia Mathematica*.

(B) *Intuitionism* (Brouwer, Heyting, Kronecker, and Poincaré): This school of thought differs from the logistic school primarily in treating mathematics as the product of a human synthetic faculty (Kant) rather than as a matter of convention, tautology, or logical reduction (Leibniz). Thus, as in the Kantian treatment of time, the mind contributes something to the reification of experience. However, rather than temporal experience, we are dealing with mathematical experience. The sense of mathematical truth is conveyed to us not by logical argument, *per se,* but by our intuitive faculty. Both the intuitionists and the formalists acknowledge indebtedness to Kantian intuitionism, but it is with the former school that the idea of mathematical faculty assumes primary emphasis.

(1) *Number:* The perhaps two most repeated quotations in the foundations of mathematics are Russell's

> "Mathematics may be defined as the subject in which we never know what we are talking about, nor whether what we are saying is true."

and Kronecker's

> "God gave us the integers, the rest is the work of man."

In the first case, we get the sense of the thesis that mathematics is tautological, analytic, nonempirical; in the other, the sense of the proposition that mathematics is a constructive enterprise beginning with intuitive non-reducible entities. Any given integer n in the succession of natural numbers "is well defined only if a method for calculating it is given" (Heyting, 1956, p. 2). Hence a major contention is that numbers and sets are constructible entities whose status is one of potentiality rather than subsisting reality. "To exist means to be constructed." Therefore, so far as any natural number or any infinite sequence of numbers is concerned, their existential status is contingent upon our devising generator functions for actually constructing such entities. Hence, infinite sets, the ordinal numbers in the series of integers, the cardinal numbers assignable to pairings of elements among corresponding sets are not subsisting entities ready to be discovered and formalized, but are purely emergent as a function of our constructive faculty.

(2) *Infinite:* As in the case of number, the concept of infinity is constructive. For the most part, nonintuitionists, and to be sure the logisticists and formalists, considered infinite sets to be complete totalities with existential status. For intuitionists, however, infinite sets take on existential status only as they are created by our constructions. Thus the meaning of infinity rests in the constructual enterprise rather than in properties we seek to discover for subsisting totalities. Therefore the concept of a set (or "spread" as Brouwer called it) is admissible, but requires, in addition to the rule of the defining property of elements of the set, a "complementary" rule for generating the elements of that set. Since these rules demand the exact construction of sets much of the Cantorian theory of the continuum, sets of subsets, infinite sets, and transfinite numbers, was rejected. The theory of transfinite numbers is built on the concept of subsets of infinite sets. Thus if $\aleph_0$ (aleph null) is the number of elements in the infinite set of rational numbers, then the number of subsets of these elements is $2^{\aleph_0}$, which is clearly greater than $\aleph_0$. But $2^{\aleph_0}$ is then the number of elements in a set, and the number of subsets of this set becomes $2^{2^{\aleph_0}}$; and so on and on to ever and ever greater infinities. But here the intuition-

ists claim that traditional enumeration leads to a series of transfinite numbers in which the constructual detail is unclear.

(3) *Proof:* According to Heyting, "A mathematical construction ought to be so immediate to the mind and its result so clear that it needs no foundation whatsoever" (1956, p. 6). And again he writes, "Logic is a part of mathematics and can by no means serve as a foundation for it" (1956, p. 6). Such statements indicate that intuitionists understand the concept of proof in other than formal terms. In logic a proposition is provable if it can be shown to be a tautology or, more generally, if it follows as a consequence of the axioms elaborated through the transformation rules. For the intuitionist the *modus operandi* of all proof and of the generation of integers is the principle of mathematical induction. Assume a propositional function $P(n)$, where n is some integer and P is some property assignable to that integer. Then if it can be shown in the set of all integers that $P(n+1)$ is the case if $P(n)$ is the case, and if it can also be shown that $P(n)$ is the case for $n=0$ then together these entail that $P(n)$ holds over the entire set of n. For the logistic school this principle is axiomatic as in the case of Peano's arithmetic axioms. But for the intuitionist, the principle of induction is implicit within the intuitive mathematical faculty. Hence Poincaré, an intuitionist in his philosophy of mathematics, writes, "Mathematical induction—i.e., proof by recurrence—is . . . necessarily imposed on us because it is only the affirmation of a property of the mind itself" (1952, p. 13). All proofs then must be constructive by virtue of generating rules and inductions. Hence, if a putative theorem T assigns some property P to the integer n, this theorem is proven only if there is a construction of a number n such that it does indeed have the property P. The distinctive feature of this rather innocuous way of stipulating what a proof should be is its nonlogistic framework.

Two implications follow for the intuitionist. One, the principle of the excluded middle in two-valued logic is rejected for mathematics (not necessarily for logic). And two, indirect proof by virtue of contradiction and the *reductio ad absurdum* is disallowed. By virtue of two-valued logic, the negation of a negative implies a positive. Thus

$$\sim(\sim p) \equiv p$$

And indirect proof that some n has some property W is undertaken by showing by way of a contradiction that it can not be the case that for any n, n has the property $\sim W$. For the intuitionist $\sim(\sim p)$ is a meaningful construction, but for mathematics at least we cannot take this as an assertion of $p;$ since as yet no direct construction is given of p.

(4) *Completeness:* Since nonconstructive proofs are not allowable, it should be apparent that the intuitionist is not disturbed by the possibility of incompleteness of his mathematical system. Mathematics is emergent, creative, constructive. Hence, by its very nature, it is incomplete. However, to the intuitionist, incompleteness as here signified is that of immaturity, that of the mere absence of constructive proofs. Incompleteness for the formalist and logistic schools becomes, as we shall see, a *logical* predicament of the logical impossibility of providing a proof. To

this extent, at least, Gödel's proof is germane to all points of view. It is the case nonetheless that intuitionists are less dismayed by unprovability or undecidability than are the formalists who make their case in terms of the adequacy of their logics.

(C) *Formalism* (Hilbert and Bernays): In some respects formalism embraces features of both logicism and intuitionism. It attempts to establish the foundations of mathematics on a secure logical base and then, agreeing with the intuitionists, it points to the ideal of constructive proofs as concerns complex statements alluding to properties of the system. Here, rather than focusing upon the concepts of number, or of the infinite as such, we turn to the character and possible extension of proof. According to Hilbert, formalism is accurately described as a theory of proof. If mathematics is to have a secure foundation in logic, and yet satisfy the ideal of constructive proof, it must show within the language of metamathematical analysis that the mathematical system, the object of inquiry, is free of inherent contradiction (consistent) and is complete in that it provides a method for deciding whether a statement is true or false within the system.

The method of formalism is metamathematical. Granting to mathematics, say, arithmetic or geometry, a unique domain of its own, then the object of critical study is analysis of the primitive theory in a formal language that assures the consistency of that theory. As Kleene (1952) points out, there is a threefold aspect to the method of formalism. First, there is the primitive or informal theory expressed in the natural language (e.g., of ordinary arithmetic, or the probability of chances, and so on). Second, there is the axiomatic theory which models, maps, or interprets the entities, operations, and inference chains of the primitive theory. And third, there is the metamathematical inquiry which establishes the relations between the informal and formal theories. It is in the metamathematical inquiry that we seek to establish the consistency and completeness of the informal theory.

(1) *Number:* While not agreeing with the logicists that the primitive concepts of number are logical concepts, the formalists do agree that in formal or axiomatic language we speak of numbers as logically constructible entities subject to the axiomatic treatment of Peano, Frege, and Russell.

(2) *Infinite:* According to the logistic school, infinite classes are regarded as totalities whose elements are assimilable within two-valued logic. Either an element has some property or it does not. Either all elements in the infinite set have a given property or there exists at least one element which does not. The difficulty here is that these are ideal statements, ideal in the sense that no means exist over infinite as against finite enumeration which allow us to verify the principle of the excluded middle. On the other hand, real statements are those which, in use, possess an immediate intuitive meaning, such as in the assignment of properties to the elements of finite sets.

This distinction between real and ideal statements within an informal system is due to Hilbert. Yet he maintains that in our capacity for utilizing ideal statements rests the strength of mathematical argument. However, to justify their use in the informal system we must show that every ideal statement which treats infinite sets as totalities, or that assigns properties over infinite sequences, is formally mappable as a finite constructive enterprise in the formal system. Again, this is to emphasize that all ideal statements, or rather their counterparts in the formal system, are free of inconsistency. By assuring consistency, the formalists hoped to overcome the paradoxes of infinite classes.

(3) *Proof:* According to the formalist, proof must be finitistic, constructive, intuitively indubitable, and it must be carried out in a way to circumvent the paradoxes of the logistic of quantification. In this he is in agreement with the intuitionist. One, any proof sequence in the formal language is a series of statements (formula) strung together by logical connectives and transformation rules such that the statement to be proved is the end statement in the proof sequence. If not that, then the statement to be proved, so to speak, must be an axiom of the system, in which case the status of proof is gratuitous. Thus if a, b, c are axioms of the system, and $(a \cap b \cap c) \supset p$, proof of p would be represented by the sequence $\{(a \cap b \cap c) \cap [(a \cap b \cap c) \supset p]\} \supset p$, in which p is the terminal statement or formula. Note that any proof sequence is necessarily finite and necessarily has a stopping state at which point the statement to be proved is a consequence of the preceding string of statements. Two, every finitistic proof procedure involving mathematical induction is recursive in nature. In order for the principle of mathematical induction to be admissible it must be shown, for example, that for any integer p, in the class of all integers, to have some given property W, there is a method by which it can indeed be verified that the property W is assignable to the definite integer p. In a sense, the principle of mathematical induction appears to assure this. However, an explicit statement of this principle is found in the definition of recursive functions. Informally stated, "A number-theoretic function is recursive if there exists an effective finite procedure for computing it" (Arbib, 1964, p. 124). The definition of a recursive function thereby stipulates the condition under which we can rely upon mathematical induction as a procedure for finite computation and proof. For example, the operation of addition can be formalized in terms of a recursive function. Let

$$\phi(0,a) = a$$

indicate the operation of adding 0 to the nonnegative integer a. Then

$$\phi(n+1, a) = \phi(n,a) + 1$$

shows us how to construct the addition of the integers $n+1$ and a by virtue of the successor function. That is to say, any sum of two integers is computable by virtue of the successor function, itself intuitively axiomatic. Other arithmetic operations can be formalized in a similar fashion (cf. Körner, 1960). We emphasize that all recursive functions are computable in a finite set of steps. Hence a proof sequence as indicated above would satisfy the conditions of a recursive function.

(4) *Completeness:* Although argument for the reasonableness of the finitistic proof procedures could be made on intuitive grounds, justification for the formalization of a mathematical theory rests on logical grounds. The system must be shown to be free of inherent contradiction and it should be complete. Significantly, Hilbert (*Grundlagen der Geometrie*) demonstrated that formalized geometry could be regarded as a consistent system, but only if it could also be shown that arithmetic is consistent. The forlorn quest for ultimate consistency, however, terminated with the appearance of Gödel's paper on undecidable propositions.

A discussion of the foundations of mathematics in terms of schools and adherents may be considered somewhat dated. Rather than credos and charisma we should focus upon the ontological status of mathematical entities as such. Thus a distinction is to be made between mathematical platonists and mathematical constructivists. Mathematical platonism is akin to philosophical realism (Bernays, 1935). It assumes subsistent status for mathematical entities, sets of sets, totalities, such that their existence is to be regarded as independent of our cognitional, constructive enterprises. Thus the nature of mathematical totalities is to be discovered, our formulations of them to be subject to truth analysis. In contrast constructivism emphasizes intuition and the constructive activities of man; statements of totalities would be meaningless without this cognitive base. Hence constructivism points toward invention rather than discovery, toward that which is in principle constructible rather than that which is subsistent, toward the potential rather than the actual. However, the old schools remain divided; the logicists and most formalists lean toward platonism, the intuitionists toward constructivism.

For an excellent discussion of this distinction and a general survey, see Parson's article "Foundations of Mathematics" in the *Encyclopedia of Philosophy,* Vol. 5 (Parsons, 1967).

Bibliographic Note:

Accounts of the various schools on the foundations of mathematics can be found in the following general references: S. F. Barker, *Philosophy of Mathematics* (1964); E. W. Beth, *The Foundations of Mathematics* (1959); M. Black, *The Nature of Mathematics* (1933, 1959); A. H. Fraenkel and Y. Bar-Hillel, *Foundations of Set Theory* (1958); S. C. Kleene, *Introduction to Metamathematics* (1952); S. Körner, *The Philosophy of Mathematics: An Introduction* (1960); H. Meschkowski, *Evaluation of Mathematical Thought* (1965); F. Waismann, *Introduction to Mathematical Thinking* (1951); R. L. Wilder, *Introduction to the Foundations of Mathematics* (1952, 1965). The Beth, Fraenkel and Bar-Hillel, Kleene, and Wilder books are outstanding but somewhat technical sources on the foundations of mathematics. All give extensive treatments of Gödel's proofs.

Logicism references: G. Frege, *The Foundations of Arithmetic* (1884, 1903); W. O. Quine, *Methods of Logic* (1950), B. Russell, *Prin-*

ciples of Mathematics, 2nd Ed. (1937), *Introduction to Mathematical Philosophy* (1919); B. Russell and A. N. Whitehead, *Principia Mathematica,* Vol. 1 (1925).

Intuitionism references: A. Heyting, *Intuitionism: An Introduction* (1956); H. Poincaré, *Foundations of Science* (1913, 1946); H. Weyl, *Philosophy of Mathematics and Natural Science* (1949).

Formalism references: R. Carnap, *Foundations of Mathematics and Logic* (1939); D. Hilbert, *The Foundations of Geometry* (1902); D. Hilbert and W. Ackerman, *Principles of Mathematical Logic* (1950).

Gödel's Theorems: An English translation of Gödel's original 1931 paper has been issued with an expository preface by R. B. Braithwaite (Gödel, 1962).

Non-technical expositions can be found in the following works: J. Findlay, Goedelian Sentences: A Non-Numerical Approach, *Mind,* 1942, 51, 259–265; H. Jeffreys, *Scientific Inference* (2nd Ed., 1957); A. Mostowski, *Sentences Undecidable in Formalized Arithmetic* (1952); E. Nagel and V. R. Newman, *Gödel's Proof* (1958); W. O. Quine, *Methods of Logic* (1950); J. B. Rosser, An Informal Exposition of Proofs of Gödel's Theorem and Church's Theorems, *J. symbol. Log.,* 1939, 4, 53–60; R. Schlegel, *Completeness in Science* (1967); R. L. Wilder, *The Foundations of Mathematics* (1965).

NOTE 5.2

Mention should be made of certain other metamathematical theorems that are relevant to the problems of reduction and explanation in psychology. Theorems of Church and Tarski followed on the publication of Gödel's famous proofs and add to our understanding of the essential incompleteness of formal systems. The Löwenheim-Skolem theorem antedates the work of Gödel, but it also foretells the incompleteness of certain well-formulated logical systems. The significance of all these theorems seems to be that there are logical reasons for rejecting the ideal of perfectible formal systems of description and computation. That being the case, there are computational acts which transcend the given system and whose description is not fully carried out within the schemata of the primary system. With Gödel's theorem we see that for a presumptively consistent system L there is a demonstrably true proposition not decidable within L itself. Church extends this qualification and Tarski ties it in with meaning and semantic systems.

To point out the significance of Church's theorem it is necessary to distinguish between "unsolvability" and "undecidability." We have seen that a proposition, a possible theorem of a formal system, is undecidable if it is neither provable nor disprovable in the formal system. We may say of a formal system that its decision problem is unsolvable if there exists no effective procedure for determining which members of a set of potential theorems of that system are decidable in the system and which are not. As we have seen, Gödel's theorem establishes that there is at least one demonstrably true statement of L which is undecidable in L itself.

Church's theorem (Church, 1936; Rosser, 1936), on the other hand, takes up the matter of general solvability. It establishes that there is no algorithm, no possible decision procedure, which will enable us to determine, by means of that procedure alone, the class of provable theorems within the set of all putative theorems.

Tarski's theorem (1939, 1956) concerns the semantic aspects of undecidability. Thus far we have been alluding to the properties decidability and general solvability within the formal system as such. Suppose now we visualize a semantic system structured on formal systems which again we assume to be consistent. Then according to our semantical conventions, we should be able clearly to define which sentences in the semantical system S are true. This we can do, but not in S. As an important adjunct of the Gödel result, Tarski was able to prove his "truth theorem," namely, that the notion of the semantic definability of truth is not itself definable in the semantic system S. Thus Fraenkel and Bar-Hillel write, "Whereas Gödel's theorem shows that the *deductive power* of any given sufficiently rich system is intrinsically limited, Tarski's theorem discloses the limitations in the *expressive power* of such systems" (1958, p. 307).

The Löwenheim-Skolem theorem (proved initially by Löwenheim, 1915, and later by Skolem, 1920) antedates the work of Gödel but is also thought to have relevance for the program of reduction (Scriven, 1960). This theorem states that any well-formed formula in the first order functional calculus which is satisfiable in an infinite domain, is satisfiable in the infinite denumerable domain of all integers; i.e., it has a countably infinite model (Fraenkel and Bar-Hillel, 1958). By "satisfiable" we mean that there are entities in the domain which render the formula true. By "the first order functional calculus" we mean the calculus utilizing the conventional logical operations including negation, conjunction, disjunction, implication, and existential and universal quantification; and by "a denumerable model" we mean that all constructible entities in the formal system can be represented, interpreted, or satisfied by a set of entities which at most are denumerably infinite.

Since, for us, the implications of this theorem are not readily apparent, let us pursue the argument along the nontechnical lines suggested by Myhill (1953). Let us visualize a formal computational act such that it is expressible in the formal language of the first order functional calculus. (We may also visualize a realization of that calculus in the language of neurophysiology; e.g., McCulloch and Pitts, 1943.) Now the fact that the formal calculus, by virtue of the Löwenheim-Skolem theorem, has a denumerable model means that its analysis of the continuum is interpretable in terms that are denumerably infinite. But according to Cantor's analysis of the continuum, a theorem of the system stipulates that the points of the continuum are nondenumerably infinite. Hence the denumerable model of our formal calculus is inadequate to enumerate all points in the infinite continuum i.e., unable to generate all points in the continuum of real numbers. As Scriven (1960) states the argument, we cannot be sure that a machine which is the realization of a calculus with a denumerable model is capable of grasping the role that the irrational numbers play in the infinite continuum. Or to phrase the predicament in another way, we are not sure how the computer with a denumerably infinite model is to generate the infinite continuum, short of the introjection of some kind of nonformal mathematical intuition.

More formally, the argument can be expressed with respect to axiomatic set theory (Kleene, 1953). If the axioms of set theory are satisfiable then, according to the Löwenheim-Skolem theorem, they are satisfiable in a denumerable infinite domain. Thus an interpretation of the theory implies that there are only a denumerably infinite number of sets. Paradoxically (Skolem's paradox) a theorem of the theory (Cantor) asserts that there is a transfinite nondenumerable number of sets of sets. Thus, comparing this paradox to Gödel's incompleteness theorem, Kleene writes:

> Thus it may be possible for the subsets of a given infinite set definable within the theory to be enumerable from without the theory, and yet be nonenumerable within the theory, because no enumerating set of corresponding pairs is among the sets definable within the theory. The construction of the enumerating set of pairs is accomplished by taking into account the structure of the axiom system as a whole, and this construction is not possible within the theory, i.e. using only the operations provided by the axioms.
>
> The situation is similar to that in Gödel's incompleteness or undecidability theorem . . ., where, if we suppose the number-theoretic formal system to be consistent, we can recognize that $A, (p)$ is true by taking into view the structure of that system as a whole, though we cannot recognize the truth of $A, (p)$ by use only of the principles of inference formalized within that system. (1953, p. 426)

The implication of this paradox is akin to that of Gödel's theorem of incompleteness. We cannot do everything within the performatory bounds of the system that we can do outside it by taking that system into our extrasystemic considerations.

Note also should be taken of the problem of unsolvability as articulated in the language of Turing machines. Recall from our discussion of Chapter 3 that a problem is solvable by a Turing machine if we can show that from its initial scanning state it proceeds computationally to a stopping state. Moreover, the program of any Turing machine can be incorporated into a universal Turing machine such that the universal machine can compute what any Turing machine can compute. Suppose we now ask of this universal machine whether it can compute a given formula (number) n. The tactic of answering such a question is for the machine to compute continuously *until* it reaches a stopping state. Hence it can effectively enumerate the set of formula for which it can indeed demonstrate stopping states. But this tactic is obviously inconclusive. Since, for some problems, the machine may go on computing forever without reaching a stopping state, the machine is unable in finite time to answer which of the problems presented to it are noncomputable. Hence it is also unable to enumerate in finite time all problems which it finds computable (cf. Davis, 1958; Arbib, 1964; Minsky, 1967).

We may visualize the problem of the stopping state as "Turing's predicament." Let us put it in the following way. Upon dying, the mathematician Ephraim finds himself in Hell where he has been sentenced to the treadmill forever. Having previously lived an exemplary life as befits a logician, Ephraim thinks his sentence unjustified and thereby importunes the Devil for redress. Lucifer, being a capital fellow, sees the point and responds that he, Ephraim, may leave Hell for Heaven, but only if he can provide "proof" for an answer to a very simple question. Then Lucifer remarks, "Now, Ephraim, it is obvious, is it not, that you will either provide the requested proof or you will not. And obviously you will either go to Heaven or you will remain in Hell. The question for which you are to provide proof is: Will you tread the mill forever?" Thus, Ephraim can provide the proof so that he can go to Heaven, but only if he remains in Hell forever.

NOTE 5.3

Thus, it seems, the score is evenly divided. There are those who imply the human computer can compute what no conceivable computer can compute. And there are those who deny Gödel's theorems establish such a proposition. The issue is still an open one. How are we to decide? Suppose we are to feed the question posed in "The Argument from Gödel" to a Turing machine. Can the machine provide an answer? One answer at least would be forthcoming if we ask the computer to compute Gödel's proof. This it will do providing we give it explicit instruction on how to convert entities in the primary logic into their corresponding Gödel numbers, along with instructions on how to proceed step by step in the argument. Such a machine will be formalized on a formal system L' and prove a theorem of the incompleteness of L. But now we must ask of the machine a question the answer of which we know from the generality of Gödel's proof: namely, "Is there a formula demonstrably true, but which is unprovable by you?" For this machine, the question is undecidable, for either it reaches a stopping state or it computes forever. But in order to reach a stopping state we know by Gödel's proof it must go from a formal system L' into another supplemented formal system L''. Yet, mark this well, our machine has a machine table sufficient only for implementing the formal system L'. Hence it must go on computing forever. And we know it, but the machine can not!

We seem to have the advantage here. But note also that the ideal of reduction and explanation is realizable. If we can explain our own deductive enterprises, we can simulate those enterprises in mechanical terms.

Another troublesome aspect of the argument from Gödel is introduced by Polanyi in his book, *Personal Knowledge*. Aside from the alternation and interaction between intuition (an important subject for Polanyi) and computation, the human problem solver has an intentional relation with his computational apparatus. Whether he makes use of computers or makes use of his own nervous system is immaterial. He makes use of his computational acts in order to achieve problem defined goals. Thus there is a tripartite system of mind, machine, and purpose entertained by mind. The computer stands in relation to the person as the homing device stands in relation to its designer. It may look as if the machine is intelligent just as it may look as if our homing missile is purposive, but it is clear that purpose and intention belong only within the province of mind.

A person "makes use of" a machine. Thus, Polanyi believes that intelligence belongs only to the person. But, of course, we might counter that machines too can "make use of" other machines. A computer which is given a problem may seek its solution by submitting it to other machines, or to subprograms. Polanyi insists that intelligent intention, however, always rests outside the machine complex.

Perhaps so, but our task is to simulate personal behavior. There is no difficulty in our simulating a limited intentional act of the kind where a machine utilizes other machines for the purpose of seeking a solution. The significance of this argument will be explored further in Chapter 6.

Finally, it should be observed that logicians themselves are often reluctant to apply their metamathematical theorems to domains outside that of formal mathematics. The results of the Gödel, Church, and Tarski theorems, for example, deal with formal systems and the concepts of representation, computability, solvability and constructive proof within those systems. It is hazardous indeed to move from formal systems of inference to representations of the processes and limitations of human thinking. Consequently it is not surprising to find that logicians such as Gödel, Church, and Tarski have not themselves engaged in the public debates over man and machine.

A recent critical article by Webb (1968) is to the point. In particular Webb attacks the argument from Gödel as presented in Lucas' paper, "Man, Machines, and Gödel" (1961), but it is obvious that much of the critique is germane to our own discussion.

For Lucas the Gödel theorems imply that man is capable of displaying a unique self-consciousness not attributable to machines. He maintains that conjointly these theorems serve to (1) refute mechanism, (2) establish grounds for distinguishing between conscious and unconscious beings, and (3) provide a nonmechanistic base for morality. Only points (1) and (2) are germane to the problem of explanation. The focal issues are consistency and self-reference.

Gödel's first theorem, that on undecidability, rests upon the premise of consistency for the formal system. But according to Gödel's second theorem, that consistency of the formal system cannot be established within the system itself; i.e., assuming consistency for the system, that consistency cannot be established as a theorem of the system. Since the assumption of consistency is necessary to the proofs of the theorems, Lucas argues that that assumption betokens self-consciousness of the human computer on the grounds of its self-reference. And more important, the substance of the first theorem itself implies self-consciousness on the part of the human computer as to the limitations of the formal system to which it has recourse. That is, it effects self-consciousness in becoming aware of the unprovability of a theorem that it knows to be true.

Thus a significant property about conscious minds (as Webb interprets Lucas) "is their ability to answer questions about themselves without becoming other than themselves . . ." (Webb, 1968, p. 163).

To the first argument, that of self-consciousness implicit in the assumption of consistency, Webb retorts that attribution of a property of mind by the tactic of making an assumption is merely question begging. The assumption of consistency is a peremptory one, neither to be proved in the formal system, nor intuited. A Gödel machine (one capable of turning out Gödel proofs) may not be able to offer reasons for adopting the assumption of consistency, but then neither can the human computer, other than its realization that the alternative of inconsistency would be cataclysmic. The assumption of consistency is as much a part of the Gödel machine as it is the human computer, in the sense that for neither theorem of Gödel is the apodosis meaningful without the conditional assumption.

I think we must agree with Webb (1968), the Lucas argument appears to be circular. The necessity of assuming consistency and the self-reflexive character of the assumption do not themselves entail our belief in any unique self-consciousness as beng indispensable to the human computer. The appropriate machine and the human computer can make the same inference. Furthermore if we suggest that the human computer recognizes the necessity for the assumption of consistency, whereas the machine does not, then we are proposing a different computational situation than that of churning out Gödel theorems.

However, it is to the issue of self-reference *per se* that Webb directs his technical critique. He argues that the Gödel sentence which asserts its own unprovability need not be interpreted as reflexive at all, but only that its own Gödel number lies in the set of Gödel numbers "refutable" in the formal system. Thus we are speaking of properties assignable to numbers definable in the Gödel systemization. It is one thing to make this clear in the metalogical system, quite another to say this formalized self-reference betokens self-consciousness in the human computer. Moreover, we may visualize the technical metatheory as providing means for generating members of a nonrecursive set of undecidable sentences, such sentences being subject to incorporation as axioms in a formal system.

But what if we grant the self-referring property of Gödel sentences [e.g., $W_q(q)$]? Nothing here attests to a Gödel machine's inability to answer questions about its own states or processes. The machine "can answer truthfully infinitely many questions about itself and needs no new parts to do it" (Webb, 1968, p. 168). Here we return to the problem of explaining *any* act of computation as against explaining *all* conceivable acts. As Lucas states the problem:

> We can see how we might almost have expected Gödel's theorem to distinguish self-conscious beings from inanimate objects. The essence of the Gödelian formula is that it is self-referring. It says that "This formula is unprovable-in-this-system." When carried over to a machine, the formula is specified in terms which depend on the particular machine in question. The machine is being asked a question about its own processes. We are asking it to be self-conscious, and say what things it can and cannot do. Such questions notoriously lead to paradox. At one's first and simplest attempts to phi-

losophize, one becomes entangled in questions of whether when one knows something one knows that one knows it, and what, when one is thinking of oneself, is being thought about, and what is doing the thinking. . . .

The paradoxes of consciousness arise because a conscious being can be aware of itself, as well as of other things, and yet cannot really be construed as being divisible into parts. It means that a conscious being can deal with Gödelian questions in a way in which a machine cannot, because a conscious being can both consider itself and its performance. A machine can be made in a manner of speaking to "consider" its own performance, but it cannot take this "into account" without thereby becoming a different machine, namely the old machine with a "new part" added. But it is inherent in our idea of a conscious mind that it can reflect upon itself and criticize its own performances, and no extra part is required to do this: it is already complete, and has no Achilles' heel. (Lucas, 1961, pp. 124-125)

We have persistently maintained throughout our discussion that a distinction is to be made between simulating *any* and *all* acts of computation. Furthermore if any given act of computation is simulatable, then all such acts are simulatable by our incorporating them into the making of a universal Turing machine. If there is any relevance to the Lucas argument it is that there is no extant universal Turing machine standing in juxtaposition to the potential-laden human computer. Perhaps so, but then the matter of potential computation is not formulatable as a question of scientific explanation. Webb, on the other hand, considers specifically the augmented formal system incorporating the "new parts" deemed (by Lucas) as essential to higher order self-interrogations. Such new parts may constitute an extension of the formal system, but in kind they are the same elements, formulae, and symbols.

In what sense is the new augmented system, and the machine of which it is the representation, a "new" or "different" system? It is the difference of computational schema, not of kind. That is to say, the content of an explanation, as a computational schema, may be altered, or extended, but in no way does the tactic of extension represent a departure from the logical rubrics established for computation. The universal Turing machine, like any Turing machine, computes within the established rubric. As in the other statements of the argument from Gödel, Lucas has alluded to a predicament and to the apparent versatility of the human computer, but the matter of the limits of mechanical explanation is left at issue.

An equally cogent, but somewhat less technical, critique of Lucas (1961) can be found in a recent paper by Benacerraf (1967). Happily it is one of the most readable essays in a difficult literature.

After a concise and clear exposition of Gödel's theorems Benacerraf takes note of the following quotation from Lucas:

Now any mechanical model of the mind must include a mechanism which can enunciate truths of arithmetic, because this is something which minds can do: in fact, it is easy to produce mechanical models which will in many respects produce truths of arithmetic far better than human beings can. But in this one respect they cannot do so well: in that for every machine there is a truth which it cannot produce as being true, but which a mind can. This shows that a machine cannot be a complete and adequate model of the mind. It cannot do *everything* that a mind can do, since however much it can do, there is always something which it cannot do, and a mind can. This is not to say that we cannot build a machine to simulate *any* desired piece of mind-like behaviour: it is only that we cannot build a machine to simulate *every* piece of mind-like behaviour. We can (or shall be able to one day) build machines capable of reproducing bits of mind-like behaviour, and indeed of outdoing the performances of human minds: but however good the machine is, and however much better it can do in nearly all respects than a human mind can, it always has this one weakness, this one thing which it cannot do, whereas a mind can. The Gödelian formula is the Achilles' heel of the cybernetical machine. And therefore we cannot hope ever to produce a machine that will be able to do all that a mind can do: we can never, not even in principle, have a mechanical model of the mind. (1961, pp. 115–116)

Observe that Lucas herein refers to the distinction between any and all computational behaviors. However it is not this which initially draws Benacerraf's attention. Rather he questions whether "the prowess *claimed* for mind is one that Gödel I precludes for machines."

. . . what is it that Gödel I precludes the machine (let's call her "Maud") from doing? Evidently it is to prove H (her Gödel formula) from *her* axioms according to *her* rules. But can Lucas do *that?* Just as evidently not. But what *can* Lucas do which Maud cannot? One thing he might be able to do is give an *in*formal proof of H: informal in the sense that it cannot be formalized in Maud's system. But is it clear that Maud cannot do this too? (Benacerraf, 1967, pp. 19–20)

Benacerraf then suggests that "proof" of the Gödel formula H follows from proving that the consistency of Maud implies H. To be sure, Lucas and Maud may utilize different tactics in proving H, but still the argument that Lucas can do something Maud cannot do would be an untenable one. However, the argument can be placed on more formal grounds. The formula H can be appropriated as an axiom of the augmented system $Maud_1$: as a consequence, ". . . H is a theorem of $Maud_1$' is provable by Maud." "So, thus interpreted, what Lucas can 'prove' does not differentiate him fom Maud." (1967, p. 21)

But now consider the argument of oneupmanship, namely, that Lucas can find a flaw, that of incompleteness, in any machine the mechanist might conjure. Does this preclude our comparing the competencies of Lucas and machine? Obviously not, for what is at stake is not one of comparing Lucas against the extant machine but one of whether there is a conceivable machine that can do what Lucas does in faulting the extant machine.

In the last section of his paper, Benacerraf formulates certain aspects of Lucas' argument in rigorous terms. In brief that argument is as follows:

Let us first stipulate my entire deductive output, that is, everything I can prove either as basic statements or as theorems derived therefrom (first order logic with identity). Call this S^*. Then I know S^* is consistent, for I cannot prove what is false. This consistency of S^* therefore is among the provable theorems in S^* (Lucas' assumption of consistency). Now if there is some recursively enumerable set W_x (i.e., some set within S^*), then that W_x is consistent and that consistency is assertable within S^*. We are now ready to stipulate the conditions for the Gödelian predicament. Suppose that there is some recursively enumerable set W_j (i.e., a Turing machine) such that:

(a) the statement "some set Q is among W_j" is within S^*. (i.e., the quoted statement is among the theorems I can prove);

(b) the statement "W_j is within S^*" is itself within S^*. (i e., the statement that the recursively enumerable set W_j is among the theorems provable by me is itself provable by me—the formal counterpart of "knowing that I know");

(c) anything provable by me, S^*, is within the recursively enumerable set W_j.

Now (a), (b), and (c) simply state the computational relations between the Turing machine W_j and myself. And (c) in particular states that I am a Turing machine. By introducng Gödel sentences and the substance of Gödel's two theorems, Benacerraf is now able to prove the inconsistency of my deductive output S^*. Hence assuming the consistency of S^*, it would appear that there is no Turing machine satisfying (a), (b), and (c). Indeed, if we were to hold that this argument implies the negation of (c) we could consider this the support of Lucas' argument, namely, I am not a Turing machine. But Benacerraf maintains that the argument implies no such thing.

> At best Gödel's theorems imply the negation of the conjunction of [a, b, and c]. They imply that given any Turing machine W_j, either I cannot prove that W_j is adequate for arithmetic, or if I am a subset of W_j, then I cannot prove that I can prove everything W_j can. *It seems to be consistent with all this that I am indeed a Turing machine, but one with such a complex machine table (program) that I cannot ascertain what it is. In a relevant sense, if I am a Turing machine, then perhaps I cannot ascertain which one.* (Benacerraf, 1967, p. 29)

He then goes on to comment:

> As things now stand, if there is a Turing machine that can prove everything my first order closure can, *then I cannot show of (any instantiation of) that machine both that it is adequate for arithmetic and that I can prove everything it can.* This result, though considerably weaker than what Lucas claimed, seems still significant. One person to whom I explained it concluded that psychology as we know it is therefore impossible. For, if we are not at best Turing machines, then it is impossible, and if we are, then there are certain things we cannot know about ourselves or any others with the same output as ourselves. I won't take sides. (1967, p. 30)

Well, if Benacerraf won't take sides perhaps neither should I. However, the note of skepticism concerning knowledge as to what kind of Turing machine am I should not come as a surprise to me. For any machine I build will be subject to the limitations of undecidability. Hence every effort to build a machine (an explanation) of what I am remains incomplete in that I can, by the appropriate Gödel proposition, show that it is incomplete. Hence I may indeed be a Turing machine, but never the one for which I formulate the program. So, granting the skepticism, the wry afterthought remains: I may in principle be explainable as a Turing machine but not by me.

> If I am Turing machine, then I am barred by my very nature from obeying Socrates' profound philosophic injunction: KNOW THYSELF. (Benacerraf, 1967, p. 30)

For his rejoinder to Benacerraf see Lucas (1968). Lucas continues to maintain that *any* machine realization of what I conceive myself to be remains essentially incomplete, in that I can do something it cannot (i.e., demonstrate the truth of the appropriate Gödel sentence). We may agree. However, I have argued that we may accept Lucas' thesis and still not be compelled to give up explaining the behavior of man, *any* behavior, in machine terms.

CHAPTER 6

The Argument from Intention

IN THE preceding chapters we have reviewed several objections to reductionism and mechanical explanation by focusing upon the issue of computability and the comparison of mechanical and human computers. We now turn to those motivational problems which, because of the unique intentional character of organismic behavior, would seem to preclude mechanical and hence reductive explanation. In substance, the argument is as follows:

Assume that there is a generic behavior language, the *B* language, sufficient to describe both the intentional and the nonintentional (objective) aspects of behavior. Assume also the physicalistic objective thing language, the *P* language. Then, according to the argument from intention, there is a subset of predicate expressions in the *B* language, not translatable in the *P* language; namely, those statements descriptive of behavioral intentions. This being the case, between the two languages a theory of behavior formalized in the *P* language will be essentially incomplete as concerns interpreting all expressions and statements meaningful in the *B* language. Thus it would appear that there are some behaviors expressible in the generic behavioral language not interpretable, hence not explainable, in the *P* language to which the methodological behaviorist is committed.

This is a somewhat formal statement of the proposition that descriptions of the intentional control and implementation of behavior are logically incompatible with descriptions expressible in the physical thing language. Predicates relating to "desire," "purpose," "reasons for," and so on, are refractory to physical description when put in the context of intentions implemented and carried out by an active agent.

In order to appreciate the argument one must entertain a certain empathy for the mentalistic connotation of an intention (cf. Note 6.1). An intention is a something, a state of mind, let us say, of which we are retrospectively more or less aware as participative agents, and which is

151

essential to the description of goal-defined acts. Although we may attempt dispositional translations of intentional terms, such as desire and expectancy, in the physical language, these translations, it is claimed, do not capture the significance or the implications of purely intentional terms in the generic language.

MEANING OF INTENTION

According to the classical doctrine of intentionality (Brentano, Husserl) a distinction is to be made between events described in intentional terms and events described in nonintentional terms. A nonintentional term simply refers to an observable event in the domain of publicly experiencable events. Thus, such terms belong to the physical language. Intentional terms, on the other hand, always entail a meaning or significance of the object to a given observer. Rather than having a simple ostensive semantic tie to an event in the world, intentional terms entail a transitive relation of aboutness. They are, in a sense, once removed; their meanings are not rendered explicit by simple object denotations. Therefore, for the experiencing subject intentional terms are connotative rather than simply denotative (cf. Note 6.2).

There is, as we shall see, a connection between classical and more recent explanatory conceptions of intention. However, these latter treatments have emerged out of philosophical analysis (Wittgenstein, 1953; Anscombe, 1957; Melden, 1961; C. Taylor, 1964; R. Taylor, 1966) and rather than focusing upon pure phenomenology, they analyze intention in terms of the ordinary language of motivation. Rather than the phenomenology of subject-object relations, they concentrate on purposive act, goal-striving, anticipation, means to ends. By intention, in this restricted sense, we mean that motivated acts have meaning for the organism (person or agent) in terms of goals or ends to be realized. And it is intention which serves to define the act as a meaningful unit of behavior.

A standard example for defining an intentional act is to be found in the distinction between "the rising of the arm" and "raising the arm" to signal a turn or to hail a friend (Melden, 1961; R. Taylor, 1966; Wittgenstein, 1953). The rising of the arm requires only a mechanical description in the physical language; it is purely objective. "The person's raising his arm to signal a turn," on the other hand, describes a meaningful act entailing an agent. The meaning of the act to the agent is expressed in terms of intentions, and in terms of the communication of those intentions. Thus we must distinguish between mere behavioral movements and behavioral acts or actions which are manifestations of intentions. An intentional description always involves describing actions in purposive contexts; it is the intention that serves to define the context and dimensions of the act.

Note that intention becomes the defining property of the act. Realizing this, we should avoid attributing to it any of the causal properties that generate the obfuscations of the mind-body problem (cf. Note 6.3). An intention is not one event and the subsequent action another, but rather it is the property that all acts have with respect to the agent. It is that which sets those acts apart from mere behavioral movements.

The substance of argument from intention, we shall see, rests in the assertion that logical or methodological behaviorism is constrained in its descriptions to consider movements only, never acts. Thus, if we can find a class of explanations dealing explicitly with acts and their intentional aspects, and which exploit specifically those intentional properties, then scientific explanation, as visualized by methodological behaviorism, is essentially incomplete. Tenability of this argument rests on the premise that we cannot provide strictly behavioral criteria for intentional acts.

But just how defensible is this premise? How refractory are intentional acts to behavioral description? Before turning to the details of the critique, we need first to review how certain methodological behaviorists have in fact analyzed purposive acts.

PURPOSIVE BEHAVIORISM

It is obvious at the outset that a critique of modern psychology cannot be based on a contention that behaviorists have failed to consider purposive activity of organisms. Almost from the outset, behavioristic psychology has focused upon the adaptive behaviors of organisms. Stimulus-response, trial and error, habit, even the lowly reflex, have all been utilized as conceptual tools for analyzing adaptive acts. Tropisms, instinct, conditioned reflex, among other concepts of behavioristics, have been utilized in the analysis of purposive activity of organisms. But whereas behaviorists have been inclined to descriptions of purposeful, adaptive activity of organisms, they have at the same time been uniformly opposed to incorporating mentalistic agents, entelechy, and other nonphysical constructs into the description and explanation of that purposeful activity. Thus, from the instinct theories of McDougall, through the formal theories of behaviorism, down to the neo-instinctive doctrines of contemporary ethologists, organismic activity has been treated as adaptive, but without recourse to extraphysical properties and laws unique to teleological explanation.

Behavioral description becomes complicated, however, when the object of study is the human organism with its capacity for self-reflection. Here the language of intention becomes germane to the description of behavior in its generic sense. There is no need for the methodological behaviorist to deny this. Since the language of purpose has traditionally been mentalistic or psychophysical, it has been necessary to give terms in the language of intention, dispositional translations in nonmentalistic behavioral language. To lend credence to a program of methodological behaviorism that eschews neither purposive acts nor intention, we need recall but a few of the efforts of behavioral scientists to find dispositional interpretations of purposive activity.

Functionalism (Dewey, Angell, Carr) antedated classical behaviorism by a few years. Unlike behaviorism, it did not make a fetish of avoiding mental constructs. But even for functionalism, such contructs were invariably interpreted in purposive behavioral contexts. Hence the interest in learning and habit. The meaningful unit of psychological description is the adaptive act; therefore, mental processes, habit, discrimination, all assume significance in the context of the act. Thus function became the key term, with its emphasis both on the process and the utility of activity. Thinking, discrimination, habit are inseparable from the basic conception of adaptive behavior. Behavior is purposive, that is its distinguishing feature. However, one can develop, indeed must develop, teleological explanations without introducing teleological principles foreign to the spirit of scientific explanation. A careful functional description of a behavioral event constitutes its explanation (Heidbreder, 1933, p. 229). Yet we must concentrate on describing the goal-oriented activity of organisms in behavioral terms, *sans* any recourse to special explanatory rubrics which would remove psychology from the purview of observational science. The concept of purpose is implicit in the adaptive act. And we must look to the behavior of the organism rather than to mediating mental states.

However, it is in behaviorism itself that we find some of the most explicit accounts of purposive behavior. For example, Karl Muenzinger (1942), an early purposive behaviorist caught up in the transition from functionalism to behaviorism, begins his systematic analysis of behavior by defining the basic unit of behavior as the purposeful act. Designate this the *S–E* unit. This unit of behavioral description is distinguished by a starting phase and an end phase, the time spread being delineated by the onset of a motivational state and by the reaching of a terminal stage of goal realization. In this conceptual frame, meticulous descriptions of performance are not essential, providing the response, whatever it is, is sufficient for goal achievement. Every *S–E* unit involves motivation, discrimination, performance, and affectivity. These concepts, as it were, establish the coordinates of behavioral description—a behavioral description, it is to be emphasized, which focuses upon molar events conceived as meaningful, adaptive acts. Note especially the concept of discrimination. What had traditionally been treated as the relatively autonomous domain of sensation and perception, now receives cognitive interpretation in terms of the goal-oriented activity of the subject. Rather than the simple input-output schema of traditional psychophysics, we conceive discrimination in terms of the relation of stimulus objects and situations to goal achievement. Again we have a systematic treatment of behavior and behavioral analysis *sans* recourse to agentry or to extraphysical teleological principles.

Doubtless the most distinguished treatment of purposive behaviorism is to be found in the systematic works of Edward Tolman. Here, concepts of sign-significance and expectancy replace the then prevailing mechanical paradigms of stimulus and response. Stimuli are signs to the organism. Hence they cannot be concretized, they cannot be isolated from their role in cognitive functions. They are meaningless apart from means-end behavioral processes. Rather than the S–R paradigm, we adopt the schema of S_1–R–S_2 (MacCorquodale and Meehl, 1953) in which a response R is made in the context of S_1 in order to realize the expectancy associated with S_2. Such a schema is clearly cognitive in its implications, for the association of S_1 and S_2 in the cognitive context of behavior is sufficient to produce R. Since the association S_1 and S_2 is cognitive, and since the occurrence of realization of S_2 is contingent upon R, one can liberally interpret R as a response defined by the intention to produce S_2. To be sure, the mentalistic overtones are excluded from Tolman's treatment of expectancy. In fact, an expectancy is conceptually nothing more than a set of physical events S_1–R–S_2 in which the pattern of expectancy is interpreted conventionally as a disposition. Under S_1 a response R produces a stimulus (environmental) situation S_2. The occurrence of R in the context of S_1 is an indicator of an expectancy of S_2. Expectancy thus receives a rigorous interpretation as an intervening variable explicitly defined in terms of situational and response characteristics.

Tolman's conceptual paradigm is clearly intentional and cognitive. An effective stimulus is always one that is the occasion for some expectancy contingent on the appropriate response. And response is always the means of the realization of some expectancy. The relation of expectancy to goal achievement, to intention, to purposeful acts is thereby obvious.

For Tolman, sign-significance and expectancy are inferred mediators. Or rather, they are constructs, for they are devoid of surmise as to how cognition and cognitive significance are to be materialized in the nervous system. Simple, straightforward, dispositional definitions will suffice. More recently, Miller, Galanter, and Pribram (1960) provide a cybernetic model for a sign-expectancy system (See Chapter 3). The feedback schema is adopted as a model of functional cognitive processes.

Recall that the test-operate-test-exit unit functions to reduce cognitive disparity between a goal state and the prevailing stimulus state. In a sense the functional unit of cognition is internalized, but it is also objectified. The comparison of an image and an input determines what response is to be emitted in order to reduce the cognitive incongruity implicit in the comparison. Not only are larger molar plans implemented by the TOTE units, but so are the molecular sequences of response which are instrumental to ultimate goal achievement.

Again we have an analysis of purposeful activity that is amenable to the language and expression of goal orientation and intention. And, remote as it is from classical behaviorism, we may emphasize that this functional analysis of behavior is consonant with classical explanatory paradigms. That is to say, the functional unit is a feedback system, which is interpretable in rubrics permitting deductivist explanations. Nothing in the conceptual system—no construct, no hypothetical entity—precludes visualizing the TOTE unit as being the interpretation of either a mechanical or formal deductive system. Indeed, it is conceived that our central nervous system is just the kind of physical system which realizes the TOTE schema of function.

Finally, mention should be made of the work of the comparative ethologists (Thorpe, 1963) who have sought to explain complex adaptive acts in terms of sequences of specific action patterns. Such adaptive behaviors are regarded as mechanical and instinctive. Of course, no intention *per se,* is involved, nor is it appropriate to suggest that goals are foreseen or anticipated, or that the organism stands at the vortex of executive decision. Still, these behaviors are adaptive. And the theory of instinctive behavior reflects the cyberneticist's prospectus, namely, that of describing behavioral function in terms of explicit mechanical systems. Schematically, the conceptual system is quite simple. Complex adaptive behaviors are to be regarded as fixed action patterns (Lorenz), incorporating rather elaborate sequential behaviors and culminating in a consummatory act. To implement these action patterns, we visualize two systems, one concerning innate reactivity, the other, stimulus release. Thus specific response is associated with specific *action potentials,* which involve both energizing and release of response patterns. The motivational level of such potentials is a function of the state of the organism. The release, or triggering off of specific response, is associated with the *innate releasing mechanism,* which in effect serves as an innate selector of stimuli. That is, specific situational stimuli then become the releasers for the specific actions. Adaptive behavior is then regarded as sequential, where, in the set of specific acts constituting the adaptive act, each specific act, as released by an appropriate stimulus, brings the organism to and prepares him for the next step in specific activation and the searching out of releasers.

An analysis along similar lines, but more adaptable to learning modifications, can be found in the work of J. A. Deutsch (1960). Details of this need not concern us here. It is significant merely that purposive behaviors can be accounted for in terms that preclude any special teleological properties or agents.

DISPOSITIONAL CONCEPTS

In the preceding discussion it was proposed that either adaptive behavior could be given an explicit mechanical description (as in the case of Tinbergen, 1951, and Deutsch, 1960) or intentional constructs could be interpreted as intervening variables or hypothetical constructs subject to dispositional translations. Although the empirical characteristics of intervening variables have been well surveyed (e.g., MacCorquodale and Meehl, 1948) and their logical characteristics fairly well detailed (e.g., Carnap, 1936; Hempel, 1958), interpretation of the dispositional term in general remains somewhat troublesome.

By a dispositional term we mean to signify a theoretical construct which has specifiable implications in the behavioral language. Let us assume a cognitive construct C. The meaning of the term is dispositional. That is to say, the construct C means that we can expect behavior R under input conditions S. But how may we express this general formula? Not as an explicit definition,

$$Cx =_{df} Sx \supset Rx$$

for the implication $S \supset R$ is itself equivalent to $\sim(S \cdot \sim R)$. Thus by definition we would attribute the disposition (construct) C to x if in fact there were no situational test [i.e., if $(\sim S \cdot \sim R)$]. To overcome this objection to giving a dispositional term an explicit definition, Carnap (1936) utilized bilateral reduction sentences to produce

$$Sx \supset (Cx \equiv Rx)$$

that is, if x is subjected to the situational test, then the disposition C if and only if R. This overcomes the objection of an empty situational test, but note now that the matter of assigning a disposition to the subject emitting a specified response in the presence of S is purely a conventional one. Thus, if an intention were to be rendered the status of C, it is reduced to the status of arbitrary response equivalence. And it is difficult to see how we would assign any explanatory significance, or, indeed, any executive significance to the idea of an intention. The fact is that intentions are essential to the description of the class of behaviors we call acts, and if actions are meaningfully distinguishable from motions, we must have some evidence or some other support for predicating intentions in those situations appropriately calling for dispositional interpretations.

Were it not for our mentalistic traditions in describing volitional acts, it is doubtful that the idea of intention would ever occur in the context of motivation. That is to say, predication of intention is contingent upon experiencing intention, however dubitable or semantically imprecise that intention might be. At any rate, we require supporting evidence, additional indicators, either intrinsic or extrinsic, as to where and in what context intention is to assume the dimensions of a significant construct.

Let us try conjoining the "evidence" (psychic or otherwise) for intention with the situational context, S. Thus Carnap's rendition of a dispositional term might more appropriately be specified

$$SxIx \supset (Cs \equiv Rx)$$

Thus in only those situational contexts that we find evidence of intention do we assign the construct intention on a response contingency. But then, evidence of what? Our dispositional translation of intention subsumes an existential status for that which we are defining in conventional terms. S–R translations of dispositional terms such as desires and intentions are clearly problematic. Our evidence for their formulation, the occasions for stipulating the particular dispositional terms, are other than the S,R observational states themselves. Etiologically, the evidence is the intention, the internal nonobjective state of the organism, a mental state if you will; and it is only through knowledge of that state, a living through it, so to speak, that we can set about defining the dispositional predicates which are appropriate to the situation.

But need this tactic be necessarily disavowed? To take a subjectivist stance, does some initial reliance upon introspection preclude this utilization of dispositional terms in the description and explanation of behavior? To deny to the objectivist the resources of any experience, both as spectator and as participant, is, as Brodbeck (1963) has suggested, to commit the genetic fallacy. In order to objectify his language, the scientist need not disavow any experience. We shall return to this point. But first we must examine the intentionalistic argument (cf. Note 6.4).

PURPOSE AND INTENTION

The argument from intention hinges upon, one, the need to stipulate the intentional property of actions as against objective motions, and two, the unique semantical reference of intentional terms (as against those in the object language).

On the first count we find Charles Taylor (*The Explanation of Behavior*, 1964) arguing that acts involving intention share a functional paradigm not to be found in ordinary behavioral description. The ordinary behavioral paradigm is that of S–R. That is, we write

$$R \equiv f(S)$$

and introducing dispositional terms for motivation or intention, we then write

$$R \equiv f(S,I)$$

That is to say, the purposive response R is a function both of the situational input S, and the mediating variable I, which carries a dispositional translation. Note here that I, being dispositional, is an indicator of what class of responses to expect contingent on given situational input.

According to Taylor, the teleological paradigm has a different structure. Rather, we write

$$R \equiv f(S,G)$$

where G, the goal state, is the object of intention; and where G is the sufficient condition for the occurrence of the goal-achieving response. But it is a mistake, Taylor argues, to fit this paradigm into the atomistic rubric of antecedent-consequent. To do so would mean explaining a response from the goal-result which follows, and this, according to the atomists (e.g., Hull, 1943) would preclude a causal explanation of response. Rather, what is involved in the teleological paradigm is the intentional definition of the goal which is both antecedent to and sufficient for the response.

This substantially is the argument of all phenomenologists who argue against the principle of mechanical and reductive explanations of behavior. The intentional description of the goal and indeed of the environment is missing from the $S\text{–}R$ paradigm. The rebuttal by the atomist or mechanist must be to show either that the two paradigms are equivalent descriptions, or that indeed an account of the teleological paradigm can be given purely in terms of the intrinsic mechanisms that operate to mediate the molar patterns of the adaptive act.

Observe now that our dispositional paradigm

$$SxIx \supset (Cx \equiv Rx)$$

adopts the convention of equating the response R to the dispositional (intentional) term, C. Thus the intention in the objectivistic behavioral system is conventionally reduced to response, and the factor I in Ix, the mental indicator of intention, is suppressed. We insert it only to indicate where dispositional terms are to be utilized in behavioral analysis. However, if we omit the conventional introduction of the dispositional term C, our paradigm becomes simply

$$SxIx \supset Rx$$

Here the phenomenological intention, in conjunction with the antecedent situational factors, becomes sufficient for the occurrence of the response. It, in effect, puts a teleological qualifier upon $S\text{–}R$ laws. Thus we find C. Taylor writing as follows:

> Thus, if a given piece of behavior is rightly classified as an action, then we cannot account for it by some causal antecedent, where the law linking antecedent (E) to behavior (B) is not itself conditional on some law or rule governing the intention or purpose. For if the law linking E to B were not dependent on some law linking E and the intention or purpose, I, to do B, then $E\text{–}B$ would hold whether or not $E\text{–}I$ held. But then B would occur on E whether the corresponding intention was present or not. And then, even when it is present, it cannot be said to bring about the behavior, so long as this is done by E. Thus to account for B in terms of E would be to offer a rival account, to disqualify B as an action. (1964, p. 34)

We need only substitute S for E and R for B to render his account in our $S\text{–}R$ terms.

Taylor goes on to argue that behavior which is classified as action and which utilizes the intentionalistic paradigm can be described only in terms which prove incompatible with methodological behaviorism. But need this be the case? To imply that an intentional description $SxIx$ is sufficient for the occurrence of a goal-directed response does not at all rule out the possibility of dispositional terms such as

$$\left. \begin{array}{c} S_1 x \supset (Cx \equiv R_1 x) \\ \cdot \qquad \cdot \\ \cdot \qquad \cdot \\ S_i x \supset (Cx \equiv R_i x) \\ \cdot \qquad \cdot \\ \cdot \qquad \cdot \\ \cdot \qquad \cdot \end{array} \right\} Ix$$

where the set of pairs S_i, R_i covers the situation-response settings for applying the dispositional term, and where Ix is simply the phenomenological source for binding the set of S_i, R_i pairs into a family setting calling for the common dispositional term or concept, C. The methodological behaviorist need not, perhaps cannot, deny the factor of phenomenological intention. But this means only that there has been some heuristic source, some private support, for his deriving and adopting the dispositional terms he finds sufficient for the task of explanation. By and large, this differs very little from how a methodological behaviorist would proceed in developing dispositional translations of the construct intelligence (Turner, 1967, p. 319), or of habit, or of any mediating variable that stands as legacy from our nineteenth-century beginnings.

Our two paradigms are, therefore, essentially equivalent expressions. In the intentionalistic paradigm, phenomenological intention is the *sine qua non* of behavioral explanation and teleological laws. In the dispositional paradigm, phenomenological intention, *per se,* is suppressed. In its place we find a dispositional concept formally equivalent to a set of complex responses but generalized over the set by virtue of insights as to the surplus meaning latent within the hypothetical constructs.

Certainly the intentionalistic paradigm is an allowable one. It is the one which emerges clearly in ordinary discourse. But since modern analysts have all but deified ordinary language as a metaphysical probe, one gains the impression (from analysts and phenomenologists as well) that ordinary language, hence intentionalistic descriptions, serve genuinely to resurrect for thoughtful people a type of explanation forgotten or overlooked by behavioral scientists. Hence it is not uncommon to hear that our two paradigms for description and explanation are logically incompatible (Anscombe, 1957; Jessor, 1958; C. Taylor, 1964; R. Taylor, 1966; Peters, 1958; Winch, 1958). However, the charge of logical incompatibility would be defensible only if we could in fact show that our two paradigms are in some sense contradictory, or that there is at least one event subject to intentional description and explanation which proves inaccessible to an explanation utilizing either explicit extrinsic descriptions or dispositional translations of mediating variables.

When one claims logical incompatibility and yet fails to formulate the argument in crisp, logical rubrics which clearly define the meaning of incompatibility (namely, proof of contradiction or incompleteness), we may suspect that we are involved in an argument over pragmatics rather than logic. It is hard to see, therefore, that the argument of the intentionalists in this context is any more than a proposal that in certain contexts of language and inquiry one type of description is preferred to some other. The preference for intentional language is doubtless justified in writing biography, historical analysis, and case studies. But certainly there is nothing incompatible with mapping an intentionalistic description with a behavioral one, even of representing a cognitive process by a mechanical one.

The substance of the deductivist's objection to the intentionalist's argument is that emphasis on the special status of intention tends to preclude physical analysis of meaningful behavioral acts. The objection is twofold. One, the intentionalist tends not to appreciate the difference between an intention's being the object of study as such, and its being the source of ideas for behavioral analysis. Two, though admitting the differences between the inner intentional vantage and the outer nonintentional vantage, the intentionalist would hold the latter at fault for not incorporating the former. On this second matter, we shall comment in some detail. But of the first, we are offered no descriptions of events which are not in principle subject to dispositional mapping,[1] nor are we shown, when we treat the two modes of expression as equivalent descriptions of the same behavioral events, why the intentional description is the more defensible one for a program of scientific explanation (cf. Note 6.5).

TELEOLOGY AND MACHINES

Thus far we have treated intentional descriptions in terms of theoretical constructs which are then subject to dispositional translations in the behavioral language. Although explanatory rubrics deriving from these constructs become problematic when we are dealing with unique events, the explanation of unique events, it should be noted, is also problematic for the phenomenologist should he emphasize the rejection of behavioral laws and general principles.

---

[1] The strong argument for the complementary character of intentional and dispositional properties (see pp. 167–169) is not made by any of the intentionalists referenced in the text.

But consider now the possibility of objectivist explanations and the explicit reduction of intentional behavior and descriptions. We might hope to achieve this reduction by devising mechanical simulators of purposeful activity. Thus we may ask: Do we provide an explanation of purposeful behavior and teleology if we succeed in designing a machine or a mechanical explanation such that our device simulates all relevant aspects of the behavior in question and without recourse to principles not realizable in the mechanical system? Actual simulation is, of course, not the issue. We are concerned only with physical explanation, and even that schematically expressed. Thus, in this context, Deutsch's theory of sequential behavior (Deutsch, 1960) constitutes a mechanical (in the broad sense) realization of adaptive, instinctive behavior (Thorpe, 1963). Much, of course, is made of purposive machines utilizing negative feedback mechanisms. For all appearances they are ingeniously purposive vehicles. But are they really purposive? The phenomenologists would contend they are not (C. Taylor, 1964; R. Taylor, 1950, 1966). According to them, Craik's promise, for example, to interpret all behavior in terms of mechanical principles cannot be realized.

Let us pick up the argument with an example offered by Richard Taylor (*Action and Purpose,* 1966). Consider a homing torpedo designed to pick up a target in its scanning device and to steer itself by feedback systems so as always to keep the target in view. Presumably, the torpedo eventually accomplishes its mission, and, speaking metaphorically, realizes its intention. Mechanically this torpedo is a realization of a self-corrective purposive machine. It fulfills the behavioral criteria for teleological entities (Rosenblueth, Wiener, Bigelow, 1943; Rosenblueth and Wiener, 1950). But is it purposive in any significant sense of intention? As applied to this machine, is this language of purpose any more than metaphor?

It is not at all difficult to detect certain disparities between this machine and a purposive organism undertaking a similar mission—let us say, a Kamikaze pilot. A malfunction of the machine means that it may fail in its mission. On the other hand, it may function properly and still fail. Indeed, by circumstances external to itself, evasion by the target, interference by the target vessel, it may indeed hunt out and destroy the launching vessel. Still the machine carries out its preprogrammed "intention" flawlessly and efficiently. The Kamikaze pilot may, of course, also make a mistake, such as in a confusion of target identification. But he is at least capable of realizing that he is making a mistake, one that is not preconceived, whereas the machine is not. The machine simply functions according to its program and its mechanical guts; there is no need for intention, real or otherwise.

But let Taylor phrase the question and provide an answer:

. . . it might reasonably be asked, if this object *behaves* like a purposeful being, if its behavior is to observation indistinguishable from that of some being which is admittedly purposeful, what reason can exist for refusing to describe it in just that way? Clearly, if the *criteria* of purposeful behavior are to be empirical or behavioral, as physical science must require in case it is to have any place for the notion of purpose at all, then no such reason can possibly exist. The answer to this is, quite simply, that there do not and logically cannot exist any behavioral criteria for purposeful behavior . . . (1966, p. 228)

Taylor then goes on to say

There is, of course, nothing the least *mysterious* about this; it is only terribly complex, and appears mysterious and wonderful only to ignorance. An engineer of suitable training can describe and explain the mechanics of such a missile without needing any concepts whatever except those of physical science, and in particular, he can give a *complete* and adequate explanation without once introducing the idea of a purpose or goal. (1966. p. 229)

Doubtless this is true, and that is only to point up to us what others have said (e.g., Nagel, 1961): it is possible to describe the functioning of purposive entities without recourse to extraphysical teleological principles. But throughout his discussion of purposive behavior, Taylor insists upon a directive agent as being indispensable to the action. The torpedo in no sense "directs itself." The executive function of the agent, the intention, the goal realization are all properties assignable to the machine's designer, but not, Taylor emphasizes, to the machine itself.

Intention rests with the designer not with the machine. To be sure, we could as well substitute another torpedo tied to the target ship, say by frogmen, such that it would float into the ship on a change in tide. The only difference between the two, Taylor maintains, is the complexity of the mechanical systems. Obviously, to attribute intention to this machine is to reduce intention to a triviality.

At first glance, Taylor's argument appears to be convincing. The machine is indeed a machine. Under malfunction it does what mechanical principles dictate; the solecism of its behavior is a matter of relevance only to the designer, not to the machine itself. A broken down car that sputters to a stop is as much an exemplar of physical law as a new machine that roars out from the assembly line. There is nothing aberrant about its behavior. Thus, in similar fashion, the homing torpedo is irrevocably committed to the laws of nature, it has no purpose, no intention; it merely performs as a mechanical vehicle and in such a way that its behavior is explainable by mechanical principles. Such a machine can never have the capacity for regret concerning its overall functioning.

The designer, however, has other potentialities. If the guidance system of the vehicle goes awry, then indeed he does have regrets. The malfunctioning machine does not fulfill his intentions. Hence in his regrets and in his knowing the machine's malfunction, he, the desinger, reveals himself to be a different kind of entity than the one he designed.

But let us see. Suppose we observe a gliding missile launched from a mother aircraft. The vehicle continually corrects its course in such a way as to home in on a target. From all appearances it is a device much like the homing torpedo. Yet on inspecting the vehicle we find not only a system of mechanical controls of aileron and rudder, but also a pigeon pecking at a constantly shifting target display which is mounted on tambours in such a way that the pigeon's pecking constantly brings the target image into his purview (Skinner, 1960). In effect, the pigeon is sitting at the controls. (If you deem a pigeon too lowly a creature to disport intention, then substitute a Kamikaze pilot of your own choosing.) But what kind of a vehicle is this? Is there an intentional agent operative in the machine or is there not? Presumably, if we followed Taylor in his argument, we would have to say there is, but that the pilot's intention of pecking at the target image, or keeping it in view, is not precisely the same intention as that of the designer of the complete vehicle. But then could we not substitute a mechanical device for achieving the same piloting function? There should be no difficulty in designing such a device. But then apparently the modified machine would have given up its intentional attribute.

So far so good. Professor Skinner has played a joke on us. But our inspection turns up intention after all. And replacing the pilot with the guidance device relegates the vehicle to a machine state.

But now suppose our vehicle is actually a man, with gliding wings attached to arms and feet, and an explosive head attached to punctuate the significance of his mission. In part, at least, he too is a mechanical device. That is, how he controls the glide, how he maintains his orientation to the horizon, the angle of glide and so on, is realized through his kinesthetic, orientative, and muscular apparatus. No need for intention in these details. Somewhere, however, we must locate the intentional pilot in him. Suppose now there is a kind of pigeon in his machine, seriously, I mean, a smaller machine that is the executive of intention. Doubtless, like the pigeon, it too will have its machine aspects, just as indeed does the pigeon. And so the regress begins, from the homunculus within the man, to the homunculus within the homunculus, and always in pursuit of the ultimate agent of intention. The agent of intention always retreats as we seek to interpolate more and more mechanical details.

The argument need not be so quaint however. We may turn our attention to a man on the way to the store, and who undertakes his mission in order to get some tobacco. We learn, however, on questioning, that he does not smoke. His wife smokes and she asked him to go to the store. So the wife stands to John as the designer does to his vehicle. And at first glance, John fares no better than the homing torpedo. Still it may be maintained that John has *his* intention. It may be just to go to the store, or to please his wife, or to get some air and please his wife, or even to help her along to a carcinogenic demise. But it is still a possibility that John is just an automaton carrying out a preprogrammed mission. From appearances we cannot tell, for it may be that John had no intentions of going to the store at all until he received instructions from his wife.

But now suppose that even his wife does not smoke. She too is under instructions, not from the self-autonomous executive agent, but from her smoking friends who are coming for dinner. There is no limit to the instructions we may insert, no limit to retreat in search of the ultimate intention. Each person is an agent to be sure, but the agent for another person, another input. For all appearances they are vehicles, in the sense that at every stage of implementing an intention we may substitute for the person a machine. To be sure we have not got rid of intention in the larger picture of this going to the store in order to get some tobacco. But we have made it clear that so long as there are instructions from without, so long as there is input, there has been no real point, no persuasive occasion for interjecting intention as a unique predicate in the description of behavioral processes.

THE TWO VANTAGES

Much, if not all, of what appears to be controversy over the nature of behavioral explanation devolves upon a distinction to be made between the inner intentional vantage and the outer objectivistic vantage. Intentional explanations focus upon the inner vantage, while scientific explanation has traditionally focused on the outer. The question then becomes one of whether behavioral science is remiss for not having broken away from its objectivist traditions. But first, let us spell out the matter of the two vantages in greater detail.

Historically, psychology has been distinguished from the physical sciences by virtue of its concern for the concept of awareness. For astronomy, physics, chemistry, even biology, the observation is from without. The object is external to the observer. The thought as such is no part of the observational datum. Thinking, to be sure, may alter the character of our observation, and of our description of the object. This we know from the conceptual account of facts (e.g., Hanson, 1958; Feyerabend, 1962, 1964; Kuhn, 1962). However, thinking and being aware in no way control or affect the behavior of the object. Thought may affect the way we describe the acceleration of objects but it in no sense affects the acceleration of the object as such. To this extent, as objectivists, we are all realists.

For psychology the case has been different. In the mediation of behavior, the thought itself as intention, desire, motive enters into a functional relation with the behavioral movements. Thinking will not alter the objects of astronomy, but in psychology, thinking becomes integral with action. Thus, as the intentionalists argue, thinking about goals, anticipating, and valuing are inseparably entwined within the action.

There is, of course, nothing in the logics of science that requires our dividing the subject matters of science into the subjective and the objective, into the intentional and the nonintentional. Nothing, other than methodological convenience, demands that we deprive psychology of its unique intentional contents. To be sure, even for the intentionalist the descriptions of behavioral events are largely behavioral, involving as they do, physical displacement, exchange of momenta, and conservational balances. What is clearly unique, however, is the intentional description of the action. There can be little question that for the participant making a choice, the deliberations, the weighing of alternatives, the intention are all very real experiences.

The question remains, however: Is that vantage indispensable to the explanation of an action? Suppose we answer affirmatively and endow the intentional setting with some kind of executive function. Let us assume that intentional processes somehow define the agent, the real executor of the action. At what point does the intentional agent enter into the execution of an action? We are at a loss to say. My thinking about my body will, of course, not alter its shape. A thought, *per se,* will not activate a neuron attuned to specific energy. Clearly there are some aspects of my bodily movements which are not affected by my thinking, all aspects, we may suspect, not associated with voluntary muscular control. But thought as the intentional agent presumably does integrate certain motor activity. At some point, thought does effect control. But at what point? That is the question that invariably prompts the intentionalist to retreat. We do not experience the causal efficacy of willing, desiring, wanting, or any other intentional state (cf. Note 6.6).

Be that as it may, there is an important sense in which the agent's thinking about his action is causally intrusive, and in a way that thinking about other physical objects is not. Thinking about myself as object alters, that is, intrudes upon, the state of the object. I cannot gain objective information about my own being in the sense that I can get objective information about another person. The paradoxes of "complementary descriptions," of the inner intrusive vantage and outer objective vantage (Popper 1950; MacKay, 1966) have not, to my knowledge, been aired by writers in behalf of intention. Yet from the vantage of the person, the possibility of complementary descriptions presents a real logical difficulty in establishing any equivalence between an objective and an intentional description of *his own* behavior. To the extent of introspective intrusion, alternative complementary descriptions are indeed required.

This is a point worth pursuing in some detail for it points up to us an important logical distinction between intentional and nonintentional descriptions. And it is one in which the tactic of dispositional translations does not obviate the need for descriptions and explanations in the purely intentional setting.

Psychology and Complementarity

It is true for psychology as it is true, doubtlessly, for many sciences that the state of the system or the state of the fundamental entity is altered by our probes, the purpose of which is to gain information on the system or entity. Thus, in effect, the probe and the pick-up turn up information on a system different from the one intended. Hence, rather than information on a system S we have information on S', a system which now includes the interference effects interjected by the probes.

This predicament is of course not confined to electrode implants, to ablation studies, to studies on drug effects, or to any other study wherein attempts to make inferences about the functioning of the system are complicated by instrumental feedback of the probe. Psychologists and philosophers long ago recognized the impossibility of getting information on pure states of introspection, without the introspector's state itself complicating the object of study. Although both types of interference, the obtrusive and the intrusive, are significant for the psychologist, it is the latter which touches most directly on the argument to be presented.

In brief the argument is as follows. The object of study is the decision-making act "entered into" by the individual. A complete description of the phenomenon, so to speak, entails all aspects, all vantages of observation. Thus, for example, a person in the act of choosing can be observed from without, and the phenomenon will be described in the familiar public observation language of choice behavior. He can also be observed from within. That is, the person making the choice includes in the domain of all possible data, those data of his personal awareness, of his feeling, willing, deciding, to which he has privileged access. But it is the inner vantage which signifies to the individual highly relevant events not to be included in the ideal set of objective descriptions. That is to say, it is not possible for the individual, determinist that he himself may be, to apply the ideal of perfect descriptions and perfect predictability to himself. Now it might be argued that, interference effects of instrumental probes aside, descriptions in the object language would well fit into our deterministic rubrics. Any indeterminancy would be purely of a technological nature and could in principle be overcome. However, when we turn to the data of the inner vantage, the effect of the probe is inescapably built into the data, and in such a way that no matter how perfect the instruments of observation, awareness of the data always entails an element of indeterminancy which cannot be written off simply as a matter of technological deficiency. Since there is something distinctively different and yet aspectually requisite as regards our two vantages of decision making, a complete description of the decision-making event results in our embracing a principle of complementarity. And since the inner vantage, so to speak, introduces an inescapable indeterminancy into the state descriptions, it is all the more clear that complementary descriptions are essential for the complete description of the event under study.

In somewhat general terms, the argument has been advanced by Niels Bohr. On one occasion, Bohr writes:

> Indeed the necessity of considering the interaction between the measuring instruments and objects under investigation in atomic mechanics exhibits a close analogy to the peculiar difficulties in psychological analysis arising from the fact that the mental content is invariably altered when the attention is concentrated on any special feature of it (1958, p. 11).

And on another occasion he writes:

> Recognition of complementary relationship is not least required in psychology, where the conditions for analysis and synthesis of experience exhibit striking analogy with the situation in atomic physics. In fact, the use of words like *thoughts* and *sentiments,* equally indispensable to illustrate the diversity of psychical experience pertain to mutually exclusive situations characterized by a different drawing of the line of separation between subject and object. In particular, the place left for the feeling of volition is afforded by the very circumstance that situations where we experience freedom of will are incompatible with psychological situations where causal analysis is reasonably attempted. (1950, p. 57)

But other than to "renounce explanatory argumentation" whenever the volitional aspects of the inner vantage are thought to be appropriate descriptions, Bohr does not detail at what point in reference descriptions in the ideal causal rubric break down.

A poignant statement of the argument comes from cyberneticist MacKay (1966). Speaking to the issue of the conscious control of action, he denies that acceptance of a psychoneurological correlation commits one to determinism.

> I believe this conclusion to be itself mistaken, for it overlooks a curious and far-reaching logical implication of that same postulated connection between brain and consciousness, irrespective of the particular form that the connection takes. The key point is that if what a man believes affects correspondingly the state of his organizing system, no complete up-to-date account of that organizing system could be believed by him without being *ipso facto* rendered out of date.
>
> By the same token, even given the most complete current data, no complete prediction of the future state of his organizing system is deducible upon which both agent and observer could correctly agree.
>
> A prediction made secretly by a totally detached (nonparticipant) observer may well be valid for him (and his fellow nonparticipants), but upon the agent himself it has no logical binding force. On the contrary, he would be mistaken if he believed it, even though the nonparticipants were correct to believe it. (1966, p. 434)

And when speaking to the issue of the "logical indeterminancy" of human choice, MacKay concludes:

The argument hinges on a singular logical consequence of the assumed correlation between conscious experience and brain activity, which does not seem to have received sufficient attention. It is shown that in the case of a typical choice, even if the human information system were physically determinate in a pre-Heisenberg sense, it is impossible in principle to deduce, from the prior state of the world including the agent's brain, a prediction of his choice upon which agent and observer would be right to agree. More strongly, but for similar reasons, no prediction of it exists which is binding equally upon the observer and upon the agent whether the agent knows it or not. In this sense, typical human choices would be "logically indeterminate" even if the flow system that mediated them were physically determinate.

It is therefore suggested that the invocation of Heisenberg indeterminancy, though potentially relevant to our picture of spontaneous human activity, is logically unnecessary in order to make room for the kind of freedom that goes with responsible choice, and that objections *a priori* to a closed-loop model of the conscious human control of action are without foundation. (1966, p. 440)

Note here that despite the kinship of complementarity and indeterminancy, Heisenbergian indeterminancy is not the issue for psychology. The psychologist who would be a determinist needs to consider all data indispensable to his ideal of perfect description. But whenever he utilizes the inner vantage, as indeed he must when he considers himself the object of prediction, the ideal of the inclusion of all relevant data is denied to him. There is therefore an inescapable indeterminancy which no self-directed objectivity can overcome.

We shall return to this argument and that of complementarity after a brief look at consciousness as it functions in a semantic system.

A Semantic Treatment of Consciousness

Doubtless a major difficulty in writing about consciousness and awareness, even at this late date, is that no one is able precisely to define what it is that either he would affirm or he would deny. For scientists, at least, it would appear that the conundrums of mind-body dualism are passé, if for no other reason than empirical tests of hypotheses are found wanting. All the same, it cannot be denied that when we as individuals say that we are conscious or that we are aware, we have something other in mind than the propositions specifying material objects or states of our nervous systems. Thus, if I say that I am seeing a round red object, I am reporting my act of observation in which the observation in its immediacy is something apart from activities of my peripheral and central nervous systems. Furthermore, when I am seeing a round red object, my observation, its act and content, is something different from the object itself, just as there is the difference between the content of experience and the objects which that content is evidence for. There is, of course, a difference between seeing a round red object and savoring a cool liquid, and there is a different difference between the round object and the liquid. What I am alluding to here is the semantic roles that consciousness, as content of experience, may play. States of consciousness differ as do the putative objects we observe. Consciousness can thus be regarded as constituting the signs for object states of affairs.

Observations are, of course, reported as statements in the physical object language. I see a round red object, but the focal point of my observation-awareness is that content of experience which I take to be the evidence for the object. Were it unnecessary to distinguish between the object in the thing-language and the evidence for it, there would be no occasion to distinguish between veridical and illusory perception. Thus, I may have images, illusory or hallucinatory, without necessarily taking them to be evidences of real objects, however we may wish to define real objects. And, if it occurs to me to report the content of my experience independently of any question of its status as evidence, I can certainly do so. That is all I intend by consciousness or awareness, and I see no grounds for denying that this is the case. If you ask me to define consciousness I can do little more than to say, "consciousness" alludes to a state which supports my capacity to report what I am experiencing (in that state) independent of any question concerning the evidential status of the content.

Here, however, I must be careful not to imply that by the content of experience, i.e., the substantive aspect of my awareness, I am alluding to anything so abstract as sense data, *per se*. In studies of perception the phenomenologists are correct. We are aware of objects and not of sense data. That is to say, the phenomenological entity is a configuration of what we may abstract as sense data, and it is the configuration which we take to be the evidence for the extraperceptual object.

I wish to maintain this distinction (i.e., that between perceptual content and object for which that content may or may not be evidence) without at the same time engaging in any argument over ontology. The distinction, it seems to me, can be retained regardless of whether a person is a pure phenomenalist or is a dualist embracing a causal theory of perception. I would avoid the ontological argument by noting that perceptual configurations, just as symbolic configurations I can print or utter, are signs. That is to say, the occurrence of configurations in perceptual experience can be regarded as consciousness-signs signifying occurrences having a status different from that of the sign itself. Appropriately, we may take the conscious configuration to be a sign for a real object. That is what is meant by "evidence for." [2] The content of consciousness is the sign which

---

[2] There is perhaps a difficulty in our taking a sign as "evidence for." Generally, we do not treat signs, *per se,* as the evidence, but rather what is signified by the sign. However, the present tactic is required by our taking the content of consciousness as a sign; its defense is best stated in terms reminiscent of syntactical physicalism

signifies the object. In this case the semantic role of consciousness seems straightforward. There is, however, a different domain of signification, and an important one, which enables us to hold a semantic thesis of consciousness without the question of the reality of the significate becoming a problem. This is the domain of neural process. Let us entertain, then, the familiar postulate of no psychosis without neurosis. Then, regardless of whether we are psychophysical parallelists, or epiphenomenalists or even interactionists, we may take consciousness to be a sign of some accompanying neural process. Thus if we could read our signs correctly, we could indicate clearly what our perceptual contents signify in the domain of neural process.

The argument here for the sign-significance of consciousness does not in any way pretend to be a resolution of the traditional mind-body problem. To say that consciousness signifies is not a matter of saying either that it is epiphenomenon, or that it is productive of neural activation, or that it intermediates between neural states. Rather what is proposed is that the utility of consciousness rests in its function of signification. Just as a sign signifies an object or an abstraction, so consciousness serves as a sign signifying what can be designated in the physicalistic language, or for that matter, in the abstract language of classes. However, note that there are two domains of objects that consciousness can be said to signify. And in this it is semantically unique. One is the real phenomenal world, the world of objects specified by our unique consciousness of them. This is the semantic of consciousness made familiar to us by phenomenalists and phenomenologists alike. We know our phenomenal world only through its signification in consciousness. The second object domain is that of neural function. That is to say, consciousness, such as seeing a red round object, is a sign not only for the object, but also for the fact of certain processes occurring within the nervous system. Here, of course, the semantic is much less precise. We seldom, if ever, know the state of the nervous system which any momentary flux of consciousness is said to signify. Although it is a challenge for the contemporary student of brain and consciousness to establish the semantic ties between sign and significate, all that is required now as a metaphysical commitment is the stipulation that there is no sign without an appropriate neural domain of signification; that is to say, no psychosis without neurosis.

If we maintain that consciousness has a two-fold semantic reference,

---

(Carnap, 1935). According to this doctrine "evidence for" would be explicated in terms of reduction of the object statement (of the thing evidenced) to a set of basic statements which are adopted conventionally (i.e., without regard to factual reference). Thus to say "A 'sign signifying a red object' is the evidence for the object" is to assert within the metalanguage that the sign properly used in conjunction with certain other premises, is instrumental in the inference of statements about the object. The inference may be incorrect, to be sure, as in the case of hallucination. But that is only to say that there are other premises and other rules which in conjunction with the sign lead to a different inference.

i.e., it signifies the phenomenal world as perceptual construction *and* it signifies the underlying neurophysiological process, then any conscious flux in the process of decision making will serve as signification for the two-fold aspect. Doubtless it is the case that of this reference the outer aspect offers the more defensible semantic. It has the advantage of public access and public agreement. However, we cannot deny that the inner aspect is significant. If consciousness is invariably a sign of neurophysiological activity, then in spite of our lack of detailed construction of that activity we know by the signification that important mediating activity is going on. To be conscious in this sense signifies that some significant neural process is going on without perhaps our being able to represent that process with a perceptual construction. If I am now committed to complete descriptions, I cannot ignore any of signs available to me. And even were I myself the object of study and a neurophysiologist with the appropriate preferences for descriptions and explanations in the physical thing-language, I most assuredly could not ignore those functional episodes in this physical process which are signified to me in my own consciousness. Thus, as the compleat neurophysiologist, I must make sure that all of that which is signified by consciousness is represented by a perceptual construction translatable and manipulatable within my formal theory—not only my observations germane to the construction of neurophysiological process and function, but also my consciousness-in-process which signifies to me that some activity is occurring at that moment in my nervous system.

Complementarity and Consciousness

We return now to the idea of complementarity. According to our semantic thesis, consciousness signifies two domains of referents. One is the world of object construction, our phenomenologically "real" worlds; the other is the underlying neurophysiological process which we may visualize, if we choose, as being indispensable to awareness. I wish to maintain that the two domains of signification, of description, if you will, are semantically complementary but syntactically incompatible. What is curious initially is that any neurophysiological description appears solely to refer to the domain of phenomenologically real objects. It is only when we utilize consciousness in the role of signification that we discover the need for complementary descriptions and the need to reject all models of determinism that might conceivably apply for our object worlds.

The predicament can be stated straightforwardly. Conceivably, it is possible to write strictly deterministic laws for the behavior of organisms when such behaviors and such organisms are exogenous to the observer. However, no such laws are applicable (i.e., the nature of predictive error and uncertainty is significantly altered) when any person, scientific observer that he may be, attempts to apply the same system of description to his own behavior. The crucial point is that of prediction. Let O be any object-person whose behavior is amenable to prediction by a set of laws L. Further let S be a person who undertakes the prediction of his own behavior. In principle, any O's behavior is predictable. As behavioral scientists, we apply to O the comprehensive set of laws such that from the complete complement of independent variables and the laws we can in principle make an exact prediction. But for S, the situation is different. The set of laws which prove comprehensive for the prediction of O does not prove comprehensive when S himself becomes the object of inference. Let S be an informed behavioral scientist. When requested to predict what he himself will do, he proceeds to treat himself as object, therefore converting his S to an O. In other words, he is to treat his own self as the object of behavioral laws. This, however, he cannot quite do. For whereas it is possible to update the complement of state variables for the prediction of O and to do so without interfering with the character of O, it is not possible to update the complement of state conditions for S, *from the vantage of S.*

Let us say, that S is to predict his own behavior. He proceeds as he does for any other O, by ascertaining the state conditions and the laws appropriate to the situation. In addition, however, he becomes conscious of this predictive complex as it applies to his object self. Thus, this consciousness signifies a state not included in the original complement of state conditions. However careful S is to include the full complement of variables in the state description, the state of apprehending them, as signified in immediate consciousness, is not included in the predictive set. This is the sign-significate counterpart of the impossibility of introspecting the contemporary act of introspection. The immanent act can be objectified only as it loses its status of immanence. The contemporary signs in consciousness signify objectifiable states only if they lose their contemporary status.

Now, any behavioral scientist observing an O remains within the causal rubric, only if he possesses the tactics for making his descriptions contemporary. To the extent that he can keep his descriptions contemporary, he can sustain his deterministic commitment. However, the point to consider is that any person, any behavioral scientist, in the role of S cannot appropriately apply deterministic models to the making of his own decisions. He is in the position of never being able to make his descriptions strictly contemporary.[3]

---

[3] "Contemporary" requires some specification. One predicts from the contemporary moment to the future. Thus the finest grain of time would require that between the contemporary moment t_0 and t_1, the moment of action in the future to be realized, there is a time difference Δt such that between t_0 and $t_0 + \Delta t = t_1$ nothing of significance occurs within the system so as to change the prediction. There is no occasion to change what is predicted of O at any time during the interval $t_0 + \Delta t$ from what is predicted of O at the time t_0. In effect, we can render Δt nonsignificant so far as concerns prediction. The argument here is that we can in principle render Δt nonsignificant so far as concerns any O. However, for any S, for any person scientifically knowledgeable and well informed about himself, Δt always entails significant events which make a putative contemporary description impossible. Thus contemporary descriptions which are essential to the premise of determinism are inaccessible to S.

CONCLUSION

It is apparent to scientist and philosopher alike, to logician and analyst, that there are alternative meanings of explanation. The philosophical analysts have performed a valuable service in reminding us of the fact. But, however helpful it is to be informed that there are many usages of a given term, it is equally important that we define the specific contexts of meaning so as not to confuse one contextual meaning with another.

Doubtless there are several meanings of "explaining behavior." No behaviorist, for example, ought to deny the relevance of a person's giving reasons for his behavior, especially if that is what he is specifically requested to do. Too often, however, the question of offering explanations is misdirected. It is addressed to a critique of what constitutes scientific explanation, rather than the more relevant issue of what type of explanatory exposition is called for and in what context.

Consider two contexts of explanation; one, the hypothetico-deductive, the other, that of giving reasons. The one context is that traditionally associated with scientific explanation; the other is associated with intentionalistic or purposive explanation. I have argued that there is no logical incompatibility between these two types of explanation. Still we are being persistently reminded that behavioral science stands in default because, in its deductive rubrics, it does not take account of intentionalistic descriptions. If it is suggested that the behaviorist may substitute dispositional terms for the language of intention, it is countered that pure cognition is logically unique and is not amenable to formalization in a theory.

But then, why should behavioral science take account of pure cognition and intention independent of their behavioral implications? The behavioral scientist follows in the tradition of physical science. He seeks explanations by deducing statements of events within a formal theory. Although there is something uniquely adaptable, flexible, deliberative in the behavior of organisms, there is no insurmountable barrier to the scientist's producing deductivistic explanations of what he observes. He, like all of us, recognizes the significance of teleological explanations of behavior in ordinary discourse, but in giving his "reasons for" some behavior in the familiar phrases of ordinary language, he also recognizes that he is not advancing statements that are necessarily useful in his scientific undertaking.

Suppose I ask of our behavioral scientist, a doctrinaire behaviorist, if such a man there be, "Why did you go to the store?" And suppose he responds either by giving a detailed neurophysiological account of input-output, feedback, and motor control, or by giving an account in terms of motivation, habit, discrimination and so on, compatible with methodological behaviorism. But then I counter: "That is not what I mean; rather I want to know your reasons for putting on your coat, leaving your study,

and walking to the store." Now, of course, a meaningful, intentional explanation can be given by our scientist friend, as meaningful to him as it is to
any teleologist. But that intentional description is not the one that he
deemed appropriate to give when he thought he was being asked to provide
a scientific explanation of his behavior. When it is called to his attention
that he has misconstrued my question, he may put his scientific portfolio
down and proceed as well as any intentionalist to give the appropriate
answer: "In order to get some pipe tobacco and a bit of exercise."

So the matter of giving an explanation comes initially to the query:
What kind of an explanation? It is little short of a game of puns for me to
ask for an explanation and, anticipating my friend's penchants, to respond,
"But that is not the kind of explanation I asked for." Like asking, "How do
you feel?" And when you answer: "Fine," I say "Incorrect: you feel with
your tactical apparatus." Or better, "Why do you feel regret over having
chosen A instead of B?" If you answer, "Because I was confronted with a
free choice, and my choice proved financially disastrous," I might call you
to task for not having provided me with a neurophysiological account of
your affective behavior. One cannot win at these games of punnery, and
the reason is obvious. Rules stipulating what constitutes an appropriate
class of answers are not made explicit in the question.

It is not an accident that many critiques of classical explanation have
capitalized upon the possibility of intentional involvements. Being involved
as the subject as well as being the object of investigation offers a predicament different from that of being merely object. It is not at all clear that
we can have a science of subjective intentional experience, or what a
science of such experience would be like if indeed we could have one. And
this is a predicament similar to the one involved in the issue of behavioral
determinism versus indeterminism. Being an object in a causal matrix and
being a free agent is not an argument of one description over another; it
is a matter of complementarity. Contextually, of course, both positions are
correct. To ask of a person, for example, our behavioral scientist: "Are
you free?" calls for the answer perspicuity dictates: "What kind of an
answer do you wish me to give?" As object, the hero of our study becomes
the antihero, he is describable in the language of a causal, albeit perhaps a
stochastic, matrix. But as subject participating in the act, he becomes hero
incarnate. He must make the choice out of his own deliberation. He can
rely on neither the fates nor his own nervous system to "make the choice."
Even as dedicated objectivist he can never fully rely upon his practiced
skills in object description. He can never attempt a contemporaneous description of himself as object, without that description being fed back into
the objective being.

I have argued that intention is not problematic for the behavioral
scientist should he give his intentional terms dispositional translations. That
is, of course, what we must do in the case of nonlingual species. There are,

of course, some difficulties. "Why did the porpoise sound?" "In order to avoid collision with the skiff." But why not, "Because it wanted to avoid dumping the captain and his crew"? Behaviorally, both intentional descriptions imply the same response. Therefore, dispositional translations, *sans* recourse to introspection, will not decide the issue. But neither will self-conscious practice in offering testimonials to *our* own intentions. What reason can the porpoise offer? None at all, for he is nonconversant.

And so, I suppose, are we all, so difficult is the task of penetrating the screens of rationalization. But even though explaining by giving reasons may be an appropriate exercise for the perceptive and articulate few, there are many species which are mute in the language of intention but which are purposive all the same. Suppose a dog to be of one such species. We can give reasons for his behavior, we may even attribute intentions to him. But this is by way of analogy, and an appropriate dispositional concept. Intention for the dog is a manner of *our* speaking. But equally important is the fact that there is nothing incompatible between my intentional description which personalizes the behavior of my dog and the scientific one which is favored in the laboratory.

Our response to the argument for the uniqueness of intentional description is thus a disarmingly simple one. Explanation is a manner of speaking. Contextually we know handily how to explain. Thus the recognition of our capacity to give reasons for our actions should not be elevated to a critique of science. There is nothing incompatible between scientific explanation and an intentionalistic one so long as we know the contextual formulation of the question. To think otherwise is merely to confuse logical incompatibility with linguistic preferences.

Finally, one looks in vain through these intentionalistic critiques for what a science of behavior would be like if we were to bring the purified language of subjective intention into the scientific theory. The most convincing exercise in the critique of a given science is to produce another science to take its place. And this of course the intentionalists have not done (cf. Note 6.7, Note 6.8). An intention is nothing if it is not translated into action. The advantage of behavioral descriptions of intentions is the obvious one of semantic precision. For us to concentrate on the intentional description of behavior need require nothing more esoteric than precise dispositional concepts (cf. Note 6.7).

NOTES

NOTE 6.1

Because of their phenomenological setting, intentions and expectations are usually considered to be purely mentalistic. But this is a mistake. Suppose I make my way through a dimly lighted room to my study, feeling the walls as I go. Suddenly I touch something soft and diaphanous, much like a cobweb. I withdraw my hand quickly, jump back; and the adrenalin flows. But why? How do I explain this behavior? One recourse is to formulate an explanation in terms of expectancy. Implicitly, as I feel my way along the walls, I expect the tactual experience of familiar painted walls. On touching the gossamer-like stuff, I meet in tactual contact something I obviously did not expect. But certainly the behavior of feeling my way is perfunctory, something I habitually do, while thinking of something else, while pursuing other intentions than that of feeling the wall. Since I am startled, I do react much as if my expectations of tactual experience were not fulfilled.

Now it cannot be maintained that my expectations were conscious. They were not. It did not occur to me what my expectations were, or how to interpret them until well after the response. In fact, on being startled, I turn on the light and go back to examine the point of my encounter with the cobweb stuff. Lo, I discover a ribbon dangling from an open cabinet above my passage.

Through all this, it must be emphasized that my expectations were unconscious, they were reflected in my behavior, and they came to the light of awareness only after the fact of my response. Still it may make sense to interject expectancy as an explanatory concept. And it does not particularly make sense to say that my expectancy was a uniquely mental process, unless I resort to the circumlocution of describing this occurrence as a psychophysical process in which the psychic component loses its identifying characteristic of awareness. But certainly, if we can dispense with awareness as the identifying characteristic of intention and expectancy we can as well dispense with mentalism, *per se*.

NOTE 6.2

The idea of phenomenological intentionality has always been difficult to grasp. The pivotal argument focuses upon the term "aboutness," and its semantic ramifications. A term in the physical thing-language takes its meaning in reference to what it denotes in the domain of object-experience. Meaning thus is a function of denotation in a *public* domain of experience. An intentional term, however, has a more complicated semantic. It too takes its meaning in what it denotes; in other words, in what it refers to. But what it refers to as the experienced object is itself a cognitive entity; i.e., an image or a cognitive construct. Hence the referent of intentional terms such as "thinking about" is once removed from the world of publicly experienceable objects. Thus the language of intentionality involves meaning relations not found in simple denotations of the thing-language. For example, we can describe a state of anger in purely objective terms, in, say, stimulus-response contingencies. But in an intentional description, we must include, not simply the stimulus input which is the occasion for anger, but the meaning of the stimulus input for the person experiencing the anger. In a word, that is what anger is all *about,* at least in psychological terms.

Still there are finer distinctions to be made. Although the literature of philosophical phenomenology does not sustain a reputation for exegetical clarity, some of the distinctions point to a rarified introspectionism in which thought, thought-of-object, and object are clearly separable. One may think of a unicorn. What is given in the thought is given by direct awareness. But in thinking of the object, one moves from the immanence of the thought to the transcendence of the object, as the object of thought. However, the transcendence need not involve physical object existence. That is to say (in the language of Brentano), the object of intentional thought is the intentionally inexistent object of thought. It exists in thought but is not an object of thought in the sense that the thought should designate some physical object. We have the immanent thought, the intentionally inexistent object transcendental to the immanent thought, and objects as such. The intentionally inexistent object differs from the physical object in that the former does not necessarily require the latter. Thus, as Nakhnikian writes:

> . . . objects do not *have* to exist. An intentional act may have as its object an existentially mind-dependent entity, for example, the *idea* of a mermaid; or its object may be something physical; or it may be an impossible thing such as the round square; or it may be something possible but unactualized, such as a golden mountain. Any mode of mentality (loving, desiring, believing) may have as its object an "intentionally inexistent" entity, namely, an entity that is neither physical nor existentially mind-dependent. The *idea* of a mermaid is, being an *idea,* existentially mind-dependent. But the *mermaid* which is the intention of the idea is neither a physical thing nor is it existentially mind-dependent. In contrast to this, no physical action requiring an object can be performed upon an intentionally inexistent entity. Kicking a football requires a football; but thinking of a football does not (Husserl, 1964, p. XIV).

In this context we should note that Husserl's notion of phenomenological reduction is somewhat like but clearly distinguishable from phenomenalistic reduction. By phenomenalistic reduction we mean the reduction of all object statements to sense-data statements. By phenomenological reduction, Husserl (1964) means the reduction of thought to what is immanently given independent of any projected object status, either as existent or inexistent object. That is, phenomenological reduction is the reduction of thought to its ultimate indubitable givenness. Whereas for the phenomenalist reduction is invariably a matter of linguistic and conceptual conventions, for the phenomenologist reduction is a matter of "pure intuition."

NOTE 6.3

In his defense of intentionalistic descriptions, Charles Taylor writes:

> The difference between those beings which are capable and those which are incapable of action thus lies in the former having an additional entity over and above their corporeal nature which the latter do not possess (1964, p. 57).

Since intentions, like corporeal objects, are experienced let us first examine this notion of "experience."

What do we mean by this term? The flux of sensory experience? The kaleidoscope of qualia generated by the person's response to his environment, including that of his own body? For the hard-data empiricist something more concrete is implied. Experience is of objects. And here one does not always differentiate clearly between what is immediately given and what is conceptualized.

First, consider experience of objects. Though given to us in the immediacy of perception, these object experiences are perceptually constructed. They emerge in the context of cognitive structuring. They are not given to us as pure phenomena, but are the functions of prior perceptual categories, either intuitively given or developmentally acquired. Still much of what is perceptually reified has an immediacy about it. Such is the pervasive character of cultural tradition. Doubtless we do perceive things as we are trained to see them (a truism fully documented by students of perception), but any obtrusive aspect of the conceptual framework of perception is in time, at least, forgotten. Let us say, then, that we learn to perceive objects from the vantage of our traditions, even though we regard such experience as indubitable in its givenness.

Second, consider experience which is more conspicuously conceptual. To a large extent causal context is conceptual. Our observations incorporate motives, forces, habits, resistances, and the like, and these are clearly conceptual. The data are selective, the perceptual construction reflects constructive inference. That is to say, we do not "perceive" forces, we see only movement; we do not perceive resistance but only changes in states. Thus learning to perceive by means of conceptual inference, leads to our "seeing" something which has no pure phenomenal counterpart. Doubtless much of perception is of this character, even that of our everyday "phenomenological" entities. In the domain of science, especially, perception is inseparable from conceptual activity. Inference and construction provide the synthesis for the pure data of sensory input.

And third, consider experience as applied to unstructured sensory input in its purest form. Although we experience objects in their phenomenological integrity, we also, it has been said, experience the qualia from which these entities are formed. To be sure, such experience is analytic. The child does not first experience redness, roundness, sweetness and then the apple, but first the apple. Nevertheless our languages of perceptual analysis have permitted us to say that we experience qualia, raw feels, sense data. We need not take up a defense of classical phenomenalism; the sense datum may indeed be an abstraction. However, raw feels appear to be indubitable; at least our pains are real.

In any event, there is a third construction we put on the word "experience"; this is the raw feel, the precipitate of the inner vantage. And it is the inner vantage that plays havoc with empiricism. Aside from the raw feels that we catalogue among our feelings and pains, it is doubtful that the inner vantage provides us with any data along pure sensory dimensions, so inseparable are object and qualia.

However, there is a more direct confrontation from the inner vantage which does indeed become puzzling for the empiricist who stresses the primacy of experience. Experience is the agent of all object perception. Experience is *of* the object experienced. But there is also the experience of the person's experiencing, of his feeling, his willing, his intending. And in this inner vantage from which such experience derives, there is neither phenomenological object nor perceptual construction. This experience, though involving the intended object, is itself not object. The question then becomes: Ought this experience be incorporated into scientific descriptions? Or to rephrase the question: Does methodological behaviorism, which restricts itself to descriptions and explanation in the physicalistic object-language, preclude treatment of some variable that is relevant to the description of psychological events?

The tactic of methodological behaviorism, of course, dissolves the problem. If our science is nonintentionalistic, if it is to deal only with objectifiable experience, experience within the inner vantage is, as such, irrelevant to scientific explanation. But the tactic is only methodological, a convenience, so to speak. Suppose intentions are relevant factors in the psychological event. What recourse is there then to counter the methodological tactic? That of objectifying the intention, one is tempted to answer. However, the intention of the inner vantage cannot be objectified. And it is not a matter of the failure of inference or of analogy. Rather it is the case that whereas I can experience my willing an action, even I cannot experience my will's effecting that action.

Here is the crux of our methodological departure. I cannot experience the efficacy of intention. There is, of course, no problem in phenomenological constructions. The phenomenological object is the object of study, and we can indeed experience the object. But what is the experience from within the inner vantage? It is the given, the immanent experience. Between immanence and transcendence, immanence and emergence, our language tends to become obscure. Therefore, to say that experience from within the inner vantage is immanent is merely to say that it is given independent of object support and construction. The redness and the sweetness as experienced, *per se,* are not objectified. If immanent experience there is, then in its own purity it is to be independent of the object, independent of the supportive substance to which we append our perceptual attributes. Clearly now, such experience is not the subject of scientific curiosity. The subject matter of science is always the object, the experience is always the experience *of*. Whatever curiosity we have of immanent experience, it is not a curiosity appropriate to science.

So what is the status of intentional analysis? There are those who argue that logical behaviorism, the methodological commitment, is inadequate to the task of psychological analysis, since it precludes from its descriptions the inner vantage of intentions. If intentions are, by virtue of this behavioristic commitment, to be introduced into behavioral descriptions, they are to be introduced only as dispositional terms translating into behavioral predicates. What is it, then, that our knowledge of subjective intentions can offer to scientific descriptions which cannot be treated by dispositional translations in the behavioral language?

Let us assume for the moment that the meaningful unit of psychological analysis is the act, having starting and ending phases and being accompanied by a subjective intention. What distinguishes human behavior from that of other species is the teleological, intentional component. Let us assume this. But, moreover, let us also predicate that this intentional component is a significant one in that we do in fact experience it. That is the point of its relevance. Yet, what is it that we experience?

Superficially at least we do experience our intentions. We have the experience of intending certain actions. According to subjective teleologists, it is this experience itself which is indispensable to the complete description of the act. Thus, if between the antecedent environmental complex and the consequent response complex we must insert the intention, then intention becomes a mediating causal variable expressible in the nonphysical language. In a word, we are confronted with the problem of interaction, or, if not that, the causal role of subjective intention.

Now, for intentions to play a causal role in scientific descriptions, they must be experienced. (The paradox of our purposefully doing what we do not intend to do belongs to unconscious action.) Of course, intentionalists, if we may call them that, insist that intentions are experienced. But again we ask, what is experienced? To say that we experience acts of intending and willing is not to be denied, but those experiences themselves are not what is required for the scientific description of a continuous behavioral event. Rather, what should be required for the complete description, and what is not experienced, is the connection between the experience of willing and the effecting the behavioral response. I experience my willing an action and I experience my action's occurring in the achievement of some goal, but I do not experience my will's actually effecting that action. The crucial component of my description, if I were to insist on subjective intentional analysis, remains undescribable—undescribable because I do not experience what is to be described. Were it otherwise, in other words, were the connection between willing and acting actually experienced, then it is apparent that mind-body dualism would never have been problematic.

Note that the problem of intentionalistic causality is not the same as that of Humean skepticism. Whereas for Hume we do not experience one phenomenally objectified event effecting a change of state in a subsequent event, we do, as a matter of fact, experience concatenation and juxtaposition in the domain of phenomenally objectified events. Our analysis of functional dependencies is limited only by practicable observational limits on the grain of time. And we do, in a sense, experience a connection between one event and another, the temporal-spatial one. This, however, is not the case as between intentions and behavioral events. Except in the crude semantic of our volitional language, we do not say that we experience an intention as a temporal process and then a behavioral event. Continuity-over-time is a property of physical events, it is not a property of intentional ones. But if intentional episodes are indeed to be interjected into the continuity of physical events, they can be treated in one of two ways: as executors (effectors), or as indicators. If intentions are effectors, they are either interposed within the fine grain of physical events, or they are concomitant with them. If they are concomitant, we may treat them simply as indicators of physical events, which is to say we may substitute dispositional translations for them. Only if intentions are in fact mediators and effectors of physical events are they indispensable to psychological description. The thesis expressed here, however, is that we have no sense as to what point in time (or space) our intentions become the efficacious effectors they are presumed to be. Although we may experience our intending and our willing from within the inner frame, we do not experience the efficacy of intending in its effecting the intended action.

Now, for the most part, the intentionalists are well aware of the problems involved in giving a causal analysis of intention. In fact, the purpose of this critique should be to point out what an intentional description is not. Thus, Charles Taylor defines intention in such a way that it is the intention itself that defines the purposive action and enables us to distinguish between movement, *per se,* and action. Richard Taylor (*Action and Purpose*) goes further—he maintains that indeed we have no experience of willing, desiring, intending as effecting an action. To imply that we should have such an experience is to misconstrue the role intention is to play in the understanding of behavior. But neither does Richard Taylor wish to treat intentions as conscious indicators of causal activity. Programmatically, at least, bodily motions constitute a closed causal system, and the purely symbolic role would render intention irrelevant. Rather, intentions are to be regarded as unanalyzable; they have the unique status of being unexplained explainers, that is to say, they both define and explain "self-originated" purposeful action. (See also Anscombe, 1957; Peters, 1958; Melden, 1961)

NOTE 6.4

Note that in our presentation of a dispositional interpretation of intention, bilateral reduction pairs (Carnap, 1936) are utilized only in those cases where there is a subjective indication of an intentional state of affairs. Hence, the behavioral analysis is tied to the phenomenology of the experiencing person. An alternative, and, in some respects, technically superior translation of dispositional properties is offered by Hochberg 1967). Let us first define our dispositional property by

$$Ix =_{df.} Sx \supset Rx$$

that is to say, an intention (of some kind) is assignable to x by definition if on exposure to stimulus situation S the response R is forthcoming. The intentional property I now becomes the concept by which we seek application of a general rule

$$(x) \; Sx \supset Rx$$

Such a rule, as it stands, however, is not useful. Its applicability is too general. We need to restrict it to just those situations we think compatible with our conceptual convention.

Our conceptual convention is that which defines I. But now we seek the inductive bridge for applying I. In other words I, though explicitly defined in S,R terms, connotes something more than explicit $S–R$ reductions. It betokens a state of the organism, if you will, indicatable by something other than the S,R states of affairs as such.

Let us now adopt the property VI, say as a verbal (introspective) indication of I, whatever I is thought now to be in terms of an open possibility of meaning. Our dispositional property then leads us to the lawful statement

$$(x) \; VIx \supset (Sx \supset Rx)$$

Note now that although I disappears from the expression of our general proposition (law), it is the vehicle (an implicit definition) by which we formulate the law, and by which we establish application of the propositional expression $(Sx \supset Rx)$. But what of nonintentional states and behaviors? This offers difficulty. According to Hochberg's treatment of dispositional pairs, the definition

$$\bar{I}x =_{df.} Sx \supset \sim Rx$$

leads by inductive gambit to

$$(x) \; \overline{VI}x \supset (Sx \supset \sim Rx)$$

But for this treatment to be useful we must clarify what we mean by $\bar{I}$, the state of nonintention. A bit of reflection indicates that $\bar{I}$ must be "to intend something other than is intended in I." In other words, $\bar{I}$ too must be an intentional state, but other than I; otherwise we must call to question our justification of the rule leading to our inferring $\sim R$ from S. If $\bar{I}$, the nonintention with respect to I, were simply the logical complement of I, we would have

$$\bar{I} =_{df.} \sim (S \supset R)$$

in other words

$$\bar{I} =_{\text{df.}} S \cdot \sim R$$

This would be unacceptable, for it states, in effect, that R cannot occur with S if not I. A response appropriate to an intention may occur in the presence of S. But it may very well occur in the absence of the intention (e.g., a perfunctory response). Hence the more appropriate definition is indeed

$$\bar{I}x =_{\text{df.}} (Sx \supset \sim Rx)$$

and $\bar{I}$ is an intentional state other than I.

Still we must acknowledge that this treatment of the dispositional term is not helpful in distinguishing between "purely dispositional terms" and "theoretical concepts." Initially the dispositional property I is conventionally defined in terms of S–R contingencies only to be transformed into a lawlike statement presumably by attributing some additional state or property (VI) to the object. But we cannot be sure whether VI, say, is some kind of inferred state (hypothetical construct, existential hypothesis) or whether it is nothing more than a logical construction based on an explicit definition and adopted for calculational convenience.

Carnap (1956), on the other hand, is careful to distinguish between those situations in which S–R contingencies formulate the explicit extensions of "purely dispositional terms" and those in which they only token partial interpretations of terms (states) in the theoretical language. He acknowledges that this distinction is closely related to that between intervening variables and hypothetical constructs (MacCorquodale and Meehl, 1948). Thus for example, a purely dispositional term may be represented by

$$Sx \supset (Cx \equiv Rx)$$

where S–R pairings are explicitly stipulated for the dispositional term C. Theoretical terms on the other hand are not fully interpreted by a set of S–R contingencies; in fact they are not logically bound to any S–R contingency. First, the set of all S–R pairings with which we associate the theoretical construct is an open one, thereby the heuristic property of theoretical terms; and second, the openness (incomplete interpretation) of the construct makes for exceptions (i.e., $S \sim R$) in those cases where the theoretic state nominally calls for R in the presence of S. In effect, it makes sense for us to qualify, to modify, or to amplify a theoretical construct where it does not make sense to do so in the case of the purely dispositional term (unless of course we are converting the status of the latter to that of a theoretical term). Thus, of purely dispositional terms Carnap has this to say:

(1) The term can be reached from predicates for observable properties by one or more steps of [operational procedure].
(2) The specified relation between S and R constitutes the whole meaning of the term.

(3) The regularity involving S and R, on which the term is based, is meant as universal, i.e., holding without exception. (Carnap, 1956, p. 66)

And regarding theoretical concepts Carnap writes:

> In contrast . . . the interpretation of a psychological concept as a theoretical concept, *although it may accept the same behavioristic test procedure based on S and R,* does not identify the concept (the state or trait) with the pure disposition. . . . The decisive difference is this: on the basis of the theoretical interpretation, the result of this or of any other test or, generally, of any observations, external or internal, is not regarded as absolutely conclusive evidence for the state in question; it is accepted only as probabilistic evidence. . . . (1956, p. 71; emphasis added)

Although it is not necessary that theoretical concepts be reductive in nature, Carnap's closing comments in this essay (1956) appear to favor the notion that such concepts be hypotheses subject to structural reification. What is clear, however, is that theoretical concepts in psychology are utilized only in $S-R$ contexts.

In our own treatment, we have adopted a somewhat looser definition of dispositional terms and dispositional translations. Under specifiable circumstances the theoretical state is sufficient for a behavioral response. And the response is necessary for the attribution of the theoretic state. However, the specification of those circumstances and responses appropriate to the theoretic state is itself incomplete. Therefore articulation of a theoretical construct becomes both an hypothetical and an empirical matter.

NOTE 6.5

I do not wish to imply that intentional descriptions are problem-free for the methodological behaviorist. But neither are they for the intentionalist who would maintain that they are epistemologically unique in the role they play in explaining behavior. Even for the intentionalist, behavioral criteria are required for stipulating the effectiveness of an intention.

Dispositionally treated, intentions have generality. They are akin to attitudes, values, desires, all of which are constructs such that for the given C there are a multiplicity of situations, $\{S_i\}$, where the given disposition specified under C is operative. But what of unique intentions? Situations that are once-in-a-life-time affairs? Two alternatives are open. We may attempt to classify the special event in larger classes of behavioral dispositions or we can resort to arbitrary behavioral translations of the unique intentional event. Consider, for example, my intention of going to Catalina Island to see the remains of an old Chinese junk. Either I elucidate this event as a member of the class of exploratory or curiosity behaviors, or I arbitrarily stipulate that my intending to go to the island to see the junk is equivalent to my actually going to the island and seeing the junk. Neither alternative here is particularly attractive. One denies the singularity of my cognitively unique intention; the other appears to be an empty exercise in substituting behavior for a mental state.

Yet these behavioral translations are what we need in order to give precise descriptions of our intentions. The phenomenologist is hard pressed to provide an alternative. Suppose now that on sighting land I discover that I have arrived at San Clemente Island rather than Catalina. Obviously something more than behavior or an expression of awareness is needed in order to describe this circumstance. The situation is complicated now, for I intended to travel to Catalina, but I actually traveled to San Clemente. Adventitious situational factors such as compass error, wind, sea-drift and so on, may be interjected. Or it may be that I was mistaken about my intention. I thought I intended to go to Catalina, but I really intended to go to San Clemente. In one case behavioral descriptions are insufficient to the task of interpreting my intentions. But then, the adventitious factors can be accommodated to my behavior and the predicament of my doing something I did not intend does not appear to offer an insuperable obstacle for the behaviorist. In the other case, we note that the phenomenologist, as well as the behaviorist, is forced to accept behavioral criteria for describing an intention.

How do we become aware that intentions of which we presumably are aware are not our real intentions? Our reflecting upon the possibility of unconscious intentions and upon a distinction between real and apparent intentions derives from our comparing phenomenological intention and real behavior. The occasion for uncertainty about an intention is dictated by inspection of behavior that is incompatible with that apparent intention. Awareness of an intention, i.e., its mentalistic specifications, is insufficient for placing an intention in an explanatory role. "Mistaken intentions," "unconscious intentions," even "diverted intentions" are meaningful expressions only if we articulate them in the context of appropriate and inappropriate behaviors.

It must be admitted, however, that notions of idiographic description and the explanation of unique action are, for the most part, incompatible with logical behaviorism. The behaviorist is deductivist in his methodology. In the face of presumptively unique actions he has no recourse but to hold to the premise of the generality of phenomena. Thus the unique event is not subject to explanation, except that we place it in the context of general behavioral classes. To be sure, any singular event can be deduced from a unique set of singular premises. But this, we are likely to feel, is a trivial kind of explanation, an empty deductive exercise that fails to satisfy the requirements of classical scientific explanation (Hempel and Oppenheim, 1948). Therefore, if we are to explain unique behaviors at all, we are forced to submit them to the mold of general behavioral laws. Uniqueness of behavior then is explainable in the context of our deriving that behavior by the unique conjunction of general laws and dispositions.

In the matter of providing causal explanations of behavior, the intentionalist hardly fares better. Still, several writers on intention (Melden, 1961; Peters, 1958; R. Taylor, 1966) have argued that intentional explanations involve providing reasons for behavior, and that "reasons for" are not the kind of reasons we look for in the rationalistic exercise of hypothetico-deductive method. In seeking a clarification of this point let us grant initially that the behavior of a subject S can be "explained" by providing intentional (nondeductivist) reasons for it. Let S be a person, and let the "reasons for" his behavior be just those that S can offer in the explanation (justification) of his behavior. Now it must be observed that the reasons-for offered by S have, at least for himself, the property of being psychologically satisfying. They are akin to what Abraham Kaplan (1964) has called "runic explanations." They form the substance of casual discourse about cause. Belonging to personalistic discourse, they are the vehicles of self-justification and rationalization. And they are useful—to the person, perhaps to his auditors. But are they useful in the context of scientific explanation?

Logical behaviorism is clear as to what constitutes an explanation. In embracing hypothetico-deductive methods, it holds that an event E is explained if the statement of E is the logical consequence of the set of statements $\{S_j\}$ consisting of laws, or a formal theory, and stipulations of the state conditions. Thus the statements consisting of the explanation, i.e., the explanans, are clearly of a different kind than statements we offer in the context of intention.

Offering reasons for events in the context of scientific inquiry reputedly reflects a different logical rubric than offering reasons-for in the context of intention. A scientific explanation is logically justifiable if the statement of the event to be explained (the explanandum) is a logical consequence of the set of statements constituting the explanation (the explanans). A scientific explanation is reasonable if it in effect presents sufficient grounds for the occurrence of the event. It is reasonable in the sense it just does provide grounds for deduction of statements appropriately describing the event.

But what, we might ask, are the reasonable grounds of explanation in intentional descriptions? Are reasons-for in this intentional context ever sufficient to explain a behavioral event without prescribing general laws relating an intentional state to behavior? Unless an intention uniformly translates into behavior, we are at a loss to explain behavior by intention. Suppose I say I went to the store in order to get some tobacco. My intention here presumably constitutes an explanation. But "in order to get tobacco" may not have been my "real" reason. Perhaps I went to the store really in order to get some exercise, or to escape the distraction of the house. Perhaps I lied about my intention. Or perhaps I really did not and do not know what my intentions are.

But then what is a real intention? What is an unconscious reason-for? Perhaps an unconscious intention is one I gain access to on some tortuous, therapeutic binge. The ensuing enlightenment offers me an acceptable reason for my behavior in that it befits its calling as a runic explanation. But is it the real reason? Or rather, we ought to ask, is it a sufficient reason-for? After all, the psychodynamics of the unconscious are such as to promote our digressions into self-deception.

What, then, constitutes the revelation of the real reason for my behavior? Accepting runic explanations, as I am prone to do, I am never reassured against the prospect that each and every runic explanation conceals an access to real reasons. Granting the dynamics of unconscious concealment, what comfort can I take in the ingenuousness with which I and the psychotherapist conspire to claim that the interrogative search is done?

It is clear that intentional reasons-for, if they are to be scientifically fruitful, require the logical imprimatur of sufficiency. Going to the store in order to get tobacco, or in order to get exercise, or in order to inhale the smog I've grown accustomed to are not sufficient conditions for my behavior, for any behavior, unless we can formulate general dispositional principles which translate dispositions into behavior.

Intentions, *per se,* are not enough. We require intentional rules (e.g., Peters, 1958; Mischel, 1964) that are remarkably like the behaviorists' dispositional translations of intention. "If an intention to get exercise under specified conditions, then a walk to the store": this is my intentional rule. And given those conditions, my rule is a sufficient reason for going to the store. Without the rule, I have no logical grounds for speaking of the sufficiency of my reason-for.

Now such rules become embarrassing to the intentionalist, for although his rule provides a logical rubric for his expectations, it differs very little from the conditional argument of a dispositional concept. Giving an intentional reason in a specified context is indeed very much like providing an explanation by recourse to dispositional terms.

In summary, if intention is to be a significant construct in scientific explanation, it needs to be formulated in terms of intentional rules. Intention alone does not provide reasons for behavior. My wanting exercise, in the purity of psychic intention, is neither sufficient nor necessary for my going to the store. If the intentionalist should retreat into a kind of uncodifiable psychic determinism, he is (as Guthrie said of Tolman in a somewhat similar context) inviting the person to remain buried in thoughtful intention. "I intended to go, but obviously I did not." Either I am misusing "intention" or intention has no relevance for the explanation of behavior.

NOTE 6.6

(a) As concerns the inevitable note on voluntarism, it should be emphasized that the foregoing argument does not entail our adopting a libertarian or free-will point of view. Just as Born, Schrödinger, and even Eddington have failed to find in indeterminancy the basis of a moral theory of free-choice, so we can find nothing in our argument to support the idea that indeterminancy for S entails S's being free. There is perhaps personal evidence for "feeling free," but, that, of course, is not what we mean by being free in the sense of transcending events in a causal rubric.

The point to consider is that in the role of S none of us can appropriately apply deterministic models to our own decision making. Feeling free in this sense of essential indeterminancy means only that we must participate immanently in the making of decisions. As an S we individually must decide what to do, not predict. In this there is responsibility. But I do not see how in this context we can any more speak of being free than we can speak of being determined. The complementary of determinism is not freedom. To say we are indeterminate is not the same as saying we are free.

(b) There are other puzzles of self-involvement; e.g., trying to introspect the act of contemporary introspection. But consider a well known drawing of Ernst Mach (*The Analysis of Sensations*), reproduced with a small but significant addition in Karl Pearson's popular *The Grammar of Science* (1892). In the sketch, Professor Mach attempts to draw faithfully what he sees with his left eye from the vantage of a reclining chair. Thus the drawing includes the eyebrow, the bridge of the nose and the moustache at closest possible range. In the foreground we see the professor's coat, vest, extended trousers, and shoes. In the background are the details of the room. In Pearson's reproduction a significant feature is added. Over the bridge of the nose appears an easel, a sketch pad and Professor Mach's hand, sketching what he sees.

Now our puzzle is this: Can Professor Mach sketch what he sees? Certainly if we were to insert a camera at the pupil of Mach's left eye we should get a faithful photographic reproduction of what he sees with that eye. Then why shouldn't he be able to draw the photographic sketch of what he sees? Let us reflect. In order to reproduce what he sees he must of course reproduce the very sketch he is making since it falls in the view of the left eye. Let us suppose that his pen rests just at the point of his concluding his sketch. In the main sketch, the one reproduced, we have a sketch of what Professor Mach sees, including the sketch pad on which the main sketch must be reproduced. Therefore, the main sketch itself must be reproduced on the drawing of the sketch pad.

But note now that what Professor Mach sees is not merely a sketch pad, but a reproduction on the sketch pad of what he sees. Since this, too, is part of what he sees, he must include it as well in his main sketch. So his main sketch must contain a sketch of itself on the sketch of the sketch pad. This too, of course, is seen and must be included not only in the main sketch but also in the sketch of the main sketch. Since the main sketch must contain the sketch itself of all that is seen, it is incomplete since it cannot sketch the relation of itself to the sketch of itself, which, of course, is something that can be seen.

Since sketching sketches may be confusing, let us try the tactic of relations. Suppose I try to do the impossible and sketch the relation of the sketch itself to what is seen. This I attempt by taking my sketch and reproducing it in miniature upon the sketch of my sketch pad. But then that sketch stands once removed in relation to the sketch of what I am sketching. Although I may attempt to sketch what I am sketching, I cannot sketch the relation of what I am sketching to what is sketched.

Thus, to reiterate, I have my main sketch and a sketch of my sketch and the one stands in the required relation to the other. But my main sketch is of what I see. So my main sketch must sketch a main sketch and a sketch of a main sketch and show that relation. But that relation too is something I see and must be included in my main sketch. And thus there is no end to my sketching. My sketch is never completed for it must always include a relation, that of itself to a sketch of itself, never included in the main sketch!

Apropos of simulation, we might assign a mechanical computer the task undertaken by Professor Mach. It too could look out from the left eye, photograph what it sees and promptly attempt to reproduce that photograph in miniature, and then insert it where we behold Mach's sketch pad. Thus we would have a photograph of what the left eye sees, and a reproduction of it, generated by a photographically guided stylus, emulating the task Mach set out for himself. But now, of course, we have a different visual display and the photograph does not record what is seen. A photograph cannot show the relation of itself to its own reproduction. Thus the simulator fails as Professor Mach fails; it cannot reproduce what it sees, if it sees its own reproduction.

NOTE 6.7

We are not at loss for critiques of classical behaviorism, nor for admonitions to utilize cognitive and intentional constructions (Rogers, 1955; May, 1963; Mischel, 1963, 1964; Ossorio, 1966). What remains unclear is how such critiques and proposals are to result in formulations that represent genuine innovation upon the deductivist paradigms of scientific explanation. Consider, for example, a paper by Mischel (1964) in which he proposes that a distinction between intentional or rule-following explanations and the more traditional nomothetic (deductivist) explanations requires that the clinician adopt tactics different from those of the traditionalist in behavioral science. The argument puts in relief the very issues we have attempted to deal with in terms of dispositional laws.

Mischel approaches the argument by means of a critical defense of Kelly's theory of personal constructs (1955). The person's behavior is anticipatory rather than reactive. Anticipation is a function of personal constructs, of how the person construes his world, individuals, and situations. But Mischel insists that personal constructs are in themselves insufficient to explain a person's action. In addition, we require a construct of evaluation and a rule which accommodates the intended action of the person. In this he is in fundamental agreement with other intentionalists.

Mischel now takes up the argument that there is something fundamentally different between inference, prediction, and explanation made from rule-following behaviors and those made from lawful or hypothetical rules. Moreover, there are allegedly logical differences between explanations in terms of personal constructs and intentions and those in terms of nomothetic descriptions and general laws (Meehl, 1954), the differences presumably resting in the idiosyncratic vantage of personal constructs. Thus Mischel writes:

> Personal constructs explain behavior not by showing that such behavior data are deducible from these constructs in conjunction with general principles, but by showing that such actions are intelligible because this would seem the right thing to do if one construed this way. Since such explanations are based on the content of the rules an agent follows in making choices, rather than on general laws connecting various kinds of happenings, they stand in no need of nomothetic laws for their justification (1964, p. 189).

and,

> . . . my argument is a defense of an idiographic approach to clinical activity in that it has tried to show that the use of personal constructs to explain individual behavior is different from, and independent of, the use of general laws (1964, p. 192).

Much of this touches upon our distinction between the two vantages. The reasons the subject may give for his behavior are of a different kind than those provided by a deductive theory. The question to be examined is whether that difference in kind is one of logic, and whether it calls for a radical innovation in the explanation of behaviors qualifying as action.

Consider first the statement: "For rules prescribing what *should be done* cannot (logically) be confirmed or disconfirmed by the facts; unlike hypotheses which describe what *is done,* they cannot be true or false" (1964, p. 184). Here a double fault is committed. One, if rule-following is to be a sufficient explanation of a person's action, even to himself, it must be just that, an inferential rule. Otherwise the rule would offer neither explanatory nor predictive base for either the person or the clinician. Thus, indeed, the efficacy of personal construct and rule-following in making behavior "intelligible" can be assessed on the grounds of the behavioral contingencies. And two, the predicates true or false are no more, no less, assignable to rule-following inference tickets than they are to general laws. In a sense, laws are not true or false, they are representations, with the matter of their extensions left open (Toulmin, 1953). We may falsify laws, to be sure; that is merely to ascertain that the law does not hold for the event or class of events in question. But rule-following too can be falsified if the action stipulated by the rule is not forthcoming. The rules are prescriptive, "they guide and direct [the person's] activity by *evaluating* certain behaviors as the right (appropriate) things to do." But so are all laws prescriptive. A physical law prescribes what a given object ought to do under given conditions. If the object fails to comply, as it were, the law is discountenanced. And so indeed is the rule if the person does not himself comply. The rule is discountenanced because it does not provide sufficient ground for the *person's* understanding why he acted as he did.

Admittedly, the problem of vantages remains. Rules specifying that I ought to do so and so because of my beliefs are formulated in an epistemological setting different from that of "rules" which objective phenomenon follow (as prescribed by our laws). But the inference chain is

just as compelling, just as logically unexceptionable, if we are to use a
rule in the rational sense of explication. A rule which one whimsically
does or does not follow, that is a rule that does not entail a given action,
is not a rule at all. It is not even a rationalization. In this context Mischel
writes:

> Because one end of the fear versus domination construct is "valued"
> over the other, the construct functions as a rule in terms of which
> I can decide what I *should do* about someone whom I have con-
> strued this way. The construct "governs" my behavior because it
> is a rule I use in deciding what the right thing for me *to do* is.
> Thus my fear versus domination construct not only leads me to
> *classify* the boss with respect to this dimension, it also leads me to
> see this dimension as the one in terms of which *I must act* . . .
> (1964, p. 185).

Now a rule which specifies what I ought to do does not entail an
action, any more than valuing an end implies that I will attempt to
achieve it. Thus, to get from *ought*, or should, to *must*, we interject the
logical convention of entailment. Our representation of the connection
between the constructs, anticipating and valuing, and the actual behavior
makes use of a logical connective, the utility of which in this setting is as
subject to falsification as any empirical law. Hence, the most preliminary
assessment of explanations, be they intentionalistic or nonintentionalistic,
is in terms of logical sufficiency. If there is something intuitively, nonlogically compelling about intentional rules, a kind of "should, therefore
must" nonlogical rule, we are at loss to make that kind of rule intelligible.

But there is another matter that we cannot lightly dismiss, and that
is the epistemological difference between an action-rule and a general
law. The methodological behaviorist must treat the problem of action and
intention by resorting to constructive dispositional laws. He cannot publi-
cize the inner vantage. This, of course, is how he treats personal constructs,
cognitive structure, intention, valuation, and so on. Such laws differ epistemologically, not logically, from phenomenological laws dealing with
observable events. They enjoy different semantic pedigrees, if you will, in
the sense that logical constructions and hypothetical constructs differ from
particular terms as to referents. But this is quite another matter than our
implying that the difference is logical. A dispositional law is syntactically
differentiable from a simple law; compare, for example

$$(x) \quad Sx \supset (Cx \equiv Rx)$$

and

$$(x) \quad Sx \supset Rx$$

But that difference is irrelevant to the explication of the compelling transformation rules which are characteristic of syntax, *per se*.

Mischel's argument ultimately devolves on the familiar problem of
nomothetic versus idiographic descriptions. The distinction between events
which are uniquely complex (idiographic description) and those which are
easily classifiable (nomothetic description) is a very useful one to make.
And it undoubtedly is the case that intentionalistic constructions of per-

sonality, that is, description from the inner vantage, may facilitate the task of unique description. However, even so fine a student of idiography as Kurt Lewin (1936) has suggested that the uniquely concrete description of the individual can only be made intelligible against a backdrop of general principles.

NOTE 6.8

Addendum on Awareness

Our discussion of mentalistic mediators has thus far been confined to the language of purpose and intention. Other mentalistic constructs, more or less related to that of intention, are attitude, value, and awareness, especially awareness of response reinforcement contingencies. Recently there have been several notable efforts to introduce awareness as a mediating variable in theories of verbal behavior. In the application of operant conditioning methodology to verbal learning tasks, descriptive behaviorism (Skinner) stipulates that the acquisition of verbal behaviors need only be contingent upon the extrinsic reinforcement schedule. Thus, in important studies in verbal conditioning, Sidowski (1954) and Greenspoon (1955) were able to demonstrate the acquisition of a free operant verbal response (e.g., plural nouns) without, apparently, the subject's being aware of the reinforcement contingency. Others have insisted that this learning without being aware is an artifact due simply to failure to probe satisfactorily the subject's cognitive orientation toward his task. Thus, with more extensive interrogation, subjects do tend to reveal cognitive orientation to the task by the development of reinforcement hypotheses. Indeed it is found that those subjects who become aware of the correct reinforcement hypothesis perform at a level superior to those subjects who remain unaware of the correct hypothesis (e.g., Spielberger, 1962, 1965, 1966; Dulany, 1962, 1968).

The issues of "what is learned" and learning with or without awareness are not crucial to our discussion. Clearly, awareness is a factor in learning, if for no other reason than the realization that if we instructed naive subjects initially that they were to give plural nouns in order to receive the reinforcers "Hm, Hm!" "Good!" and so on, their rates of correct response would immediately approach an asymptote. For these informed subjects we would simply create a response set that would affect their subsequent behavior. Doubtless we would obtain different learning rates between a group of informed subjects and a group of noninformed subjects.

Granting the significance of awareness in the acquisition of verbal habits, the question then becomes: How are we to incorporate the variable of awareness into the conceptual fabric of a theory? Spielberger (1965) recognizes a need for such conceptual mediators, and quotes Chomsky (1959) approvingly on the need to make inferences concerning mediating structures on the basis of the observation of overt response. He does not undertake any systematic effort to incorporate awareness into the propositional structure of a well-formed theory, but he does stress an important epistemological distinction between cognitive theories and descriptive behaviorism. According to descriptive behaviorism, awareness, if it is to be incorporated into our descriptions at all, is included among the dependent variables. It may emerge along with response patterns, but it is not essential in any way to the explanation of response acquisition. However, according to cognitive theories, awareness becomes one of the independent variables upon which the dependent variables, type and rate of response, are contingent. Thus awareness, conceptually, must be incorporated into our behavioral theory. However, as to how awareness is to be fitted into the theory, Spielberger is not clear. He merely differentiates between subjects who are aware and those who are not.

A more systematic effort to incorporate awareness into a theory of verbal conditioning is undertaken by Dulany (1968). In his speculations, awareness becomes a theoretical construct in a "propositional" argument. By "propositional control" Dulany intends to formulate a propositional network which, incorporating constructs of cognition and intention, will ensure a logical inference chain between expressions of independent and dependent variables. The propositional argument therefore represents a syntactical maneuver, one which permits Dulany to set up the rigorous inference chains that we expect of formal theory. Thus he overcomes the difficulties raised in Note 6.4. (Incidentally, an excellent presentation of this "propositional argument," but not in the same terms, is to be found in two works by Stephen Körner, 1964, 1966.)

In outline, Dulany's network theory utilizes the following propositional forms:

$$R = \text{response (response class)}$$
$$RHd = \text{hypothesis of the distribution of reinforcement}$$
$$RHs = \text{hypothesis of the significance of a reinforcer}$$
$$RSv = \text{subjective value of the reinforcer}$$
$$BH = \text{behavioral hypothesis}$$
$$MC = \text{motivation to comply}$$
$$BI = \text{behavioral intention}$$

where values assignable to the forms (from $+1$ to -1) range over the continuum of "supposed to do—not supposed to do." Since some of these forms are subject centered and some are object (predicate) centered, a relational metric can be established between subjective belief, intention, and actual experimental contingencies. In brief, a subject should do what he intends to do, i.e.,

$$R = f(BI)$$

But behavioral intention itself is expressed by the complex function:

$$BI = f(RHd, RSv, BH, RH, MC)$$

in which the values of independent variables are either inferred or are operationally assigned. Granting that assignment of value of these variables is operationally sound, then the question becomes one of relating intention to response.

Dulany now asserts that the propositional argument follows laws of logical and quasilogical inference. Thus, in the system of beliefs, a proposition that expresses cognizance of the consequence of a response, and another that expresses a positive value of that consequence to the subject, should imply that the subject intends the action producing the response. But "should" here is open to question. Ability to effect a response and the positive value of the consequence of that response do not logically entail intending the response. As reasonable as the inference chain is, the epistemic bonding of intention to response is either the product of an arbitrary rule, or it gains support on an experiential basis. In either case, we may render intention dispositional.

As troublesome as the logical connections between beliefs, values, and intentions are, that between intention and response is perhaps more problematic. Consider now the propositional argument that if $p \supset q$, and q is what I want, then I will try to implement p, p being in my intentional control. Here p is a response and q, a positive subjective valuation, is the consequent of p. But note that q does not imply p; there is nothing logically compelling about my carrying out an act associated with my subjective intention. For example, I may forget to do what I intended, I may be prohibited from carrying out the act, I may make a mistake by performing some act other than the intended one. I may simply not do what I intend, period! Recognizing these possibilities, Dulany adopts a weaker chain of inference which he calls quasilogical. So the "must" of logical inference is replaced by "should" or "ought" or "frequently does" or any number of other qualifiers on the condition of necessity. Logic, *per se,* he feels will not bridge the mediational gap between intention and response. Thus he must fall back on convention, or on empirics. But in either case, the argument is formulated in dispositional terms. And the logical bridge will be adopted, not because intention somehow transmutes into response, but because there appears to be good pragmatic justification for adopting dispositional translations of the concept of intention.

It is not clear what a quasilogical rule of inference is; what it is, for example, for a rule to resemble yet not be a logical rule. By quasilogical rule it might appear that Dulany is simply adopting the pragmatic tactic of the operationalized, psychophysical relation. The rule itself is, as all rules are, a compelling one. The question of its scientific utility, however, is one of empirical evaluation.

The issue that Dulany attempts to skirt is the old one of the mental and the physical. Regardless of the putative propositional status of the argument, there is an implied ontological commitment involved in his formulation of M (mentalistic mediator) and R (response) propositions. One can, of course, justify propositional arguments on logical grounds, pure and simple. But what is the justification of quasilogical arguments? One might answer, "A conventionalistic justification"; but only if he can get others to adopt his rules of the game. That can be done by giving some conventional interpretation of his propositional forms; or, one might add, by virtue of correlations between supportive empirical observations. In either case Dulany cannot avoid an ontological commitment. The tactic of formulating the argument in terms of syntactical conventions, or in terms of correlated measures does not obviate in any way the questions we may raise concerning propositional designata. For Dulany it appears that $M–R$ propositions are neither mere tautologies nor nonreferential conventions. Propositional forms of M and R have their respective domains of reference. To be sure, that is the case if we treat M propositions as designating something other than verbal reports.

Let us assume for the moment that M and R propositions do have different domains of reference, mind and body. Then $R–R$ propositional complexes are not problematic, for the relations they express pertain to the physical domain. Thus, within the context of Humean skepticism, we may adopt such propositional forms to express our "causal" relations. And presumably the individual may undertake an analogous mapping of his mental experience by complexes of $M–M$ propositions (even though foes of private language may doubt this). But it is not at all clear what an $M–R$ propositional form would designate since the referential domains of M and R differ.

Eschewing the tactics of a dispositional M language in which there are presumptively no mental designata, *per se,* we are forced back on the old formulations of mind and body. We deal with the problem of reference by resorting to parallelism, interactionism, or epiphenomenalism. However, both parallelism and epiphenomenalism render nondispositional M propositions dispensable. And interactionism, we have seen, is suspect even among philosophical intentionalists. Thus, without denying the two domains of events, mental and physical, our defensible recourse is to render M propositions constructual and dispositional.

One suspects the introduction of quasilogical inference to be gratuitous, an effort to exploit the merits of the dispositional conditionals while seemingly paying respects to the relics of dualism. Dulany's propositional argument can of course be a sound one. Admitting operational assessments of the variables contributing to intention, the refinements of prediction and explanation will be contingent upon how explicit we can make our interpretation of intention in purely response terms.

Maltzman (1966) has argued for a strict operational or dispositional interpretation of any putative mentalistic construct. Kanfer (1968) in this context argues against dualism and the mentalistic interpretation of the mediating constructs. And Osgood (1967) offers the telling suggestion that we distinguish between quasilogical rules as heuristic devices and such rules as fundamentally explanatory in an ontological sense. All of these criticisms devolve on the special status of the mentalistic propositions in Dulany's argument. Giving up the ontology, and relying upon conventional dispositional interpretations of such constructs as behavioral-intention, there is no fundamental incompatibility between his position and that of the logical empiricists. One can, of course, appreciate the possibility that the immediacy of awareness, the being-in-ness of his own intentions, feelings, awareness, may provide Dulany the epistemic source for his mediating constructs. The logical empiricist might then counter, however, that the being-in-ness of awareness has no part in scientific argument.

At no place in this work do I wish to argue that consciousness or awareness is unreal, nor to deny the pervading phenomenology of experience. Rather it is a question of how, if at all, we can incorporate phenomenology, *per se,* into our scientific endeavours. Our phenomenology of experience is the source of scientific descriptions and constructions, yet in no context do we incorporate the intrinsic substance of phenomenology, the awareness *per se,* into the scientific description. Thus I have adopted a two-fold semantic of consciousness. Consciousness constitutes the symbolic substance of the world we live in, and consciousness indicates to us that something is going on within the organism, that, in fact, we are viable. This two-fold semantic indeed makes consciousness, or awareness, indispensable to scientific understanding. Being aware of something defines our phenomenological uniqueness apart from the thing of which we are aware; but there is no aspect, no property of our immanent investiture in the phenomenological predicament which can be unambiguously incorporated into scientific description.

Consider, again, the idea of behavioral intention (e.g., Dulany, 1968). Here behavior is to be correlated with, that is, inferred from, a measure of behavioral intention. The tactic of methodological behaviorism is to treat intention as a mediational construct with dispositional properties. Thus from a measure of intention we infer specified behavioral states. And the measure of the intention comes by way of introspective verbal reports in situational contexts. Here the mentalism of intention is nothing more than the heuristic context in which we obtain useful measures for a propositional argument. So long as we argue causally for intention, this is about all we can claim. Intention is a dispositional construct explicitly, *though not implicitly,* interpretable in a physicalistic language. Attempts to incorporate implicit interpretations of intention into the propositional arguments of science are bound to fail.

Consider now the relation of intention to behavior. Dulany, for example, visualizes a measure of behavioral intention which translates causally into expressions of behavior. The relationship, however, as we might expect, is a probabilistic one. So long as intention is inferred from verbal report and situational factors, we have little difficulty with the argument. But suppose we are to imply that there are implicit properties of intention which are causally operative in behavior. Difficulties arise in our analysis.

Dulany (1968), for example, argues that if a person knows what to do in some response contingency situation and if he is motivated to comply, he ought then to intend a specific response. And if physical impediments are removed he should then tend to do what he intends to do. This is all very well if we are dealing with observable and explicit constructs. "Should" and "ought" are then terms that we can translate into functional (logical) relations. On the other hand, we are on unsure grounds if "ought" and "should" are to be handled in a purely mentalistic context.

Consider now some relation expressible as

$$P(R|BI)$$

i.e., the probability of a response of class *R*, given some behavioral intention *BI*. This simple probability function can be made explicit by incorporating *R* and *BI* measures, however derived, into a correlational matrix. But suppose we insist upon an implicit interpretation of *BI*. How do we make sense of a probabilistic relation between the compelling oughtness of an intention and a response class? Several alternatives can be suggested:

(1) *BI* is really only a measure or estimate of a true intention and hence subject to error.

(2) True intentions, indicated by *BI*, may or may not lead to behavior, and the probability function is a measure of the relative frequency with which they do.

(3) A given intention is connected to more than one response class and the probability function is the response weighting function for the given intention.

(4) Intentions are really only partially causal and the probability function is a measure of the partial connection.

Against the possibility of extrinsic interpretations of both *R* and *BI*, none of these alternatives are attractive. Alternatives (2), (3), and (4) do violence to the ideas of oughtness and volitional control inherent in the notion of implicit intention. And alternative (1) can be readily handled by the logico-empiric tactic of dispositional interpretation, *sans* any of the hazards of dualistic ontology.

NOTE 6.9

Bibliographic note:

The phenomenological treatment of intentionality can be found in an increasing number of works including: M. Farber, *Naturalism and Subjectivism*, (1959); M. Farber, *The Foundations of Phenomenology*, (1962); E. Husserl, *The Idea of Phenomenology* (translated by W. P. Alston and G. Nakhnikian) (1964).

For a more recent treatment of intentionality in the context of modern empiricism and logical analysis see: W. Sellars, and R. M. Chisholm, Intentionality and the Mental in H. Feigl, M. Scriven, G. Maxwell (editors) *Minnesota Studies in the Philosophy of Science*, Vol. II (1958); G. Bergmann, *Logic and Reality* (1964).

For a review of Brentano's classical definition of intentionality see: J. J. Sullivan, Franz Brentano and the Problems of Intentionality in B. Wolman (editor), *Historical Roots of Contemporary Psychology* (1968).

Treatment of intention in the tradition of philosophical analysis can be found in the following works: G. E. M. Anscombe, *Intention* (1959); S. Hampshire, *Thought and Action* (1959); A. I. Melden, *Free Action* (1961); R. S. Peters, *The Concept of Motivation* (1958); C. Taylor, *The Explanation of Behavior* (1964); R. Taylor, *Action and Purpose* (1966); P. Winch, *The Idea of a Social Science* (1958); L. Wittgenstein, *Philosophical Investigations* (1953).

For articles critical of the intentionalists' treatment of methodological behaviorism see: M. Brodbeck, Meaning and Action, *Philosophy of Science* (1963), 30, 309–324; D. Davidson, Actions, Reasons, and Causes, *Journal of Philosophy* (1963), 60, 685–700.

Both of these closely reasoned critiques are included in M. Brodbeck (ed.) *Readings in the Philosophy of the Social Sciences* (1968). This admirable collection also includes an extensive bibliography on the nature of human action.

CHAPTER 7

The Argument from Mentalism

IN THIS chapter we deal briefly with mentalism and its role in psychological explanation. To the extent that descriptions of mental processes are to be incorporated into causal rubrics and to the extent they are either semantically or ontologically unique, they obviously become problematic for behaviorism and reductionism. If we adopt reduction as a tactic of explanation, mental predicates are admissible only insofar as they are interpretable or replaceable by predicates in the languages of behavior and neurophysiology.

In the preceding chapter we have seen that intentions are conceived by some to be the defining properties of action. Implicit within the meaning of the action is the intention. Thus, intentional behavior stands uniquely apart from behavioral motions or responses. Since intentions are the interpretive element of actions, they constitute the conceptual framework for cognitive, purposeful explanation. Such intentional explanations are clearly separable from causal explanations. The language of intention being indispensable to the description of the action itself, the intention, as a construct, clearly cannot be distinguished from the action as some kind of mental or physical occurrence participating in a causal rubric. That is to say, an action intentionally described cannot be regarded as being logically independent of the (intentional) conditions which are the occasion for the action. Therefore, as Melden (1961) and Taylor (1964) argue, intentional actions are not amenable to empiricistic causal analysis, i.e., to the Humean paradigm of the concatenation of logically independent events.

There is reason, I believe, to reject this argument on its own presumptions. Fodor (1965, 1968), for example, has argued that, one, there is nothing logically objectionable in treating intentions as causes of action, and two, the Humean conditions of logical independence between a cause and an effect are unrealistically restrictive. On entirely different grounds, we have examined the methodological alternative to the intentionalists'

200

arguments by treating intentions as dispositional terms subject to interpretation in the observational language. Thus the scientific explanation of behavior can be regarded as complementary to the intentional explanation. However, none of our previous arguments has considered the possibility of utilizing mental entities as causal agents or even of utilizing mental constructs to refer to mediational processes that are causal in character.

There is nothing logically proscriptive about introducing mental entities (e.g., willing) into causal rubrics (cf. Eccles, 1953). Indeed, there is nothing objectionable to formulating these mind-body relations as contingent, empirically decidable propositions within deductivist theories of behavior (cf. Luce, 1960). The tactic of reductionism might therefore be a necessarily restricted one, but nothing in mentalistic determinancy itself would prevent articulating the mind-body aspects of behavior and behavioral interpretation in reductive terms. We would simply have to make room for the mentalistic variable that would then be as admissible to the language of neurophysiology as it is to volitional behavior theory.

There is, however, a more serious challenge offered by mentalism. The semantic of our mentalistic language may provide us access to states not readily interpreted in physical terms but which all the same might prove fruitful when incorporated as constructs in psychological theories. Indeed, if we examine classical theories of learning and perception, it is difficult to separate the physical and mental referents of many theoretical terms. What, if any, is the referent, or complex of referents, of the cognitive structure?

First, let us concede that classical treatments of mind and body are somewhat irrelevant to the issues of reducibility. Whether one embraces epiphenomenalism, or materialism, or parallism, or even dualism, there is no clear objection to his objectifying descriptions. His theory of behavior will in fact include objectivistic descriptions of events to the extent those events participate in the action; the mental entities, if required at all (as perhaps in dualism), will then be accommodated as another set of variables to be included within process functions. Difficulties arise, however, on the issue of mentalism as such. Granting mental events and mental terms, either the mental language is dispensable in scientific explanation, or it is not. And granting that it is not dispensable, its indispensability suggests one of two possibilities. Either mental events are independent causal entities, or they somehow betoken underlying processes which are inaccessible to public observation.

Consider first the possibility that mental events are independent causal entities. We have acknowledged that if such entities are indeed causal mediators, the psychologist and neurophysiologist will need in one way or another to take them into consideration. If "having an intention to do R" is the cause of "doing R," a statement relating to having an intention ought to be included in the theoretical explanation of "doing R." However, a description of having an intention may or may not be independent of a description of doing the intended R. In the case that it is not logically independent, then obviously we may resort to a dispositional formulation of the implications of the mental property. This in fact is frequently how we interpret mentalistic terms, as signifying behavior taking place under some state of mind. But what of logically independent mental entities? In this case, intention and behavior are logically separable. Then, according to our Humean skepticism, it would be conceivable that we may intend to do R, and, without behavioral constraints of any kind, fail to do R. We may account for the failure of a physical cause to produce a physical effect by our failing to enlist sufficient factors in the causal complex, or by our not detailing the physical mediational bridge between the onset of a cause and its predicted effect. But what would it mean to request that we account for the failure of an intention to produce the intended behavior if we say the organismic-environmental setting is free of constraint?

But what is equally distressing is that the intention we live through and, by virtue of referential language, are acquainted with is ontologically different from the physical states of the organism. We may understand the causal association between two physical states, or perhaps between two phenomenal mental states, but it is not clear how we can causally associate a mental and a physical state when the two are both logically and ontologically independent. In this case it is less than reassuring to suggest that we can associate the two as empirical contingencies, for how can we be assured that the experiencing of "now do R" and the "doing of R" are ontologically independent events? As I have argued earlier, to experience a mental event causing a physical event, it is not enough to suggest that the two are temporally related. We must experience the two as separable events not only in time, but as distinguishable entities.[1]

"Intending R" and "doing R," if they are to assume roles in a causal rubric, must be distinguishable events. Yet how does one ensure this? Either intending R is immanent or it is known by acquaintance (an argument we need not resolve). In either case it is difficult to describe how "intending R" is epistemologically (and ontologically) separable from "doing R." This is not to say that the task is logically impossible, but as yet no one has succeeded in systematizing a method of self-report which would ensure us that reports of "intending R" are semantically independent of

[1] The point is that an "empirical association" of "intending to do R" and "doing R" is a truly contingent one only if in fact "intending to do R" and "doing R" are referentially independent. In arguing earlier that we do not experience the causal efficacy of "intending to do R," I was suggesting that we are unable in experience to isolate "intending to do R" and "doing R" so as to render them independent separable occurrences. According to the Humean paradigm I do experience the impact of one billiard ball "causing" another to move. But I do not experience intention causing my behavior, even though the two may appear to be juxtaposed. Intention being a mental event and my behavior being physical, I must interpose the mental event of my intention's causing the action. And this experience I do not have.

reports of "doing *R*." Perhaps the failure to achieve this is symptomatic of our intrinsic incapacity to experience an intention independent of the behavior in which it is invested.

MENTALISM VERSUS BEHAVIORISM

There is, however, the other aspect of the argument: mental constructions are methodologically essential to the development of theories in psychology. In a sense this turns the usual methodological argument around. Rather than restricting ourselves to terms with objective observational implications, and to do this for reasons of public agreement, we resort to mental constructions in order to establish mediational bridges over processes for which we can provide no physical detail. We might say that personal motives and intentions are just such mental constructions which, without specifying physical referents, do indeed serve to mediate causally between states of publicly observable events. It may be the case, as perhaps it is in a theory of speech perception or one of problem-solving, that we are unable to specify any material referents for such mental constructs as recognizing or seeing relations. For example, if we should consider as essential to our theory that we postulate some process to cover the activity of recognizing, it may not be possible to specify all members in the myriad of configurations that provide templates for recognition. Recognizing just may be the capacity to see the general in the particular, or to see the particular as exemplification of the general without existentially detailing what the general is.

This is rather a more restrained argument than that of dogmatic phenomenology, which asserts either that there is a logical incompatibility between psychological explanation and physical explanation, or that there are some mental events not in any way representable by a set of behavioral events.

Let us call this the argument of methodological mentalism: namely, there are processes inaccessible to all but direct introspective observation. Represented as mentalistic constructions, these processes function as mediators between publicly observable states in what otherwise would be regarded as classical explanatory paradigms. There are two immediate implications of this doctrine: one, the reduction of psychological theories is, in principle, conceivable; but two, the conceptual focus of psychology is to make psychological explanations general in a way not easily accommodated by theories of specific neural activity. Thus methodological mentalism may admit reductionism in principle, but reject it as a tactic for theories of complex behaviors such as speech, problem solving, and perception.

FODOR: *PSYCHOLOGICAL EXPLANATION*

A well-reasoned defense of methodological mentalism is sustained by Fodor in his recent book, *Psychological Explanation* (1968). This is an excellent work and its argument warrants careful study.

Fodor begins by rejecting the arguments of the analyst Ryle (1949) and the intentionalist Melden (1961). Intentions are something other than criterial catalogues of performances; they do have a real mental status. And intentions may be formulated in such a way as to play a causal role in the explanation of actions. Intentional actions may indeed be more than concatenations of motions, but the purposeful nature of an action is as readily indicated by the nature of its causal constructs as it is by any unique, intentional interpretation of action as independent of causal notions. Thus psychological explanation of intention is possible within the classical paradigms of scientific explanation.

Fodor then proceeds to an examination of behaviorism as a comprehensive tactic of explanation. Ultimately he rejects behaviorism as Procrustean. Some mentalistic constructs are refractory either to behavioral or to neurophysiological reduction.

Now for behaviorism to offer comprehensive explanations of behavior, it must replace all mentalistic predicates with physicalistic ones. Under some circumstances the behaviorist tends to take the substitution of physical predicates for mentalistic ones as logically necessary, under some circumstances as inferential, under still others as empirical. It is necessary initially to distinguish between the logical and the empirical aspects of any putative reduction of mentalistic predicates.

Fodor begins his analysis by stipulating what we may call the *behaviorist postulate:*

> For each mental predicate that can be employed in psychological explanation, there must be at least one description of behavior to which it bears a logical connection (1968, p. 51).

This is a proposition which expresses a logically necessary truth, but the applicability of the proposition may or may not be a necessary truth. That is to say, under some formulations of behaviorism, the truth of the proposition itself may be regarded as analytic, whereas under some other formulations the truth of the proposition may only be contingent. It is essential initially that we distinguish between these formulations.

First consider formulations that postulate the behaviorist proposition as itself being necessarily true. These might take two forms. One is metaphysical behaviorism which asserts that mental states just are physical states, hence an equivalence of mental and physical predicates. This has been a difficult doctrine to defend for two reasons: one, it is *prima facie* indefensible, and two, as the philosophical phenomenologists have insisted, intentional and physical terms have different semantical structures.

But there is another formulation of behaviorism that treats the behaviorist proposition as a necessary truth, that of radical behaviorism. And this Fodor examines in some detail. First, one may adopt a strong form of radical behaviorism and insist that all mental predicates be defined in terms of physical predicates. Hence any mediational "mental" state would be definable as an intervening variable. Thus

$$Sx \supset (\psi x \equiv \phi x)$$

would exemplify such a treatment.

But there is a weaker form of the position in which one may specify both sufficient and necessary behavioral conditions covering the assignment of mental predicates. Whereas etiologically the stronger definitional defense of the behaviorist proposition may be heuristic and conventional, the weaker resort will not be. The mental language is behaviorally contaminated. For example, it is said that one "vacillates in indecision," "bubbles with enthusiasm," "writhes with agony," and so on. Hence the defense of this radical reduction, if any is called for, is just the postulated inseparability of mentation and behavior (cf. Note 7.1). The object of radical behaviorism is to free us of the need to interpret response states in other than behavioral terms. Hence, for the generic description of "writhing with agony" we substitute a description utilizing behavioral predicates only.

It is obvious from this that any expression of radical behaviorism is a denial of mentalism *per se*. Granting mental and physical predicates to be logically different types, then either mental predicates are meaningless as such, or they are clearly dispensable. But now, is not this radical position a significantly restricted one? Not all behavior follows immediately upon the onset of an action-defining situation. One perceives, cogitates, reminisces, recognizes, and so on,—all these experiences occurring, as it were, while behavior is in abeyance. As Fodor writes, ". . . some patterns of explanation require the hypothesizing of psychological events and processes that may be arbitrarily remote from behavior" (1968, p. 86). We need, therefore, to have a closer look at mentalism.

Here Fodor adopts the ingeniously simple tactic of defining mentalism as the denial of the behaviorist postulate. Thus a person must either be a "behaviorist" or a "mentalist." What is striking is that although behaviorism and mentalism are incompatible, mentalism and materialism need not be. How do we square these seemingly contradictory assertions?

Fodor first observes that mental and behavioral predicates are logically different types. This allows him to formulate the behaviorist postulate. But whereas dualism requires differentiable domains of reference, monism does not. "To maintain that statements about minds and statements about behavior are logically independent is fully compatible with maintaining that mental and behavioral predicates apply to substance of the same kind—for example, either to persons or to physical objects" (1968, p. 58). This being the case, then mentalism is compatible with the ontological doctrine that all substance is material substance. What is logically differentiable are the mental and physical representations of material substance. And since mental and behavioral predicates apply to substance of the same kind, we find compatible "the doctrine that mind states and brain states are contingently identical" (1968, p. 57) (cf. Note 7.2).

We are now ready for crucial stock-taking. Fodor writes:

> The compatibility of mentalism with materialism permits a mentalist to agree that there may be some behavioral events in whose causal explanation mental events figure—for example, because the behavior is the effect of the neurological causes with which, on the materialist's account, mental events are to be identified. But it by no means follows from this that, if materialism were true, considerations of simplicity would require the elimination of mental language from psychological theories. Even on the view that mind states and brain states are in fact identical, the propositions that assert such identities are surely only contingent. Hence, on the assumption that materialism is correct, it would still be the case that there are some true, contingent propositions that cannot be formulated unless mental language is employed: namely, all the propositions that assert of specified mental states that they are identical with specified physiological states. (1968, p. 60)

It seems to me that this is an eminently plausible analysis of mentalism. I find it compatible with our earlier treatment of consciousness as fulfilling a twofold semantic function. Awareness is the vehicle for the ascription of behavioral and other physical predicates, but awareness, as such, also signifies that the brain function is a viable process. This being the case then, certainly we ought to explore the possibility that awareness and the mental language may provide us means for predicating processes inaccessible to observation, but essential to the explanation of both mental and behavioral states. However, Fodor (1965, 1968) has argued that neither behaviorism nor reductionism is a reasonable tactic for psychological explanation. To pursue this argument we need to look at methodological behaviorism.

Methodological behaviorism, as visualized in the present essay, differs from radical behaviorism in that, one, it makes no commitment to the metaphysical identification of the mental and the physical, and two, any postulate that restricts the data language of psychology is at most a procedural one. Although methodological behaviorism rejects dualism, it admits that mental predicates and constructs are allowable as a heuristic resource—but only if it is the case that the hypothesis generated in the mental language has implication in the physical language. Thus Fodor's expression of the behaviorist's postulate is an acceptable one, but only as criterial and prescriptive for ultimate formulation of theoretical constructs. It is important to distinguish between applications of this postulate in our two formulations of behaviorism, for there is a difference between merely accommodating to the embarrassment of mentalism on one hand, and making use of mentalism as a heuristic resource on the other.

But let us turn again to Fodor's argument. As propaedeutic to his own discussion of methodological behaviorism, Fodor examines the idea of skepticism. In the strong form of skepticism, we assert "that we can never have reasons for supposing that mental predicates apply to persons other than ourselves" (1968, p. 61). This is the familiar expression of skepticism, germinal in the writings of Berkeley and critically scrutinized in the modern treatises on "other minds" (Wisdom, 1952; Austin, 1956; Ayer, 1946). As Fodor points out, the concepts of "having reasons for" and "knowing" as concerns the contents of other minds are subject to ambiguity. Hence, he proposes a less dogmatic form of skepticism. By "minimal skepticism" he means the doctrine that one "cannot know with certainty what mental state someone else is in" (1968, p. 61). And more explicitly, "there are some statements about minds, the truth of which is logically independent of the truth of any statement about behavior" (1968, p. 62). Assuming the behaviorist postulate, the implications of minimal skepticism for behaviorism are obvious:

> What behaviorism asserts and mentalism denies is that there must be logical connections between any mental ascriptions and some behavioral ascriptions. If we assume with the mentalist that, for at least some predicates, no such connection need obtain, and if we agree to the usage according to which we "know with logical certainty" that someone is in such and such a mental state *only* when the fact that he is in that state is logically implicated by facts about his behavior, it follows immediately that there must be conceivable cases in which we could not know with logical certainty what mental state someone is in. (1968, p. 62)

It also follows that we cannot necessarily determine behavioral or physical states from knowledge of a mental state. Hence, according to the skeptic, inference between mental and physical states is at least in some cases contingent, and therefore logically fallible.

It is this logical fallibility that weakens the behaviorist's position. The behaviorist may adopt as necessary rules of inference logical equivalences or implications between ascriptions of mental and physical states (as indeed his methodological tactic dictates) but the applicability of the rule is itself contingent. Thus the logical instructions of his tactic are clear-cut: for mental states we may substitute physical states. But the success of this tactic is not itself a matter of logic, it is assessable only as an empirical contingency.

Just as in the case of Fodor's treatment of mentalism and materialism, this seems to me to be an eminently satisfactory argument. The methodological behaviorist is bound by his logical conventions for connecting descriptions of mental and physical states. But whether his physicalistic reduction is complete, whether there remain physical lacunae accompanying the description of mentalistic mediation, is a question for empirical assessment. Recall from an earlier discussion that a paradigm for the dispositional interpretation of a mental predicate is:

$$SxIx \supset (Cx \equiv Rx)$$

Here we insist that an indication of the intentional state I is empirically indispensable to our defining the situational conditions in which the response complex R is to implicate the mental construct C. The occurrence of the intentional state I, in conjunction with situational conditions S is sufficient for invoking our conventional rule. But obviously the rule applies only if the response R occurs. The adequacy of the tactics of methodological behaviorism, like this one of the behavioral translation of dispositional terms, is contingent upon whether, for all meaningful states I, there are conventional physicalistic translations to render the languages of mentalism and physicalism coextensive.

Fodor's analysis is thus a poignant one for any tactic of methodological behaviorism. It is essential that we separate the logical aspects of the behaviorist postulate from the empirics of its tactical application. The question of the comprehensiveness of behaviorism then becomes an empirical matter. This, then, is the crux of the matter: Are there mental states which in fact are intractable to the tactics of methodological behaviorism? Fodor believes that there are. Even accepting materialism, he believes that some constructs in the mental language are conceptually indifferent to assimilation within the behaviorist postulate. Two issues must now be confronted. In light of minimal skepticism, how can we be assured of the reliability of mentalistic reports? And what precisely are examples of mental predicates or mental constructs that are refractory to behavioristic paradigms?

First consider the question of the reliability of mentalistic reports. Fodor adheres to the tradition of deductivistic and causal explanations for psychology. Thus, if mental constructs are essential to psychological explanation, and if we are to attest to their reliability, say, by recourse to the behaviorist postulate, they must be ascertainable by direct apprehension. In the face of skepticism Fodor now resorts to what he calls "moral certainty."

> In short, then, the minimal skeptic and his mentalist ally need not admit that, because we are often certain what mental state someone is in when we have observed his behavior, there must therefore be a logical connection between behavioral and mental ascriptions. The dilemma that the behaviorist poses for the skeptic—either there is a logical connection between mental and behavioral predicates, or else our certainty about some mental ascriptions is inexplicable—may properly be said to rest upon an insufficiently subtle appreciation of the varied ways in which such words as "certain" work. (1968, p. 66)

Moral certainty is a matter neither of formal nor informal logics. Just as a person is certain about his marital status, date of birth, and his own visual imagery, so he is certain that "truth of statements of one sort should provide reasons for believing statements of another sort." As to the connection between mental states and physical states, we cannot be logically certain, nor even empirically certain, for mental events are the subject of minimal skepticism. But we can be "morally certain": one, there is direct access by me to my mental states; two, contingent relations can be provisionally established between mental and physical states; and three, I can express the proposition that there is reason for inferring a mental state without stating that "being in a physical state" logically entails "being in a mental state." Fodor is able to establish the reasonableness and the utility of psychophysical propositions without succumbing either to skepticism or to a restrictive objectivism.

This less-than-logical "certainty," which incidentally the methodological behaviorist might also accept, should then not prove restrictive if for all mental states we have reason for inferring physical states, and vice versa. However, although we may have reasons for inferring the state of a person's mind from a set of organic and physical conditions, it by no means follows that it is always possible to find those relations which enable us to establish logical rules relating mental statements to physical ones. Thus it may be that not all mental statements are directly interpretable in terms of physical statements. And mental predicates themselves may stand as uniquely indispensable to psychological explanation. Possible examples occur in the case of utilizing mental states as mediators between physical states of the organism or between other mental states, themselves less remote from physical affairs than the mediator. Hence mediational theory, as in the case of verbal learning or speech perception, may utilize mental constructs that are only remotely related to isolable physiological or behavioral states.

Thus Fodor writes:

> For example, if it is possible to demonstrate the occurrence of psychological phenomena for which the simplest available explanation requires us to hypothesize the occurrence of mental events that do not exhibit behavioral correlates, then, since even the weakest variety of behaviorism requires at least that such correlates exist for each type of mental event, we shall be in a situation of forced choice. In particular, we shall be required either to abandon the explanation or else to abandon the methodological principle that forbids explanations of that type. (1968, p. 79)

As a case in point Fodor chooses the example of speech perception. The flow of a familiar language is perceived not as a torrent but according to a generally specifiable pausal structure. In explaining this fact one postulates "very abstract and complex mental operations." "Although these operations are of course inferred from their behavioral effects (e.g., from the data about where pauses are perceived), there is no serious possibility of assigning individual behaviors as criteria, or even as correlates, to each such operation." (1968, p. 81)

Now according to the theory Fodor presents, the perception of pausal structure in speech is a function of the "constituent structure" of the sentence at the point of the pause and is independent of the acoustical properties of the speech itself. Hence, pauses tend to be heard between words rather than within words, between well-grouped phrases rather than within phrases, and so on—and this, in spite of the novelty of the sentence. Groupings, for example, are heard according to subject, transitive verb, transitive verb and object, where the groupings are determined by the "constituent boundaries." Sentences are frequently novel, and for experimental purposes may even be contrived as nonsensical; still, they are perceived with constituent structure. Something more than familiarity and learning are involved.

According to the theory, the constituent structure of a sentence is "specified by the rules of certain sorts of grammars." The familiar language incorporates these grammars. "In particular, understanding a sentence in one's native language involves using such rules to assign appropriate constituent analysis and it is that assignment, in turn, that dictates the perceived pausal segmentation the sentence bears." (1968, p. 83) These rules are superimposed on the perception of speech, simply because they are in accord with how individuals do in fact perceive speech. They are not, however, rules of which the person is aware. Nor is the person aware of how he applies such rules in the perception of speech. Hence there is the need to postulate unconscious operations and a kind of unconscious inference.

> More to the point, it is clear that there are no behavioral *correlates* for such operations and *a fortiori* no behavioral *criteria* for them. That is, just as it is patently false to assume that each assignment of brackets to some stretch of a sentence is associated with some disposition to provide a verbal report of that assignment, so it is also false to assume that such bracketings are associated with characteristic forms of nonverbal behavior. Behavior is produced when the sentence is understood, if it is produced at all; thus, individual mental operations are related to behavior only via the entire computational process of which they form a part. The justification for positing such operations in a psychological explanation can be, then, neither that subjects report their occurrence nor that some nonverbal behavioral index of their occurrence has been observed. Rather, we posit such operations simply because they are required for the construction of an adequate theory of speech perception. (1968, p. 84)

The conclusion we may draw from Fodor's analysis of the psychological explanation is obvious. We must adopt constructs of mental operations not meaningfully reducible either to behavior or to neurophysiology.

COMMENT

In the preceding pages we have reviewed Fodor's critique of behaviorism, as I understand it. It makes the crisp differentiation between rules as logical structures and rules as pragmatic instruments. It formulates the behaviorist postulate to serve either as a metaphysical or as a methodological precept. And it states clearly the conditions that must be met if mentalism and the language of mental predicates are to be accommodated within the tactics of behaviorism. The substance of the critique, however, is that there are some mental predicates, and some hypothetical processes which are essential to some classes of psychological explanation but which remain refractory to any behaviorist program of reduction.

Initially, let us agree that linguistic behavior, perception of speech, perceptual invariance are complex processes indeed. As yet we have little confidence that they will succumb either to behavioristics (Chomsky, 1959, 1967) or to the electrode implant and the polygraph. Still, we may have reservations that mental constructions themselves will prove edifying. Mental processes are either hypothetical or they are known existentially by a vague sense of being aware. If the former, they are hypothetical constructs. As such they are no more ontologically significant, no more precedental than those we wistfully postulate for neurophysiological theory. If they are the latter, they will be edifying only if we can tie them to familiar models of functional inference.

(1) First let us consider unconscious processes and unconscious inference. Fodor is primarily concerned with theories of linguistic behavior and the perception of speech. Here, as Chomsky (1959, 1962, 1967) has indicated, the perception and understanding of speech is a complex process in which unconscious operations are involved. The constructs we utilize are mentalistic in at least two senses: one, they deal with the understanding of signs and syntactical structures that are only latently, if at all, involved with conspicuous behavior, and two, they are associated with some vague apprehension that we have of unconscious inference.

Now it seems to me that "unconscious inference" is constructually just where all mentalistic theories are weak. What clearly distinguishes unconscious or tacit (Polanyi) inference from conscious or explicit inference is that we just do not know, we cannot detail any explicit sets of inferential procedures that lead to the intelligent understanding. Generally throughout the history of psychological theory the resort to unconscious inference has in effect been to insert a place-holder in theoretic explanation, an opaque device to somehow account for the *a priori* capacities of the organism to process input. The "somehow" however is the somehow of our ignorance. As a construct, unconscious inference signifies the hiatus in the theoretic understanding. It is the provisional hypothesis, not as to *how* some inferential process is implemented, but only as to the fact that some such process *is* implemented.

There is an important corollary to this predicament. Just as in unconscious inference we have some vague awareness that cognitive structuring is emergent, so in some types of problem solving we have a salient yet vaguely specifiable sense of insight—awakening to the renowned "aha" experience. Thus it is often thought that introspection and the predicates of a mental language are indispensable to the explanation of problem solving. Yet here again, all that we have is an indication of a hiatus in our understanding. The sense of having the insight, the aura of the pervasive "aha," may indeed indicate to us that insight has been achieved, but in no way does it provide a sense of understanding *how* that insight is realized. Introspection in this case informs us that insight has been achieved in problem solving, but it remains uninformative, all the same, unless it reveals the cognitive procedures by which problematic inference is implemented.

To be sure, reports of the "aha" experience and descriptions of the unpredictable flash of insight that play such an important role in the anecdotal accounts of creative thinking will not be helpful to biophysicists who visualize problem solving and ratiocination as being realizable as nerve networks. For the biophysicists, the mechanics of unconscious inference must be detailed. But, on the other hand, perhaps insight and intuition just are processes not representable by inferential schemata, at least not by ones known to us in formal logic, computer technology, or heuristics. If this is the case, then there are two obvious alternatives open to us: one, we can leave the matter ensconced in ignorance; viz., there is some inferential process which in principle is opaque to understanding; or two, we can proceed to the task of generating theoretical constructs for the purpose of explaining what as yet we do not understand. The first alternative is defeating. The second alternative will get no help from a self-inspection which is limited *only* to knowing that insight has occurred.

I would propose therefore that as a matter of theoretic tactics we should agree to exploit our recourse to introspectionism and to mentalism. But the hypothesis we find accessible by such a route will prove fruitful to understanding only as it relates to possible physical systems. Accepting materialism, as Fodor appears to do, this seems to be a reasonable tactic. Fodor is right in suggesting that the proper role of the psychologist is to develop rigorous "phase-one theories," and where fruitful, by recourse to mental predicates. However, it is difficult to see how such phase-one theories will contribute to any enduring understanding unless they also provide hypotheses as to reductive, phase-two theories. What should discourage us from uniquely mentalistic constructs and theories is not that mental data, *per se,* are unreal or illusory, or for that matter intractable to public verification, but that, in themselves, these data provide us no information as to how insight, intuition, knowing, perceiving, sensing, and so on, take place.

Only when we put mentalism to work, so to speak, can we hope to achieve an understanding of mental processes. There is substantial evidence from perception, epistemology, and scientific understanding to indicate that the *a priori* is indispensable to structuring of experience and knowledge. Two alternatives are then open to us. We can accept Kantian skepticism in the belief that *a priori* structuring of experience is inexplicable, or we can follow Craik, among others, in the belief that *a priori* structuring itself is subject to understanding by "mechanical" explanation.

(2) And what should we say of "moral certainty"? If we can be morally certain without the logical sanctions of certainty, why not utilize this kind of certainty to support our rules of inference? That is to say, if we can be morally certain about contingent associations between mental and behavioral states, why should we not adopt the tactic of the dispositional translation of mental terms and thereby utilize conventional rules in the assignment of mental constructs? In this way the behaviorist may assimilate mentalism without the explicit denial of mental constructs. Nor need he then deny mentalism as an important epistemological resource.

For Fodor, this tactic is unsatisfactory. If these coventional rules are to be useful they must be of a form such as "if X causes pain to Y, then Y is disposed to avoid X," or "if S intends Y, then S is disposed to do Y." He maintains that despite such rules no description of behavior, as such, will entail a dispositional description such as "S is disposed to do Y." The behavioral description necessarily requires mentioning S's being in a mental state. Thus, in Fodor's argument, the behavioral description, to be purely behavioral, would have to describe a disposition without reference to mentalistic states that are essential for defining how phenomenal input is to be structured into the configurations that are supportive of the behavioral data. If Fodor is correct, we must then substitute for "S is disposed to do Y" some expression purely of physical phenomena without reference to "doing," or even to "Y," if by "Y" we designate a meaningful behavioral action taking place.

I do not believe this criticism proves particularly damaging to the tactics of methodological behaviorism unless perhaps we assume that there is, or should be, a neutral behavioral data language independent of our conceptual focus. Although Fodor is inclined to accept the possibility of such a data language, I think this assumption is quite unrealistic. What any psychologist, behaviorist or not, brings to observation is a conceptual bias. His observations are the product of input processed by perceptual schemata. Hence behaviorists are molar or molecular, as the case may be, purposive, reflexive, contiguity or reinforcement oriented. What is perceptually reified as behavior is clearly a function of how the investigator is prepared to process and structure his sensory input.

Granting that behavioral language is conceptually contaminated, I see no difficulty in establishing the connection between having a mental state about doing something and the doing of that something, where the latter is intentionally defined. Nor does Fodor, for that matter. But then, need we accept the appraisal that intentional descriptions of response prove an embarrassment to the behaviorist? What the methodological behaviorist insists upon is that the construct language, as well as data language, should be amenable to physicalistic reduction. He need not deny, nor be embarrassed by, the mentalistic overtones of his epistemology. Like the methodological solipsists of the Vienna Circle days, he may well insist that methodological behaviorism is the tactic for publicizing what etiologically is a matter of private access. But in converting what is private and what is mental into matters of public understanding he is, in fact, achieving an understanding in no way made explicit within mentalism itself.

(3) Finally, there is the point at which Fodor's efforts to put methodological behaviorism into a neat logical rubric lead to some mistaken critiques. A strict application of the behaviorist postulate, even if methodological, leads to the elimination of all constructs not reducible to observational terms. So restricted, all such constructs would be treated as intervening variables, and so-called mediators without explicit reductions would be eliminated. In this context, Fodor alludes to verbal conditioning, where remote associations presumably are mediated by implicit responses, or by s–r constructs. According to him, the methodological principle is limited by our not being able to translate into strictly observational terms the implicit s–r elements. (On the other hand, if these s–r elements are represented as hypothetical constructs, then, to be sure, their significance is not exhausted by any rules we may adopt for tying them to sets of observable responses.)

This, however, is unnecessarily restrictive of the methodological argument. Just as one can appreciate the Russell precept to replace all hypothetical constructs by logical constructions (i.e., intervening variables), so also can he emphasize that the hypothetical aspects of his constructs present the heuristics for amplifying possibilities as to surplus meaning. It is a mistake to insist that hypothetical constructs are denied to the methodological behaviorist just as it is a mistake to confuse theoretic with construct reduction (Turner, 1967). By construct reduction we mean the explicit reduction of any theoretical term to observational terms; hence the primacy of the intervening variable. By theoretic reduction, on the other hand, we mean the reduction of theoretical terms in one science to terms in a reducing science. Thus in the case of theoretic reduction, hypothetical constructs assume a preeminent role. Being "hypothetical" in character and having an openness of meaning, they serve as hypotheses as to the structure of mediation.

To be sure the behaviorist has been taken to task for his insistence upon constructual reductionism just as he has been taken to task for a rigid operationism. But we should not censure by appellation. A credo that embraces the behaviorist postulate as the reductive goal does not preclude the utilization of open hypotheses as to what might be the details of the mechanisms supporting the reduction. If we are to deny to the methodological behaviorist this recourse, we deprive him of his method. We would demand of all objectivists that they be dogmatic radical behaviorists. And from the tradition of "behaviorism" we would necessarily exclude such exemplars as Lashley, Hull, Spence, Hebb, Osgood, Krech, and many others not nameable at all if not as methodological behaviorists. The point is that we should not deny to the methodological behaviorist the option of incorporating hypothetical constructs into his explanatory rubrics.

In summary, we can agree with Fodor that mentalism is problematical to the methodological behaviorist, if for no other reason than that the latter's prospectus calls for reducing, by logical conventions, all predicates and constructs in the mental language to those in the physical language. But it is one thing to have a prospectus and a credo, and another to adopt heuristic tactics to achieve one's goals. Having accepted materialism, Fodor ironically makes one of the strongest possible cases for mentalism. Yet it is the ontology which weakens the case for the irreducible uniqueness of mental constructs. If indeed the mental and the behavioral language superimpose disparate descriptions on the same fundamental domain of referents, there remains a touch of plausibility in the assumption that the languages yield compatible descriptions. There is substance to the argument that mental constructs are incompatible with behavioral descriptions, in the sense that one conceptual framework may be functional whereas the other is mechanical (cf. Note 7.3). Still, function and the description of functional process provide hypotheses as to underlying mechanics. It may be that a cognitive, personalized language is not altogether consonant with the language of physical explanation, such is the nature of ordinary language. But that is not to say that mental constructions need be "ordinary." Certainly "unconscious inference" and "*a priori* structuring" are not. What makes this mental language significant is that it provides hypotheses as to how we might visualize mechanical systems in a way that a purely physicalistic language does not.

NOTES

NOTE 7.1

As to this type of reduction Fodor writes:

> It is evident that the behaviorist's position will be most defensible (and least interesting) if he permits as behavioral descriptions such

locutions as "eating hungrily," "writhing with agony," or "smiling happily," for it is hardly to be doubted that "writhing in agony" is logically related to "being in agony." Writhe as one may, one is patently not writhing in agony unless it is agony that is causing one to writhe." (1968, p. 53)

This is a curious statement, for indeed agony and writhing are logically related—they are logically related because the mental and empirical referents are inseparable (as anyone who has passed a kidney stone is likely to testify). In the example of writhing in agony, it is not, I believe, a case of a mental event being the occasion or cause for writhing. Even granting their separability as types of predicates, which I find doubtful, they clearly refer to the same event in time (e.g., passing the kidney stone).

But should we not look at agony and writhing as separable "events," *per se?* The plausibility of the behaviorist postulate in this context, and the weakness of Fodor's argument rests in our inability to describe putative mental events precisely in terms of mental predicates. Writhing in agony is like contorting in pain or, let us say "contorting in the presence of pain." Can we then say that pain is separable from the contorting? If so, what is the set of predicates you would use to describe the pain, such that they may be logically independent of predicates in the physical language? To say that a pain is that which hurts or is painful is less than edifying.

Fodor does maintain that causal relations need not entail logically independent events. This is why in fact he can insist upon a causal role for agony or for intention. In the same context, however, this lack of logical independence is the very reason why the behaviorist may think the behaviorist postulate an essential one.

NOTE 7.2

Fodor argues that mental and physical statements, though of logically different types, express representations of material substance. Thus, his ontology is materialistic and monistic; and, initially, it would appear to be compatible with various expressions of the "mental-physical" identity hypothesis (Place, 1956; Smart, 1959, 1963; Feigl, 1950, 1958). To be sure, there are similarities between Fodor's argument and the identity hypothesis, but there are also important differences. Whereas Fodor is critical of methodological behaviorism and reductionism, the identity hypothesis leaves the issues open.

By and large, Place, Smart, and Feigl agree on the identity hypothesis: there are mental statements and there are physical statements; and, though of different logical types, they have common referents. The identity is between a mental process, as reported in the language of awareness and consciousness, and a brain process. But when we say a "mental process is a brain process," we are appropriating the "is" of composition, not the "is" of definition (Place, 1956). The identity is synthetic or empirical, not analytic identity (Feigl, 1958). Although we may hold the identities to be "strict identity" as a working hypothesis, the tenability of that hypothesis is subject to empirical explorations (Smart, 1959). The hypothesis of mental-physical identity thereby presents a prospectus for empirical studies as to correlations between mental and physical descriptions.

Still we must not think that this doctrine lends credence to a naive conception of reductionism. For one thing, mental predicates and physical predicates are of logically different types. Mental descriptions do not logically reduce to physical descriptions. When I say, "I am in pain," I am reporting something irreducibly psychical. Yet concomitant with the raw quality of pain are physical processes describable either as behavioral processes or brain processes. The sentient raw feel we know "by acquaintance," corresponds with the physical process we know "by description (Feigl, 1958). "I am in pain" does not, of course, mean the same thing as "I am having a brain process"; the two expressions have different intentions. On the other hand, there is nothing contradictory in my denying dualism or in my asserting that consciousness *is* a brain process. The difference in the logical types of our two sets of statements does not entail an ontological difference in their referents. Indeed, there is identity in the world referents, an identity in world happening. Hence, as Smart suggests, the having a visual experience is "like what is going on" when I have a brain process appropriate to the world condition of such an experience. And a person may report his having a visual process without at the same time having knowledge of his brain process, even though there is an identity bond between the two processes.

Yet, whereas logical or ontological reduction may not be feasible, it by no means follows that methodological behaviorism or methodological reductionism, as expressed in the body of our text, is likewise infeasible. Because of their privacy, mental descriptions present "nomological danglers," not subject to public verification except through incorporation into the nomological network appropriate to physical descriptions over the common identity bond. Because of the identity of referents, mentalistic descriptions may provide access where physical descriptions are missing. The nomological rigor of our descriptions is secured by the prospects of finding physical constructions over the domain of world happenings identical for logically disparate descriptions. In a word, there is no incompatibility between the identity hypothesis and the notion that mental descriptions provide a heuristic for physicalistic descriptions acceptable to the methodological behaviorist.

In a reference to the identity hypothesis, Fodor (1968, p. 112) is critical of Place's notion of "compositional" identity. One cannot, he argues, establish the empirical identity between a mentalistic statement of a psychological function and statements of material process. The one is functional and the other mechanical. And although functional descriptions of motives, intuitions, strategies, and the like do not preclude adducing functional constructions of neurological processes, these pescriptions do not entail that there must be microanalyses of the functional concepts in neurophysiological terms.

Fodor is, of course, correct. But to stress the logical independence between functional and mechanical descriptions appears to suggest that psychology need not be bound by any commitment to realism. The identity theory can hardly be so indifferent, for it stipulates that mental statements and physical statements have a common referent. Hence the pragmatics of our merely adducing workable mentalistic hypotheses independent of the referent common also to a physical process will not suffice. Without the common anchoring, mental constructs are subject to elimination in all those cases where reductive or verificatory criteria can be utilized to sharpen Occam's razor.

Although identity theorists are critical of naive conceptions of microreduction, just as Fodor is, they must admit the relevance of the empirical search for an identity base between the mental and physical. And it is hardly to be questioned that the conceptual framework generated in the mental language will facilitate that search for the corresponding physical process.

This point is nicely adumbrated in a reference Place (1956) makes to certain comments of Sherrington (1947). Sherrington suggested that the impossibility of accounting for conscious process in terms of the properties of the nervous system stems from the fact that such properties do not accommodate the phenomenological experience of the perceiving self. That, however, is just the point; the conceptual framework of simple physical processes in Sherrington's time was insufficient to the task of reifying complex critical processes. Recent developments concerning the nature of cortical function clearly suggest that crisp descriptions of mental functions have facilitated the empirical search for brain processes.

NOTE 7.3

A feature of Fodor's argument that we have not stressed is the distinction he makes between phase-one, functional explanations, and phase-two, mechanical ones.

Consider first the argument he undertakes in his 1965 article "Explanations in Psychology." In this work Fodor initially concurs with the idea of alternative explanatory rubrics for behavioral analysis, but he rejects reductionism as the proper calling of psychologist *qua* psychologist. First he distinguishes between the explanation of molar behavioral actions and the causal analysis of molecular movement. One domain of explanation properly belongs to psychology, the other to neurophysiology. As concerns reductive explanations of behavioral actions he states " . . . though such reduction is not possible in principle, this fact nevertheless is compatible with the unity of science" (1965, p. 161). It is not altogether clear what the unity of science is in this context other than concerted agreement as to a material world known through diversified empirical methodologies. But the rejection of reductionism is clear-cut. The language of psychology and the language of neurophysiology deal with separable "events."

As to the character of psychological explanations Fodor proposes that we go to the texts. "Psychological explanations are what psychology texts supply. If you want to know what a psychological explanation is, go and look." (1965, p. 163) Such a look will reveal that these explanations are often functional in nature. But Fodor has more in mind that the standard texts. He also refers to the literature of intention (Hamlyn, 1962) wherein an explanation of behavior invokes a reason for the action and hence an interpretation of physical events in other than strictly objectivistic terms. "Roughly: the appropriateness of our explanation is determined not by the phenomena it seeks to account for but by the question it seeks to answer." (Fodor, 1965, p. 165)

Between psychology and its putative reduction, the distinction is to be made on functional dimensions. A behavioral act is describable according to its molar functional properties. As such it is conceptually defined within the behavioral system. In this context, " . . . *not even so basic a notion as that of a response can be characterized in terms of movements alone."* (1965, p. 168) But then Fodor returns to the traditional critique of reductionism. One may utilize constructs of "internal states" to develop a functional theory of behavior without these constructs being reducible to physiological states. The two languages do not have a common conceptual base.

Fodor then distinguishes two phases in psychological theory: phase one concerns functional analysis, a second phase concerns a model, the physiological interpretation, of a theory adopted in phase one. As to phase one Fodor writes:

> Phase-one psychological theories characterize the internal states of organisms only in respect of the way they function in the production of behaviour. In effect, the organism is thought of as a device for producing certain behaviour given certain sensory stimulations. A phase-one psychological explanation attempts to determine the internal states through which such a device must pass if it is to produce the behaviour the organism produces on the occasions when the organism produces it. . . . It follows too that the evidence to be adduced in favour of the claim that such states exist is just that assuming they do is the simplest way of accounting for the behavioural capacities the organism is known to have.
>
> It should be noticed that explanations afforded by phase-one theories are *not* causal explanations, although a fully elaborated phase-one theory claims to be able to predict behaviour given sufficient information about current sensory stimulations. Phase-one explanations purport to account for behavior in terms of internal states, but they give no information whatever about the mechanisms underlying these states. (1965, p. 173)

Although Fodor does not then go so far as to agree with J. A. Deutsch (1960) "that the production of phase-one theories exhausts the psychologist's professional responsibilities" (1965, p. 175), he clearly feels that the responsibility for modeling the psychological theory in neurophysiological terms is that of the physiologist, not the psychologist. After all, "a characteristic feature of phase-one explanations is that they are compatible with indefinitely many hypotheses about the physiology of the organism." (1965, p. 174)

So far as one admits the role neurophysiology plays in "modeling" the psychological theory, I find nothing particularly exceptionable in this account of psychological explanation. Indeed, it is conducive to pointing up a heuristic symbiosis between the two disciplines, psychology and neurophysiology.

What is exceptionable is Fodor's apparent equivocation as to whether neurophysiology can accommodate the functional constructs and observation language of behavioral analysis. We have shown clearly, I think, that intentional and other motivational constructs are susceptible to dispositional translations. Moreover, it is the dispositional term that encourages us to look for appropriate functional systems in the structures and processes of neural function. It would be unwarranted simplification to assume that neurophysiology must be restricted to elemental causal rubrics, to reflex chains. And it is a misconstruction of the functional argument to say that "the explanation of behavior requires reasons while causal explanations provide not reasons but causes" (1965, p. 170). To be sure, we may offer reasons for behavior, but surely nothing in the language of psychology prevents our providing (phase-one) functional descriptions over the domain of events for which we may offer "reasons." And in turn, there is nothing to prevent our providing neurophysiological theories to model the phase-one theory.

But there is a more immediate objection to Fodor's argument. The assertion that there are "indefinitely many hypotheses about the physiology of the organism" implies that basic language of physiology is independent of that of psychology. Should we then not say, on similar grounds, that there are indefinitely many biochemical hypotheses about biogenetics independent of molar Mendelian genetics? For is it not true that the concept of the genotype is epistemologically independent of biochemistry? The point worth considering is that the hypothesis of neurophysiology, just as the hypothesis of biochemistry, would be sterile indeed if it were constricted by our vision that neurophysiology is an independent, autonomous discipline. I am arguing, of course, that the hypothesis of neurophysiology is not at all independent of that of psychology. Histology might prosper without the theoretic lucubrations of the psychologist, but not, I think, a viable neurophysiology.

In effect Fodor offers us three alternatives for explanation: intentional explanation ("reasons for" behavior); functional explanation (psychological); and reductive explanation (neurophysiological). In context each of these forms of explanation offers unique response to an appropriate inquiry. Yet even in their uniqueness, I would maintain, these responses offer compatible explanations. And they may be interdependent as well. Both psychology and neurophysiology may profit by exploiting this conceptual interdependence.

Another aspect of Fodor's argument should be noted. He proposes that both the theory and the metatheory of psychology are subject to empirical disconfirmation. Generally there is little question concerning a scientific theory; a viable theory must be subject to disconfirmation (Popper, 1935). But what of metatheoretical questions? Assume some general metatheoretical proposition, P; one, for example, that asserts that all that which we regard to be behavior is drive reductive. Fodor wishes to claim that such propositions as *P* are subject to disconfirmation.

> I want to claim that not only psychological theories, but also the metatheory of psychology may, in the relevant sense, be subject to empirical disconfirmation. To show that learning can occur without reward is to show both that some behaviour is *not* directed towards the reduction of drive and that an account of psychological explanation according to which explaining learned behaviour invariably consists in showing how it affects drive reduction is an inadequate account. (1965, p. 164)

Thus Fodor goes against the tradition that metatheoretical questions are analytic, subject to arbitration perhaps but not resolvable as candidates for empirical disconfirmation. So long as we confine the discussion to theories of a given kind; e.g., drive reduction theories, there is some justification for the argument. For example, the metatheoretical hypothesis that a reward is necessary for response acquisition initially appears to be open to disconfirmation.

However, two comments on this argument: one, it is not clear that the metatheoretical hypothesis (postulate) is subject to disconfirmation, and two, metatheoretical questions deal as much with what kinds of explanatory rubrics are to be allowable as they do with types of theoretical constructs. Of the first comment no better case in point could have been chosen than that of reward and drive reduction. Witness how inconclusive were the experiments in latent learning, and how facile our improvisations of implicit processes that serve to keep the metatheoretical hypothesis intact.

However, I believe the second comment to be the more telling one. We do in fact establish canons of theoretic explanation. For science these traditionally have been the canons of deductivist explanation. And we do in fact maintain the integrity of such canons by arbitrarily excluding all nondeductivistic paradigms of explanation—not necessarily by claiming the latter to be nonsensical, but by attributing a different semantic to their languages. One can, of course, opt for expanded canons of scientific explanation so as to include explanations in the ordinary language of intention. But what is the advantage—or perhaps better, what of the disadvantage? So long as we can contrive reductive rubrics to accommodate observable behavior as intentionally defined, then the pressure upon us to augment our traditional objectivistic tactics is not at all a compelling one.

CHAPTER 8

Conclusions

IN THE foregoing chapters we have examined some objections to the idea of reductionism raised on logical grounds. Both in the argument from Gödel (simulation) and in the argument from intention we are presented with descriptions of contemporaneous action that prove refractory to reduction in the language of neurophysiology. We have found, however, that, though problematic, neither of these arguments succeeds in disqualifying the tactics of reductionism as meaningful for the scientific explanation of behavior. Nor do these arguments define problems that are irresolvable within the purview of reductionism.

There have been two aspects to our assay. On one hand, reductive explanation is a reasonable tactic on grounds of scientific realism. On the other hand, difficulties raised by the logical critique of reductionism are methodologically surmountable.

I know of no better statement of this first point than is to be found in the writings of Mario Bunge (1963, 1964, 1967). Aside from radical descriptivism, which Bunge (1967) rejects for obvious reasons, the question of scientific tactics focuses on the issue of explanation. Laws and theories explain, but what kind of laws, what kind of theories should we seek? Those scientific rubrics that bind together phenomenological descriptions into functional relations constitute our phenomenological theories, in Bunge's terms, black-box theories. Such rubrics can then be divided into *phenomenological* theories, with truly opaque black-box mediation, and *representational* theories, with translucid black-box mediation. It is Bunge's point, and a point of this essay, that translucid black-box (i.e., representational) theories are to be sought at least to the extent that the logical limits of representation permit (cf. Note 8.1).

Purely phenomenological descriptions may be undertaken without reference to any mediational mechanics. Thus, as between input and output, the black-box theory may express perfect transmission, damping effects, or amplifying effects over the possibilities of constant, sudden, or periodic input (Bunge, 1963). The relations are purely functional, but they are expressed without our taking cognizance of what it is that is functioning (Bunge, 1964).

Representational theories, on the other hand, are translucid in the sense that they offer hypotheses as to the functional details of the black box. Thus, rather than relying solely upon mathematical relations between input and output, or upon intervening variables which are logical constructions upon input and output variables, they offer hypotheses (hypothetical constructs) as to unobserved entities and processes mediating between the two sets of variables. Representational theories offer the promise of mediational reification.

There is then this initial call to scientific realism, resting as it does on the pervasive plausibility of mediational descriptions. I have argued that psychology cannot be indifferent to this task of carrying theory development to its representational level. Phenomenological (Bunge's sense) psychology is both rubric and heuristic for physiological psychology.

But there is another aspect of scientific realism. One not only seeks explanations of individual events, but also explanations of lawful relations. If laws are offered as explanations of events, the laws themselves are subject to explanation. Bunge also accommodates this problem within the analysis of black-box systems. For any such system, output is a function of input and the mediational state of the system. Thus, of the three transactional problems (prediction, retrodiction, and explanation) it is explanation especially that directs attention to mediational detail. One can predict effectively without detailing mediational structures; the emphasis is upon the workability of constructions we put upon the data. In retrodiction, we may again focus upon pragmatic constructions of the hypothetical inputs. But explanation stands apart. Given the input and the output, given the phenomenological law, we seek to determine the mediational properties of the system which make the law a factual one.

But it is the second aspect of this assay that has been our primary concern. Although the argument from Gödel and the argument from intention raise logical difficulties for reductive explanations, these difficulties are not insurmountable.

In the argument from Gödel we have found that although any given act of human computation is in principle simulatable, not all acts of human computation are simulatable by a realizable computer system. Acceptance of the predicament is contingent upon our acceding to our limited conceptions of what computer systems and computer descriptions must be. But even the acceptance of this predicament need not disqualify reductionism as a comprehensive scientific tactic. We are concerned with the adequacy of tactics for explaining *any* act of "human computation," not *all* acts in some single rubric. For any given act of human computation, including that of Gödel's proof, we may offer a legitimate explanation of the act if in principle it is a simulatable act. No implication of Gödel's proof discounts the prospects of simulation. No implication of the theorems of incompleteness discounts our sanguine prospects of reductive explanation. The task of scientific explanation is to explain the computational act as such, not to explain the *significance* of such acts for all computational endeavor.

However, our taking simulation as a prospectus for reductive explanation leads us also to the problem of intention. Robots that embody our prospecti do not cogitate and intend precisely in the way that a person cogitates and intends. A machine is the product of a human designer, "it does what it is programmed to do." And yet the human designer stands apart from his machine with a distinguishable intention of his own not simulatable by that extant machine which has emerged from his drawing board.

This much we must concede: the designer cannot build a machine that simulates himself now in the act of designing that very machine. The puzzles of self-reference are not to be circumvented. But troublesome as the issue appears, it does not foreclose the prospects of explanation through simulation. The designer may not design the machine that simulates his contemporary behavior, but that fact does not preclude his recording his present behavior, formulating a new prospectus, and designing a new machine which indeed simulates that "present" behavior. One can very well design a machine capable of designing other functional machines, providing he can detail step-by-step procedures by which the computational act is carried out. In principle, if any creative, intentional act can be fully described, then there is a conceivable machine which will be a material representation of this description. In this matter, reference to the machine is dispensable, it is the description that counts. And if we should take recourse to intuition as the source of human inventiveness, this will not discount the argument. An intuition that is nondescribable is in no communicable sense explanatory of behavior.

The predicament we are ultimately forced into is the one of simulating, hence explaining, not the "present" but the contemporary act. This is an old problem, as old as introspectionism itself. But the fact that it is logically, not just empirically, impossible to represent and to explain the contemporary act is not the same as saying there are no contingencies under which we can describe and explain purposive, creative acts that take place in the present. The intentionalist critic of reductive explanation tends to focus upon the contemporary act. And he is correct in maintaining a logical difference between himself and a machine he conceives to simulate himself. But he is not thereby correct in maintaining that this predicament precludes his offering an explanation of his behavior in terms amenable to simulation. After all, explanation is all we can ask of science. Any act is explainable if it is possible for us to conceive circumstances under which we can fully describe the act.

If this qualifier "fully" should bother us, if contemporary description is indeed what we must insist upon, then to be sure let us admit that we have a puzzle. But it is a puzzle for the parlor, not for the laboratory. And by airing it let us recognize that we have succeeded only in contriving circumstances in which the demand for a scientific explanation is not an intelligible one.

Nor need we be frightened by that scarecrow admonition: "a machine can only do what it is programmed to do." [1] The term "program" may be anathema to our sense of option, but the language of instruction, rules, and programs is in no way incompatible with a person's making choices, solving problems, and fulfilling intentions. In the same vein, we should not lose sight of the program aspects of the genetic code or the sequential patterning of instinctive acts. Gunderson (1968), neither friend nor foe of the robot, has argued effectively that "being guided by a program" is not sufficient grounds for denying feelings or consciousness to the programmed entity.

We should not be frightened by the denigrating connotations of "the program." Still, there is something uniquely human about intention. Intentional behavior involves cognition, anticipation, valuation, and goals, all of which involve the activity of foreseeing not quite like the functions we visualize for machines. We are, after all, *in* our respective selves, in a way which precludes our being in the representations of ourselves. However, the question of scientific explanation is a directed one: Can we offer objectivistic explanations of any behavior whatsoever? We may indeed utilize our inner resources for defining meaningful behavioral acts; but once defined, is it not always the case that we may interpret our intentions as behavioral dispositions? Need we exclude intentional acts from the purview of traditional scientific explanation?

But let us take for granted that there are intentional descriptions of behavior and there are objectivist descriptions of behavior; that there are noncausal intentional explanations and there are traditional, "causal" ones. The question then is not whether the domains of intentional and nonintentional description are contradictory or mutually exclusive, but whether the two are in some sense complementary. The literature on intention abounds with claims for the subjective uniqueness of its descriptions. Yet in no place are we presented with argument that the behavioral scope of the intentional act is intractable to explanation in objectivistic terms.

To be sure, intentional descriptions may utilize the idiosyncratic, personalistic language. Point of reference renders the private and the public languages incompatible. However, the conceptual identification of an

---

[1] For example, Paul Ziff writes: "MacKay has pointed out that any test for mental or any other attributes to be satisfied by the observable activity of a human being can be passed by automata. And so one is invited to say what would be wrong with a robot's performance. Nothing need be wrong with either the actor's or the robot's performance. What is wrong is that they are performances" (1959, p. 67).

226 REALISM AND THE EXPLANATION OF BEHAVIOR

intention does not preclude its analysis in behavioral terms. It is simply the case that the intention we may know directly, intentionally, must now be reformulated as a dispositional construct. The empathetic understanding from our inner vantage must necessarily be omitted from the meaning of the scientific language. We thereby admit the possibility of complementary descriptions.

However, affirmation of the possibility of objectivistic explanation is seen to obviate the issue in contention. It directs itself not to the possibility of uniquely complementary descriptions but rather to the possibility that for every intentional act, so conceived, there is also a rubric for describing and understanding the behavioral act in causal terms. If it is the case that all behaviors, whether intentional acts or not, are subject to causal interpretation, the intentionalistic critique of "behaviorism" is largely irrelevant. Just as one may give a causal account of a phenomenon "complementary" to perceptual phenomenology, so he may give a causal account of a phenomenon "complementary" to an intentional action. Behaviorists may be obtuse to intentionality, as many doubtless are, and they may be the poorer psychologists for it, but they cannot reasonably be criticized for not incorporating complementary descriptions, *per se,* into a unified scientific discipline. Complementary descriptions are just that, somewhat autonomous descriptions that complement one another in differentiable domains of understanding (cf. Note 8.2).

Critics, both from without and within psychology, have observed that there are different types of explanation. There is hypothetico-deductive explanation that forms the credo of the experimental scientist. And there is empathetic explanation that seemingly transcends traditional logical schemata and offers a personalized understanding of behavioral involvement. The distinction is well made. For we do not ask of the novelist or the clinician that he explain behavior as the consequence of laws and sets of theoretical constructs. In each case the person describes from within, as it were. He establishes an identification with the object-person, the character or the client, and thereby empathizes with the intentions and valuations of the active agent. He comes to understand the object-person not by explaining the latter's behavior within a hypothetico-deductive schema, but by participating in the intentional character of that person.

There is therefore no preemptive claim on the meaning of explanation. Those who would maintain that there are alternative forms and alternative meanings of explanation are clearly within their exegetical rights. The rights are faulted only if one conflates the meanings of explanation. But leaving it at this I would reiterate: one cannot hold behavioral science accountable for not doing what is not within its purview.

Among other reactions, it may be felt that this essay constitutes an attack upon all forms of personology that stress the participative role of the ego, or that it is hostile to cognitive sensibilities, to intuition, insight, purposive involvement, or that it rejects all forms of awareness. Such reactions are a misreading of its intentions. I have no quarrel with the clinician or the moralist, no grudge against the expositor who attempts to record the conflict of life from the actor's inner vantage, and certainly no disagreement at all with the partisan of ineluctable focal awareness. But the activities of pure introspective understanding, meaningful and valuable as they are, belong to a domain other than that of scientific discipline.

Of this distinction as to domains of understanding, we can offer no better example than the difference between "explaining a choice" and "making a choice." On one hand, the choice is explainable in terms of process functions and deductive rubrics, subject to determinacy within our conceptual and observational limits. On the other hand, in making a choice, the executor is the free agent, caught up in his reflective awareness of goals, anticipation, expectancy, remorse, the whole panoply of intentional experience. It has often been the fault of the uncritical behaviorist that he has engaged in public disavowals of the legitimacy of this private domain of experience. Yet the intentionalist becomes equally uncritical and equally at fault if he insists that what one does experience privately, what the phenomenologists may allude to as the world of intentional inexistence, must be incorporated into the descriptive and formal languages of our scientific disciplines.

Finally, it would be a mistake to construe our argument for reduction as a fully committed attack on mentalism. Intentional experience is, and ought to be, the epistemic resource for mediational constructs. Phenomenological descriptions are essential to the task of explicating the complex relations between behavioral situations and behavior itself. But we need not be encumbered by the logical uniqueness of intentional terms, as such; nor need we feel embarrassed by the behavioral vagaries of ordinary language. Both ordinary language and that of pure intention are septic probes at best.

Let us reiterate: the question before us is not whether all explanatory language, all paradigms, can be reduced logically to basic sets of statements in the heirarchy of sciences, but whether meaningful acts as described in intentional terms can be interpreted in a language conducive to reduction. Our beliefs in the inseparability of the mental and the physical in general, and of intention and behavior in particular, are traditional ones. And they are beliefs that make the idea of reductionism a suitably comprehensive one.

NOTES

NOTE 8.1

The language of representation can be misleading. If by representation we insist upon pictorial as well as process representation, we become encumbered at the limits of observation. Thus, as Bunge (1967) points out, in microphysics we are driven to symbolic rather than iconic representations. Naive mechanism and pictorial realism fail us in the case of our representations of the aether and the atom. Indeed, in the case of the atom we may enter into the ethereal domain of mathematical realism (Dirac, 1947), where it is inconceivable that we represent events in classical pictorial terms.

The observational argument, however, it not germane to the logical arguments against reduction as expressed in this book. For example, to the extent that we say intention is not representable in behavioral terms, we are alluding to a putative semantic difference between a behavioral term and an intentional term, not a difference or a difficulty in the domain of physical observation.

Failure to distinguish between semantic limitations and semantic differences has led to what in an important sense is a misapplication of the principle of complementarity to psychology. In Chapter 6, we have seen that complementary descriptions can be adopted to accommodate a juxtaposition of subjective-objective (inner-outer) descriptions. In a sense one complements the other. And both are required for a complete description of events if by complete we insist upon the subjective complementation of scientific descriptions.

Yet Bohr himself (1950), in attributing his principle of complementarity to the predicament of the inner and outer vantage, failed to observe the difference between complementarity as applied to physics and complementarity as applied to psychology. In physics, complementary descriptions relate two phenomenal representations under different conditions of objective observation. Hence, the wave-particle duality. But in psychology, complementary descriptions relate to disparate domains of observation. Complementarity is between the inner and the outer vantage, and not between sets of alternative descriptions within the domain of objective observation.

NOTE 8.2

We have admitted the possibility of complementary explanations. But if intentional and nonintentional explanations complement one another, why not go all the way and admit all alternative explanations as epistemically complementary. And why insist upon the constraints of a reductive program?

To take an example offered by Fodor (1968), the act of purchasing a sketch is subject, among others, to aesthetic, economic, psychological, physiological, and physical explanations. In each case the explanation will be unique to the context of inquiry. This we must agree. But then we may also insist that there are no incompatibilities between these alternative explanations; they are complementary, not contradictory. And reduction between any two of the explanations affords a bridge which may be something more than an epistemological curiosity.

The issue is especially germane to the reduction of psychological explanations. Assume for the moment a psychological explanation utilizing intentional or other mentalistic constructs. And assume further that a program for reducing these constructs within the language of neurophysiology is a plausible one. If we insist upon the systemic integrity of the psychological theory as independent of neurophysiology, then we may effect control of the organism by manipulating variables within the conceptual framework of psychology itself. But assuming the plausibility of reduction, we may also effect control by manipulating related complexes of variables within the domain of neurophysiology. The argument as to effective control of behavior would then be a pragmatic one as to which class of controls proves to be more easily manipulatable. Thus aesthetic and economic behavior may be readily controlled by psychological manipulations; e.g., by rather elementary operant conditioning techniques.

Perhaps in this case these exercises should be left to the utopiates. However, the possibilities for behavioral control become significant alternatives when we consider functional disorders. Functional disorders in behavioral pathology are distinguishable from organic disorders in just this way: organic disorders are explained as a function of neurophysiological mediators, whereas functional disorders are explained as a function of "psychological" mediators. If this distinction is correct, the tactics and strategy of behavioral control will themselves be a function of the type of disorder. But if reduction of functional disorders is initially plausible and if it indeed proves achievable, the question of tactics becomes one of practical judgment. The question of whether the patient goes through psychotherapy or takes a pill will indeed be more than academic. The ontological debate as to the nature of functional disorders will yield to the debate over pragmatics.

REFERENCES

ACKERMAN, W. See Hilbert and Ackerman, 1950.

AMASOV, N. M. *Modelling of thinking and the mind.* (translated by L. Feingold) New York: Spartan, 1967.

ANSCOMBE, G. E. M. *Intention.* (2nd edition) Ithaca: Cornell University Press, 1957.

ARBIB, M. A. *Brains, machines, and mathematics.* New York: McGraw-Hill, 1964.

ARKADEV, A. B. and BRAVERMAN, E. M. *Computers and pattern recognition.* (translated by W. Turski and J. D. Cowan) Washington: Thompson, 1967.

ASHBY, W. R. *Design for a brain.* London: Chapman and Hall, 1952.

ASHBY, W. R. *An introduction to cybernetics.* London: Methuen, 1956.

ATTNEAVE, F. *Applications of information theory in psychology.* New York: Holt-Dryden, 1959.

AUSTIN, J. L. Other minds. *Proc. Arist. Soc. Suppl.,* 1946, 20, 148–157. Also in J. L. Austin, *Philosophical papers.* Oxford: Clarendon Press, 1961.

AYER, A. J. Other minds. *Proc. Arist. Soc. Suppl.,* 1946, 20, 188–197.

BAERNSTEIN, H. D. and HULL, C. L. A mechanical parallel to the conditioned reflex. *Science,* 1929, 70, 14–15.

BAERNSTEIN, H. D. and HULL, C. L. A mechanical model of the conditioned reflex. *J. gen. Psychol.,* 1931, 5, 99–106.

BAR-HILLEL, Y. See Fraenkel and Bar-Hillel, 1958.

BARKER, S. F. *Philosophy of mathematics.* Englewood Cliffs: Prentice-Hall, 1964.

BARTLETT, F. C. *Remembering.* Cambridge: Cambridge University Press, 1932.

BELOFF, J. The identity hypothesis: a critique. In J. R. Smythies (editor), *Brain and mind.* London: Routledge and Kegan Paul, 1965.

BENACERRAF, P. God, the Devil, and Gödel. *Monist,* 1967, 51, 9–32.

BERGMANN, G. *Philosophy of science.* Madison: University of Wisconsin Press, 1957.

BERGMANN, G. *Logic and reality.* Madison: University of Wisconsin Press, 1964.

BERNAYS, P. Sur le platonisme dans les mathématiques. *L'Enseignment Mathématique,* 1935, 34, 52–69. English translation (C. D. Parsons), On Platonism in mathematics. In P. Benacerraf and H. Putnam (editors), *Philosophy of mathematics: selected readings.* Englewood Cliffs: Prentice-Hall, 1964.

231

BETH, E. W. *The foundations of mathematics.* Amsterdam: North Holland Publishing Co., 1959; Rev. ed., 1964. Reprinted New York: Harper Torchbooks, 1966.

BIGELOW, J. See Rosenblueth, Wiener, and Bigelow, 1943.

BIRKHOFF, G. D. and LEWIS, D. C. Stability in causal systems. *Philos. Sci.,* 1935, 2, 304–333.

BLACK, M. *The nature of mathematics.* London: Routledge and Kegan Paul, 1933. Reissued Paterson: Littlefield, Adams, 1959.

BLOCK, H. D. Learning in some simple non-biological systems. *Amer. Sci.,* 1965, 53, 59–79.

BOHR, N. On the notions of causality and complementarity. *Science,* 1950, 111, 51–54.

BOHR, N. *Atomic physics and human knowledge.* New York: Wiley, 1958.

BOOTH, D. A. Vertebrate brain ribonucleic acids and memory retention. *Psychol. Bull.,* 1967, 68, 149–177.

BORING, E. G. Mind and mechanism. *Amer. J. Psychol.,* 1946, 59, 173–192.

BORKO, H. (editor), *Computer applications in the behavioral sciences.* Englewood Cliffs: Prentice Hall, 1962.

BOWER, G. H. See Hilgard and Bower, 1966.

BRADNER, H. A. A new mechanical 'learner.' *J. gen. Psychol.* 1937, 414–419.

BRAITHWAITE, R. B. *Scientific explanation.* Cambridge: Cambridge University Press, 1953.

BRAITHWAITE, R. B. Models in empirical science. In E. Nagel, P. Suppes, and A. Tarski (editors), *Logic, methodology, and philosophy of science.* Stanford: Stanford University Press, 1962.

BRALY, K. W. See Katz and Braly, 1935.

BRAVERMAN, E. M. See Arkadev and Braverman, 1967.

BRIDGMAN, P. W. Remarks on the present state of operationism. *Sci. Mon.,* 1954, 79, 224–226.

BROAD, C. D. The relation between induction and probability. *Mind,* 1918, 27, 389–404; 1920, 29, 11–45.

BRODBECK, MAY, Meaning and action. *Philos. Sci.,* 1963, 30, 309–324.

BRODBECK, MAY, (editor). *Readings in the philosophy of the social sciences.* New York: Macmillan, 1968.

BRONOWSKI, J. The logic of mind. *Amer. Sci.,* 1966, 54, 1–14.

BRUNER, J. S. and GOODMAN, C. C. Value and need as organizing factors in perception. *J. abn. soc. Psychol.,* 1947, 42, 33–44.

BUNGE, M. A general black-box theory. *Philos. Sci.,* 1963, 30, 346–358.

BUNGE, M. Phenomenological theories. In M. Bunge (editor), *The critical approach to science and philosophy.* Glencoe: Free Press, 1964.

BUNGE, M. *Scientific research II, the search for truth.* New York: Springer-Verlag, 1967.

CAMPBELL, N. R. *Physics, the elements.* Cambridge: Cambridge University Press, 1920. Also published as *Foundations of science.* New York: Dover, 1957.

CARMICHAEL, L., HOGAN, H. P. and WALTER, A. A. An experimental study of the effect of language on the reproduction of visually perceived forms. *J. exp. Psychol.*, 1932, 15, 73–86.

CARNAP, R. *Philosophy and logical syntax.* London: Kegan Paul, 1935.

CARNAP, R. Testability and meaning: I, II. *Philos. Sci.*, 1936, 3, 419–471; 1937, 4, 1–40.

CARNAP, R. Foundations of mathematics and logic. *International Encyclopedia of Science.* Chicago: University of Chicago Press, 1939.

CARNAP, R. The methodological character of theoretical concepts. In H. Feigl and M. Scriven (editors), *Minnesota studies in the philosophy of science,* Vol. I. Minneapolis: University of Minnesota Press, 1956.

CHOMSKY, N. *Syntactic structures.* 'S-Gravenhage: Mouton, 1957.

CHOMSKY, N. Review: Verbal behavior (B. F. Skinner). *Language,* 1959, 35, 26–58.

CHOMSKY, N. Explanatory models in linguistics. In E. Nagel, P. Suppes, and A. Tarski (editors), *Logic, methodology, and philosophy of science.* Stanford: Stanford University Press, 1962.

CHOMSKY, N. Recent contributions to the theory of innate ideas. *Synthese,* 1967, 17, 2–11.

CHURCH, A. A note on the Entscheidungs-problem. *J. symbol. Log.,* 1936a, 1, 40–41; 101–102.

CHURCH, A. An unsolvable problem of elementary number theory. *Amer. J. Math.,* 1936b, 58, 345–363.

CLACK, R. J. Can a machine be conscious? *Br. J. Philos. Sci.,* 1966, 17, 232–234.

CLARK, W. A. and FARLEY, B. G. Generalization of pattern recognition in a self-organizing system. *Proceedings 1955 Western joint computer conference.* New York: IRE, 1955, 86–91.

COULSON, W. R. and ROGERS, C. R. (editors). *Man and the science of man.* Columbus: Charles Merrill, 1968.

CRAIK, K. J. W. *The nature of explanation.* Cambridge: Cambridge University Press, 1943.

CRAIK, K. J. W. *The nature of psychology.* (edited by S. G. Sherwood) Cambridge: Cambridge University Press, 1966.

CRUTCHFIELD, R. S. See Krech and Crutchfield, 1948.

DAVIDSON, D. Actions, reasons, and causes. *J. Philos.,* 1963, 60, 685–700.

DAVIS, M. *Computability and unsolvability.* New York: McGraw-Hill, 1958.

DE NIKE, L. D. See Spielberger and De Nike, 1966.

DEUTSCH, J. A. *The structural basis of behavior.* Cambridge: Cambridge University Press; Chicago: University of Chicago Press, 1960.

DINNEEN, G. P. Programming pattern recognition. *Proceedings 1955 Western joint computer conference.* New York: IRE, 1955.

DIRAC, P. A. M. *The principles of quantum mechanics* (3rd edition). London: Oxford University Press, 1947.

DUDA, W. See Rochester, Holland, Haibt, and Duda, 1956.

DUHEM, P. *The aim and structure of physical theory* (1914, 2nd edition, translated by P. P. Wiener). Princeton: Princeton University Press, 1954. Also New York: Atheneum, 1962.

DULANY, D. E. Awareness, rules, and propositional control: a confrontation with S–R behavior theory. In D. Horton and T. Dixon (editors), *Verbal behavior and general behavior theory*. Englewood Cliffs, Prentice-Hall, 1968.

DULANY, D. E. The place of hypothesis and intentions: an analysis of verbal control in verbal conditioning. In C. W. Eriksen (editor), *Behavior and awareness*. Durham: Duke University Press, 1967.

DUNCKER, K. On problem solving. *Psychol. Monogr.,* 1945, 58, No. 270.

ECCLES, J. C. *The neurological basis of mind*. London: Oxford University Press, 1953.

ECCLES, J. C. (editor). *Brain and consciousness*. New York: Springer-Verlag, 1966.

ELLSON, D. G. A mechanical synthesis of trial and error learning. *J. gen. Psychol*. 1935, 13, 212–218.

FARBER, M. *Naturalism and subjectivism*. Springfield: Charles Thomas, 1959.

FARBER, M. *The foundations of phenomenology*. New York: Payne-Whitman, 1962.

FARLEY, B. G. See Clark and Farley, 1955.

FEIGENBAUM, E. A. *An information processing theory of verbal learning*. Santa Monica: Rand, 1959.

FEIGENBAUM, E. A. and SIMON, H. A. *Performance of a reading task by EPAM*. Santa Monica: Rand, 1961.

FEIGENBAUM, E. A. and FELDMAN, J. (editors). *Computers and thought*. New York: McGraw-Hill, 1963.

FEIGL, H. Operationism and scientific method. *Psychol. Rev.,* 1945, 52, 250–259.

FEIGL, H. The mind-body problem in the development of logical empiricism. *Revue Internationale de Philosophie,* 1950, 4, 64–83. Reprinted in H. Feigl and M. Brodbeck (editors), *Readings in the philosophy of science*. New York: Appleton-Century-Crofts, 1953.

FEIGL, H. The "mental" and the "physical." In H. Feigl, M. Scriven, and G. Maxwell (editors), *Minnesota studies in the philosophy of science,* Vol. II. Minneapolis: University of Minnesota Press, 1958.

FESTINGER, L. *A theory of cognitive dissonance*. New York: Harper and Row, 1957.

FEYERABEND, P. K. Explanation, reduction, and empiricism. In H. Feigl and G. Maxwell (editors), *Minnesota studies in the philosophy of science* Vol. III. Minneapolis: University of Minnesota Press, 1962.

FEYERABEND, P. K. Realism and instrumentalism. In M. Bunge (editor), *The critical approach to science and philosophy*. Glencoe: Free Press, 1964.

FEYERABEND, P. K. On the 'meaning' of scientific terms. *J. Philos.*, 1965, 62, 266–274.

FINDLAY, J. Goedelian sentences: a non-numerical approach. *Mind,* 1942, 51, 259–265.

FODOR, J. A. Explanation in psychology. In M. Black (editor), *Philosophy in America.* Ithaca: Cornell University Press, 1965.

FODOR, J. A. *Psychological explanation: an introduction to the philosophy of psychology.* New York: Random House, 1968.

FRAENKEL, A. H. and BAR-HILLEL, Y. *Foundations of set theory.* Amsterdam: North Holland Publishing Co., 1958.

FREGE, G. *The foundations of arithmetic.* (original 1844, translated by J. L. Austin) Oxford: Blackwell, 1950.

GAITO, J. and ZAVALA, A. Neurochemistry and learning. *Psychol. Bull.,* 1964, 61, 45–62.

GALANTER, E. *Textbook of elementary psychology. S*an Francisco: Holden-Day, 1966.

GALANTER, E. See Miller, Galanter, and Pribram, 1960.

GAULD, A. Could a machine perceive? *Br. J. Philos. Sci.,* 1966, 17, 44–58.

GEORGE, F. H. *The brain as a computer.* New York: Pergamon Press, 1961.

GERBRANDT, L. K. See Hudspeth and Gerbrandt, 1965.

GERLERNTER, H., HANSEN, J. R. and LOVELAND, D. J. Empirical explorations of a geometry theorem machine. *Proceedings Western joint computer conference,* 1960, 17, 143–150.

GIBSON, J. J. The reproduction of visually perceived forms. *J. exp. Psychol.,* 1929, 12, 1–39.

GIBSON, J. J. The concept of stimulus in psychology. *Amer. Psychol.,* 1960, 15, 694–703.

GLICKMAN, S. E. and SCHIFF, B. B. A biological theory of reinforcement. *Psychol. Rev.,* 1967, 74, 81–109.

GÖDEL, K. *On formally undecidable propositions of Principia Mathematica and related systems.* (translated by B. Meltzer; introduction by R. B. Braithwaite). Edinburgh: Oliver and Boyd, 1962.

GOODMAN, C. C. See Bruner and Goodman, 1947.

GREENSPOON, J. The reinforcing effect of two spoken sounds on the frequency of two responses. *Amer. J. Psychol.,* 1955, 68, 409–416.

GREEN, B. F., JR. *Digital computers in research: an introduction for behavioral and social scientists.* New York: McGraw-Hill, 1963.

GREGORY, R. L. The brain as an engineering problem. In W. H. Thorpe and O. L. Zangwill (editors), *Current problems in animal behavior.* Cambridge: Cambridge University Press, 1961.

GUNDERSON, K. Robots, consciousness, and programmed behavior. *Br. J. Philos. Sci.,* 1968, 19, 109–122.

HAIBT, L. See Rochester, Holland, Haibt, and Duda, 1956.

HAMLYN, D. W. Behavior. In V. L. Chappel (editor), *The philosophy of mind.* Englewood Cliffs: Prentice-Hall, 1962.

HAMPSHIRE, S. *Thought and action.* London: Chatto and Windus, 1959.

HANSEN, J. R. See Gerlernter, Hansen and Loveland, 1960.

HANSON, N. R. *Patterns of discovery.* Cambridge: Cambridge University Press, 1958.

HAWKINS, D. *The language of nature.* San Francisco: Freeman, 1964.

HAYEK, F. A. *The sensory order.* London: Routledge, 1952.

HEBB, D. O. *The organization of behavior.* New York: Wiley, 1949.

HEBB, D. O. A neurophysiological theory. In S. Koch (editor), *Psychology: a study of a science,* Vol. 1, *Sensory, perceptual and physiological formulations.* New York: McGraw-Hill, 1959.

HEBB, D. O. *A textbook of psychology.* (2nd edition) Philadelphia: Saunders, 1966.

HEIDBREDER, E. *Seven psychologies.* New York: Appleton-Century-Crofts, 1933.

HEIDER, F. Attitudes and cognitive organization. *J. Psychol.,* 1946, 21, 102–112.

HELSON, H. Adaptation level theory. In S. Koch (editor), *Psychology: a study of a science,* Vol. 1, *Sensory, perceptual and physiological formulations.* New York: McGraw-Hill, 1959.

HEMPEL, C. G. The theoretician's dilemma. In H. Feigl, M. Scriven, and G. Maxwell (editors), *Minnesota studies in the philosophy of science.* Vol. II. Minneapolis: University of Minnesota Press, 1958.

HERBART, J. F. *A textbook in psychology.* (translated by Margaret K. Smith, 1834 edition) New York: D. Appleton, 1896.

HESSE, MARY B. Models in physics. *Br. J. Philos. Sci.,* 1953, 4, 198–214.

HESSE, MARY B. *Models and analogies in science.* London: Sheed, 1963.

HEYTING, A. *Intuitionism, an introduction.* Amsterdam: North Holland Publishing Company, 1956.

HILBERT, D. *Grundlagen der Geometrie.* Stuttgart: Teubner, 1899 (1956).

HILBERT, D. and ACKERMAN, W. *Principles of mathematical logic.* New York: Chelsea Publishing Co., 1950.

HILGARD, E. R. *Theories of learning.* (3rd edition with G. H. Bower). New York: Appleton-Century-Crofts, 1948, 1956, 1966.

HOCHBERG, H. Dispositional properties. *Philos. Sci.,* 1967, 34, 10–17.

HOGAN, H. P. See Carmichael, Hogan, and Walter, 1932.

HOLLAND, J. See Rochester, Holland, Haibt, and Duda, 1956.

HOVLAND, C. I. Computer simulation of thinking. *Amer. Psychol.,* 1960, 16, 687–693.

HOVLAND, C. I. and HUNT, E. B. Computer simulation of concept attainment. *Behav. Sci.,* 1966, 5, 265–267.

HOVLAND, C. I. See Hunt and Hovland, 1961.

HUDSPETH, W. J. and GERBRANDT, L. K. Electroconvulsive shock: conflict, competition, consolidation and neuroanatomical functions. *Psychol. Bull.,* 1965, 63, 377–383.

HULL, C. L. *A behavior system.* New Haven: Yale University Press, 1952.

HULL, C. L. *Principles of behavior.* New York: Appleton-Century-Crofts, 1943.

HULL, C. L. See Baernstein and Hull, 1929, 1931.

HULL, C. L. See Krueger and Hull, 1931.

HUNT, E. B. and HOVLAND, C. I. Programming a model of human concept formation. *Proceedings 1961 Western joint computer conference.* New York: IRE, 1961.

HUSSERL, E. *The idea of phenomenology.* (translated by W. P. Alston and G. Nakhnikian) The Hague: Martinus and Nijhoff, 1964.

JEFFRESS, L. A. (editor). *Cerebral mechanisms in behavior.* New York: Wiley, 1951.

JEFFREYS, H. *Theory of probability.* London: Oxford University Press, 1939.

JEFFREYS, H. *Scientific inference* (2nd edition). Cambridge: Cambridge University Press, 1957.

JESSOR, R. The problem of reductionism in psychology. *Psychol. Rev.,* 1958, 65, 170–178.

JOHN, E. R. *Mechanisms of memory.* New York: Academic Press, 1967.

KANFER, F. H. Verbal conditioning: a review of its current status. In D. Horton and T. Dixon (editors), *Verbal behavior and general behavior theory.* Englewood Cliffs: Prentice-Hall, 1968.

KANTOR, J. R. *Problems of physiological psychology.* Bloomington: Principia Press, 1947.

KAPLAN, A. *The conduct of inquiry.* San Francisco: Chandler, 1964.

KATZ, D. and BRALY, K. W. Racial prejudice and racial stereotypes. *J. abn. soc. Psychol.,* 1935, 30, 175–193.

KELLEY, G. *The psychology of personal constructs.* New York: Norton, 1955.

KEMENY, J. G. *A philosopher looks at science.* Princeton: Van Nostrand, 1959.

KEMENY, J. G. and OPPENHEIM, P. On reduction. *Philos. Studies,* 1956, 7, 6–19.

KENDLER, H. H. "What is learned?"—a theoretical blind alley. *Psychol. Rev.,* 1952, 59, 269–277.

KENDLER, H. H. The structure of psychology. Presidential address, Division 1, American Psychological Association, 1968.

KENDLER, H. H. and KENDLER, T. S. Vertical and horizontal processes in problem solving. *Psychol. Rev.,* 1962, 69, 1–16.

KENDLER, T. S. See Kendler and Kendler, 1962.

KESSEN, W. and KIMBLE, G. A. "Dynamic systems" and theory construction. *Psychol. Rev.,* 1952, 59, 263–267.

KEYNES, J. M. *A treatise on probability.* London: Macmillan, 1921.

KIMBLE, G. A. See Kessen and Kimble, 1952.

KLEENE, S. C. *Introduction to metamathematics.* Princeton: Van Nostrand, 1952.

KOFFKA, K. *Principles of Gestalt psychology.* New York: Harcourt Brace, 1935.

KÖHLER, W. *Gestalt psychology.* New York: Liveright, 1947.

KÖRNER, S. *The philosophy of mathematics: an introduction.* London: Hutchinson, 1960. Reprinted New York: Harper Torchbooks, 1962.

KÖRNER, S. Deductive unification and idealization. *Br. J. Philos. Sci.,* 1964, 14, 274–284.

KÖRNER, S. *Experience and theory: an essay in the philosophy of science.* London: Routledge and Kegan Paul, 1966.

KRECH, D. and CRUTCHFIELD, R. S. *Theory and problems of social psychology.* New York: McGraw-Hill, 1948.

KRUEGER, R. G. K. and HULL, C. L. An electrochemical parallel to the conditioned reflex. *J. gen. Psychol.,* 1931, 5, 262–269.

KUHN, T. S. *The structure of scientific revolutions.* Chicago: University of Chicago Press, 1962.

LANDAUER, T. K. Two hypotheses concerning the biochemical basis of memory. *Psychol. Rev.,* 1964, 71, 167–179.

LEWIN, K. *Principles of topological psychology.* New York: McGraw-Hill, 1936.

LEWIS, D. C. See Birkhoff and Lewis, 1935.

LINDSLEY, D. B. Higher functions of the nervous system. *Annu. Rev. Physiol.,* 1955, 17, 311–338.

LIPPMANN, W. *Public opinion.* New York: Macmillan, 1922. Also New York: Penguin, 1946.

LORENTE DE NÓ, R. Analysis of the activity of the chains of internuncial neurones. *J. Neurophysiol.,* 1938, 1, 207–244.

LOVELAND, D. J. See Gerlernter, Hansen, and Loveland, 1960.

LUCAS, J. R. Mind, machines, and Gödel. *Philosophy,* 1961, 36, 112–127.

LUCAS, J. R. Satan stultified: a rejoinder to Paul Benacerraf. *Monist,* 1968, 52, 145–158.

LUCE, D. R. The action of mind on body. *Philos. Sci.,* 1960, 27, 171–182.

LUCHINS, A. S. and LUCHINS, E. H. *Logical foundations of mathematics for behavioral scientists.* New York: Holt, Rinehart, and Winston, 1965.

LUCHINS, E. H. See Luchins and Luchins.

MACCORQUODALE, K. and MEEHL, P. E. On a distinction between hypothetical constructs and intervening variables. *Psychol. Rev.,* 1948, 55, 95–107.

MACCORQUODALE, K. and MEEHL, P. E. Preliminary suggestions as to a formalization of expectancy theory. *Psychol. Rev.,* 1953, 60, 55–63.

MACH, E. *The science of mechanics.* (translated by T. J. McCormack; original 1883) La Salle: Open Court, 1906.

MACH, E. *The analysis of sensations.* (original 1897) La Salle: Open Court, 1914.

MACKAY, D. M. Mindlike behavior in artefacts. *Br. J. Phil. Sci.,* 1951, 2, 105–121.

MACKAY, D. M. Mentality in machines. *Proc. Arist. Soc. Suppl.,* 1952, 26, 61–86.

MACKAY, D. M. The use of behavioral language to refer to mechanical processes. *Br. J. Philos. Sci.,* 1962, 13, 89–103.

MACKAY, D. M. Cerebral organization and the conscious control of action. In J. C. Eccles (editor), *Brain and conscious experience.* New York: Springer-Verlag, 1966.

McCULLOCH, W. and PITTS, W. A. A logical calculus of ideas immanent in nervous activity. *Bull. Math. Biophys.*, 1943, 5, 111–133.

McCULLOCH, W. *Embodiments of mind.* Boston: M.I.T. Press, 1965.

McCULLOCH, W. S. See Pitts and McCULLOCH, 1947.

McGUIRE, W. J. The current status of cognitive consistency theories. In S. Feldman (editor), *Cognitive consistency.* New York: Academic Press, 1966.

MALTZMAN, I. Awareness: cognitive psychology vs. behaviorism. *J. exp. res. Person.*, 1966, 1, 161–165.

MAY, R. Intentionality: the heart of human will. *J. human. Psychol.* 1965, 5, 202–209.

MEEHL, P. E. See MacCorquodale and Meehl, 1948.

MEEHL, P. E. See MacCorquodale and Meehl, 1953.

MELDEN, A. I. *Free action.* London: Routledge and Kegan Paul, 1961.

MESCHOWSKI, H. *Evolution of mathematical thought.* (2nd edition translated by J. H. Gayl) San Francisco: Holden-Day, 1965.

MILLER, G. A. What is information measurement? *Amer. Psychol.*, 1953, 8, 3–11.

MILLER, G. A. (editor) *Mathematics and psychology.* New York: Wiley, 1964.

MILLER, G. A., GALANTER, E., and PRIBRAM, K. H. *Plans and the structure of behavior.* New York: Wiley, 1960.

MILNER, P. M. The cell assembly: Mark II. *Psychol. Rev.*, 1957, 64, 242–252.

MINSKY, M. Steps toward artificial intelligence. *Proceedings IRE,* 1961, 49, 8–30.

MINSKY, M. L. *Computation: finite and infinite machines.* Englewood Cliffs: Prentice-Hall, 1967.

MISCHEL, T. Psychology and explanation of human behavior. *Philos. Phenom. Res.*, 1963, 23, 578–594.

MISCHEL, T. Personal constructs, rules, and the logic of clinical activity. *Psychol. Rev.*, 1964, 71, 180–192.

MOSTOWSKI, A. *Sentences undecidable in formalized arithmetic.* Amsterdam: North Holland Publishing Co., 1952.

MUENZINGER, K. F. *Psychology: the science of behavior.* New York: Harper and Row, 1942.

MYHILL, J. R. On the ontological significance of the Löwenheim-Skolem theorem. In M. White (editor), *Academic freedom, logic, and religion.* American Philosophical Association. Philadelphia: University of Pennsylvania Press, 1953.

NAGEL, E. The meaning of reduction in the natural sciences. In R. L. Stauffer (editor), *Science and civilization.* Madison: University of Wisconsin Press, 1949.

NAGEL, E. *The structure of science.* New York: Harcourt, Brace & World, 1961.

NAGEL, E. and NEWMAN, J. R. *Gödel's proof.* New York: New York University Press, 1958.

NAGEL, E. and NEWMAN, J. R. Putnam's review of *Gödel's Proof. Philos. Sci.,* 1961, 28, 209–211.

NEUMANN, J. VON. The general and logical theory of automata. In L. A. Jeffress (editor), *Cerebral mechanisms in behavior.* New York: Wiley, 1951. Reprinted in J. R. Newman (editor), *The world of mathematics,* Vol. 4. New York: Simon and Schuster, 1956.

NEUMANN, J. VON. *The computer and the brain.* New Haven: Yale University Press, 1958.

NEWELL, A., SHAW, J. C. and SIMON, H. A. Empirical explorations of the logic theory machine. *Proceedings Western joint computer conference.* New York: IRE, 1957, 218–230.

NEWELL, A., SHAW, J. C. and SIMON, H. A. Chess playing programs and the problem of complexity. *IBM J. Res. and Dev.,* 1958, 2, 320–335.

NEWELL, A., SHAW, J. C. and SIMON, H. A. A report on a general problem-solving program. *Proceedings international conference on information processing.* UNESCO, 1959, 256–265.

NEWELL, A. and SIMON, H. A. GPS, a program that simulates human thought. In H. Billing (editor), *Proceedings of a conference on learning automata.* Karlsruhe, Germany, 1961a.

NEWELL, A. and SIMON, H. A. The simulation of human thought. In *Current trends in psychological theory.* Pittsburgh: University Pittsburgh Press, 1961b.

NEWELL, A. and SIMON, H. A. Computers in psychology. In R. D. Luce, R. R. Bush, and E. Galanter (editors), *Handbook of mathematical psychology* Vol. I. New York: Wiley, 1963.

NEWMAN, J. R. See Nagel and Newman, 1958.

NEWMAN, J. R. See Nagel and Newman, 1961.

OPPENHEIM, P. See Hempel and Oppenheim, 1948.

OPPENHEIM, P. See Kemeny and Oppenheim, 1956.

OSGOOD, C. E. A behavioristic analysis of perception and language as cognitive phenomena. In *Contemporary approaches to cognition.* Cambridge: Harvard University Press, 1957.

OSGOOD, C. E. Toward a wedding of insufficiencies. In D. Horton and T. Dixon (editors), *Verbal behavior and general behavior theory.* Englewood Cliffs: Prentice-Hall, 1968.

OSGOOD, C. E. and TANNENBAUM, P. H. The principle of congruity in the prediction of attitude change. *Psychol. Rev.,* 1955, 62, 42–55.

OSSORIO, P. *Persons.* Boulder: Linguistic Research Institute, 1966.

PARSONS, C. Foundations of mathematics. In P. Edwards (editor), *Encyclopedia of Philosophy,* Vol. 5. New York: Basic Books, 1967.

PEARSON, K. *The grammar of science.* (original 1892) London: Dent, 1937.

PETERS, R. S. *The concept of motivation.* London: Routledge and Kegan Paul, 1958.

PITTS, W. and MCCULLOCH, W. S. How we know universals: the perception of auditory and visual forms. *Bull. Math. Biophys.,* 1947, 9, 127–147.

PITTS, W. A. See McCulloch and Pitts, 1943.

PLACE, U. T. Is consciousness a brain process? *Br. J. Philos. Sci.*, 1956, 47, 44–50. Reprinted in V. C. Chappell (editor), *The philosophy of mind.* Englewood Cliffs: Prentice-Hall, 1962.

POINCARÉ, H. *Science and hypothesis.* (translated by W. J. G., original 1905) New York: Dover, 1952.

POINCARÉ, H. *The value of science.* (translated by G. B. Halstead; original 1913) New York: Dover, 1958.

POINCARÉ, H. *Foundations of science.* Lancaster: The Science Press, 1913.

POLANYI, M. *Personal knowledge.* Chicago: University of Chicago Press, 1958.

POLANYI, M. "Tacit knowing": its bearing on some problems of philosophy. *Reviews of Modern Physics,* 1962, 34, 601–616.

POPPER, K. R. Indeterminism in quantum physics and in classical physics, I, II. *Br. J. Philos. Sci.*, 1950, 1, 117–133; 173–195.

POPPER, K. *The logic of scientific discovery.* London: Hutchinson, 1959; New York: Wiley, 1961. (original *Logik der Forschung,* Vienna: Springer, 1935.)

PRIBRAM, K. H. A review of theory in physiological psychology. *Annu. Rev. Psychol.,* 1960, 11, 1–40.

PRIBRAM, K. H. Interrelations of psychology and the neurological disciplines. In S. Koch (editor), *Psychology: a study of science,* Vol. 4. New York: McGraw-Hill, 1962.

PRIBRAM, K. H. See Miller, Galanter, and Pribram, 1960.

PURTILL, R. L. Discussion: Kuhn on scientific revolutions. *Philos. Sci.,* 1967, 34, 53–58.

PUTNAM, H. Minds and machines. In S. Hook (editor), *Dimensions of Mind.* New York: New York University Press, 1960a. Reprinted New York: Collier Books, 1961.

PUTNAM, H. Review: Nagel and Newman, *Gödel's proof. Philos. Sci.,* 1960b, 27, 205–207.

QUINE, W. O. *Methods of logic.* New York: Henry Holt, 1950.

RAZRAN, G. Russian physiologists' psychology and American experimental psychology. *Psychol. Bull.,* 1965, 63, 42–64.

REITMAN, W. Programming intelligent problem solvers. *IRE Transactions Human Factors Electronics,* 1961, 2, 26–33.

REITMAN, W. R. Personality as a problem solving coalition. In S. S. Tomkins and S. Messick (editors), *Computer simulation of personality.* New York: Wiley, 1963.

REITMAN, W. R. *Cognition and thought.* New York: Wiley, 1965.

ROCHESTER, N., HOLLAND, J., HAIBT, L. and DUDA, W. Test on a cell assembly theory of the action of the brain, using a large digital computer. *IRE Transactions Information Theory,* 1956, 2, 80–93.

ROGERS, C. Toward a science of the person. In T. Wann (editor), *Behaviorism and phenomenology.* Chicago: University of Chicago Press, 1964.

ROSENBERG, M. J. Discussion: simulated man and humanistic criticism. In S. S. Tomkins and S. Messick (editors), *Computer simulation of personality*. New York: Wiley, 1963.

ROSENBLATT, F. The perceptron. *Psychol. Rev.*, 1958, 65, 386–408.

ROSENBLATT, F. Recent work on theoretical models in biological memory. In J. T. Tou (editor), *Computer and information sciences—II*. New York: Academic Press, 1967.

ROSENBLUETH, A., WIENER, N. and BIGELOW, J. Behavior, purpose, and teleology. *Philos. Sci.*, 1943, 10, 18–24.

ROSENBLUETH, A. and WIENER, H. Purposeful and non-purposeful behavior. *Philos. Sci.*, 1950, 17, 318–326.

ROSSER, J. B. Extensions of some theorems of Gödel and Church. *J. symbol. Logic.*, 1936, 1, 87–91.

ROSSER, J. B. An informal exposition of proofs of Gödel's theorem and Church's theorems. *J. symbol. Log.*, 1939, 4, 53–60.

ROZEBOOM, W. W. Ontological induction and the logical typology of scientific variables. *Philos. Sci.*, 1961, 28, 337–377.

RUSSELL, B. *Introduction to mathematical philosophy*. New York: Macmillan, 1919.

RUSSELL, B. *Principles of mathematics* (2nd edition). New York: Norton, 1937.

RUSSELL, B. *History of western philosophy*. London: George Allen and Unwin, 1946.

RUSSELL, B. See also Whitehead and Russell, 1925, 1927, 1962.

RYLE, G. *The concept of mind*. London: Hutchinson, 1949.

SAMUEL, A. Some studies in machine learning using the game of checkers. *IBM J. Res. and Dev.*, 1959, 3, 210–229.

SAYRE, K. M. and CROSSON, F. J. (editors). *The modeling of the mind*. Notre Dame: University Notre Dame Press, 1963.

SCHIFF, B. B. See Glickman and Schiff, 1967.

SCHLEGEL, R. *Completeness in science*. New York: Appleton-Century-Crofts, 1967.

SCRIVEN, M. The compleat robot: a prolegomena to androidology. In S. Hook (editor), *Dimensions of mind*. New York: New York University Press, 1960. Reprinted New York: Collier Books, 1961.

SCRIVEN, M. The limits of physical explanation. In B. Baumrin (editor), *Philosophy of science: the Delaware seminar, Vol. II*. New York: Wiley, 1963.

SCRIVEN, M. The essential unpredictability in human behavior. In B. Wolman and E. Nagel (editors), *Scientific psychology: principles and approaches*. New York: Basic Books, 1965.

SELFRIDGE, O. G. Pattern recognition and modern computers. *Proceedings 1955 Western joint computer conference*. New York, IRE, 1955.

SELLARS, W. The language of theories. In H. Feigl and G. Maxwell (editors), *Current issues in the philosophy of science*. New York: Holt, Rinehart and Winston, 1961.

SELLARS, W. and CHISHOLM, R. M. Intentionality and the mental. In H. Feigl, M. Scriven, and G. Maxwell (editors), *Minnesota studies in the philosophy of science*, Vol. II. Minneapolis: University of Minnesota Press, 1958.

SHAFFNER, K. F. Antireductionism and molecular biology. *Science,* 1967a, 157, 644–647.

SHAFFNER, K. F. Approaches to reduction. *Philos. Sci.,* 1967b, 34, 137–147.

SHANNON, C. E. and WEAVER, W. *The mathematical theory of communication.* Urbana: University Illinois Press, 1949.

SHAW, J. C. See Newell, Shaw, and Simon, 1957, 1958, 1959.

SHEFFLER, I. *Science and subjectivity.* New York: Bobbs-Merrill, 1967.

SHERRINGTON, C. *The integrative action of the nervous system.* Cambridge: Cambridge University Press, 1947.

SIDOWSKI, J. B. Influence of awareness on verbal conditioning. *J. exp. Psychol.,* 1954, 48, 355–360.

SIMON, H. A. See Feigenbaum and Simon, 1961.

SIMON, H. A. See Newell, Shaw, and Simon, 1957, 1958, 1959.

SIMON, H. A. See Newell and Simon, 1961a, b, 1963.

SKINNER, B. F. Are theories of learning necessary? *Psychol. Rev.,* 1950, 57, 193–216.

SKINNER, B. F. Pigeons in a pelican. *Amer. Psychol.,* 1960, 15, 28–37.

SLAGLE, J. R. A heuristic program that solves symbolic integration problems in freshman calculus; symbolic automatic integrator (SAINT). *MIT Lincoln Lab. Report.* 56–0001, Lexington, Mass., 1961.

SLUCKIN, W. *Minds and machines.* Harmonsworth: Pelican Books, 1954.

SMART, J. J. C. Sensations and brain processes. *Philos. Rev.,* 1959, 68, 141–156. Slightly revised in V. C. Chappell (editor), *The philosophy of mind.* Englewood Cliffs: Prentice-Hall, 1962.

SMART, J. J. C. *Philosophy and scientific realism.* London: Routledge and Kegan Paul, 1963.

SPIELBERGER, C. D. The role of awareness in verbal conditioning. In C. W. Ericksen (editor), *Behavior and awareness.* Durham: Duke University Press, 1962.

SPIELBERGER, C. D. Theoretical and epistemological issues in verbal conditioning. In S. Rosenberg (editor), *Directions of psycholinguistics.* New York: Macmillan, 1965.

SPIELBERGER, C. D. and DE NIKE, L. D. Verbal operant conditioning. *Psychol. Rev.,* 1966, 73, 306–326.

STELLAR, E. Physiological psychology. *Annu. Rev. Psychol.,* 1957, 8, 415–436.

STEVENS, J. M. A mechanical explanation of the law of effect. *Amer. J. Psychol.,* 1929, 41, 422–431.

SULLIVAN, J. J. Franz Brentano and the problems of intentionality. In B. Wolman (editor), *Historical roots in contemporary psychology.* New York: Harper and Row, 1968.

TANNENBAUM, P. H. See Osgood and Tannenbaum, 1955.

TARSKI, A. On undecidable statements in enlarged systems of logic and the concept of truth. *J. symbol. Log.,* 1939, 4, 105–112.

TARSKI, A. *Logic, semantics, metamathematics.* (translated by J. H. Woodger) Oxford: Clarendon Press, 1956.

TAYLOR, C. *The explanation of behavior.* London: Routledge and Kegan Paul; New York: Humanities Press, 1964.

TAYLOR, R. Comments on mechanistic conception of purposefulness. *Philos. Sci.,* 1950a, 17, 310–317.

TAYLOR, R. Purposeful and non-purposeful behavior: a rejoinder. *Philos. Sci.,* 1950b, 17, 327–332.

TAYLOR, R. *Action and purpose.* Englewood Cliffs: Prentice-Hall, 1966.

THOMPSON, D. Can a machine be conscious? *Br. J. Philos.* Sci., 1965, 16, 33–43.

THORPE, W. H. *Learning and instinct in animals,* (revised edition). London: Methuen, 1963.

TINBERGEN, N. *The study of instinct.* Oxford: Clarendon Press, 1951.

TOLMAN, E. C. Prediction of vicarious trial and error by means of a schematic sow-bug. *Psychol. Rev.,* 1939, 46, 318–336.

TOLMAN, E. C. Discrimination vs. learning and the schematic sow-bug. *Psychol. Rev.,* 1941, 48, 367–382.

TOMKINS, S. S. Simulation of personality: the interrelationships between affect, memory, thinking, perception and action. In S. S. Tomkins and S. Messick (editors), *Computer simulation of personality.* New York: Wiley, 1963.

TOULMIN, S. *The philosophy of science.* London: Hutchinson, 1953.

TURING, A. M. On computable numbers, with an application to the Entscheidungs problem. *Proc. London Math. Soc.* 1937, 42, 230–265. Reprinted in M. Davis (editor), *The undecidable.* Hewlett, N. Y.: Raven Press, 1965.

TURING, A. M. Computing machinery and intelligence. *Mind,* 1950, 59, 433–460. Reprinted as "Can a machine think?" In J. R. Newman (editor), *The world of mathematics.* New York: Simon and Schuster, 1956.

TURNER, M. B. *Philosophy and the science of behavior.* New York: Appleton-Century-Crofts, 1967.

WAISMANN, F. *Introduction to mathematical thinking.* (translated by T. J. Benac) New York: Frederich Ungar Publishing Co., 1951. Reprinted New York: Harper Torchbooks, 1959.

WALTER, A. A. See Carmichael, Hogan, and Walter, 1932.

WALTER, W. GREY. *The living brain.* London: Duckworth, 1953.

WATANABE, S. Comments on key issues. In S. Hook (editor), *Dimensions of mind.* New York: New York University Press, 1960. Reprinted New York: Collier Books, 1961.

WATSON, A. Conditioning illustrated by an automatic mechanical device. *Amer. J. Psychol.,* 1939, 42, 110–117.

WATSON, J. D. *The double helix.* New York: Atheneum, 1968.

WEAVER, W. See Shannon and Weaver, 1949.

WEBB, J. Metamathematics and the philosophy of mind. *Philos. Sci.,* 1968, 35, 156–178.

WERTHEIMER, M. *Productive thinking.* New York: Harper and Row, 1945.

WEYL, H. *Philosophy of mathematics and natural philosophy.* Princeton: Princeton University Press, 1949.

WHITEHEAD, A. N. and RUSSELL, B. *Principia Mathematica.* 3 Vols. (2nd edition) Cambridge: Cambridge University Press, 1925, 1927, 1927.

WHITEHEAD, A. N. and RUSSELL, B. *Principia Mathematica: to *56.* Cambridge: Cambridge University Press, 1962.

WIENER, N. *Cybernetics.* New York: Wiley, 1948.

WIENER, N. See Rosenblueth, Wiener, and Bigelow, 1943.

WIENER, N. See Rosenblueth and Wiener, 1950.

WILDER, R. L. *Introduction to the foundations of mathematics,* (2nd edition). New York: Wiley, 1965.

WINCH, P. *The idea of a social science.* London: Routledge and Kegan Paul, 1958.

WISDOM, J. O. The hypothesis of cybernetics. *Br. J. Philos. Sci.,* 1951, 2, 1–24.

WISDOM, J. O. Mentality and machines. *Proc. Arist. Soc. Suppl.,* 1952, 26, 1–25.

WISDOM, J. T. W. *Other minds.* Oxford: Blackwell, 1952.

WITTGENSTEIN, L. *Philosophical investigations.* (translated by G. E. M. Anscombe) Oxford: Blackwell, 1953.

WOODGER, J. H. *Biological principles.* London: Kegan Paul, 1929.

WOODGER, J. H. *Language and biology.* Cambridge: Cambridge University Press, 1952.

YOUNG, J. Z. *A model of the brain.* Oxford: Clarendon Press, 1964.

ZAJONC, R. B. The concepts of balance, congruity and dissonance. *Public Opinion Quarterly,* 1960, 24, 280–296.

ZAVALA, A. See Gaito and Zavala, 1964.

ZIFF, P. The feelings of robots. *Analysis,* 1959, 19, 64–68.

NAME INDEX

SUBJECT INDEX

as intervening variables, 205
sans physical correlates, 209–210
Mentalism, 227
argument from, 200–221
and behaviorism, 203, 211, 215
Fodor's views, 205–210
and materialism, 205–206
mental reports, 208
methodological, 215
reduction of, 200–201, 203, 204
and simulation, 92
Metamathematics, 138, 141–144
Metatheory, disconfirmation of, 220–221
Microreduction, 31–32, 44
and instrumentalism, 12–13
Mind-body, 7, 196, 209
conscious machines, 93
identity hypothesis, 216–217
neurophysiology, 54
reduction, 201
Pribram's views, 54
Missiles, "intentions" of, 97
Missionary-cannibal problem, 89–108
Models,
analogy of, 58
cybernetic, 55–56, 59–60
denumerable, 142–143
mathematical, 10–11
physical vs. abstract, 28–29
structural theory, 62
Modus ponens,
mapping of, 121
in proof, 135
"Moral certainty" (Fodor), 208–209, 213

Nature of Explanation (Craik), 56–59
Nature of Psychology (Craik), 71
Nervenets, 60–61, 74, 79
Neurological Basis of Mind (Eccles), 50
Neurophysiology,
mind-body, 54
and psychology, 45–48
reduction, 30
Nomological net, 34
Nonnormal class, 117
Normal class, 117
Normal science, 6
Number,
formalism, 138
intuitionism, 136
logicism, 134
transfinite, 136–137

Observation,
pragmatic theory, 36–37
Operant conditioning, 10

Operationism, 5
"Other minds," 94–95

Paradigm, 5–6
crucial experiments, 9
and mathematics, 11, 22
priority of, 6
and psychology, 2, 7–12
teleological, 158–161
"Paradigmettes," 8, 9
Paradox,
Russell's 117–118
Skolem's, 142–143
Parameter identification, 46–47
Performatory criteria, 91–92, 96–97
Personality, stimulation of, 104–108
Phenomenology, 177–179
of awareness, 197
and explanation, 203
Gestalt, 19
of intention, 160
Physicalism, 1
Plans, 72, 74
Plans and the Structure of Behavior
(Miller-Galanter-Pribram), 71–74
Platonism, 140
Pragmatism, 12–16
and observation, 36–37
Prediction and indeterminancy, 172–173
Principia Mathematica (Russell-White-
head), 117, 125, 128, 135
Problem Solving,
explanation of, 212
simulation, 132
unconscious inference, 211–212
Process function, 25–26, 49–50
Proof, mathematical, 115, 138–140
intuitionism, 135–138
logicism, 135
Proof schema (Gödel), 121–122
Properties, dispositional, 182–185
Provability, 121–122
Psychological Explanation (Fodor), 204–
210
Psychology,
and complementarity, 167–169
historical continuity, 10
instrumentalism, 12–16
mathematical, 21–22
and neurophysiology 44–48
paradigms of, 7–12, 17–21
as science, 7–8
Psychophysical parallelism, 25
Public Opinion (Lippmann), 20
Purpose,
and behaviorism, 153–156
and intention, 158–161